"Ed Feld shows us how ancient revolutions impacted biblical revelations and how we can make religious meaning out of historical findings. Through deft and scrupulous analyses of the Bible's law codes, he uncovers what for many will be surprising connections between biblical law and biblical prophecy, demonstrating how the latter helped shape the former. Readers of all backgrounds and textual skill levels will be guided to new understandings by a gifted teacher and writer."

— SHAI HELD, author of *The Heart of Torah*

"I loved this book. It beautifully succeeds in its ambitious task of retelling the Tanakh's history of biblical Israel as the weaving of a tapestry out of the many strands of God-seeking. Feld passionately argues here that a multiplicity of interpretations and experiences is the most reverential way to seek the Divine. And it really is a page-turner, but the kind that doesn't just engage you in the moment: it lingers on as an invitation and a challenge to us in the present."

— GORDON TUCKER, vice chancellor for Religious Life and Engagement, Jewish Theological Seminary

The Book of Revolutions

University of Nebraska Press   Lincoln

The Book of Revolutions

The **BATTLES** of **PRIESTS,**
PROPHETS, and **KINGS**
That **BIRTHED** the **TORAH**

EDWARD FELD

The Jewish Publication Society   Philadelphia

All rights reserved. Published by the University of
Nebraska Press as a Jewish Publication Society book.
Manufactured in the United States of America.

Library of Congress Cataloging-in-Publication Data
Names: Feld, Edward, 1943– author.
Title: The Book of Revolutions : the
battles of priests, prophets, and kings that
birthed the Torah / Edward Feld.
Description: Lincoln : University of Nebraska Press;
Philadelphia : Jewish Publication Society, 2022. |
Includes bibliographical references and index.
Identifiers: LCCN 2021060243
ISBN 9780827615229 (paperback)
ISBN 9780827618961 (epub)
ISBN 9780827618978 (pdf)
Subjects: LCSH: Jewish law—Interpretation and
construction. | Bible. Pentateuch—Criticism, Textual. |
Bible. Pentateuch—Criticism, Narrative. |
Revolutions. | Jews—History—1200–953 B.C.
Classification: LCC BM521 .F45 2022 |
DDC 296.1/8—dc23/eng/20211223
LC record available at https://lccn.loc.gov/2021060243

Designed and set in Merope by L. Auten.

For Merle

The simple meaning of the text is constantly unfolding.

SAMUEL BEN MEIR (twelfth century)

Contents

List of Illustrations xi

Acknowledgments........................... xiii

Introduction xv

PRELUDE: Origins of the People Israel 1

PART I. Revolution in Northern Israel

1. Elijah's Victory 15

2. The Covenant Code.......................... 31

3. The Heritage of the Covenant Code 41

FIRST INTERLUDE: In Judea................... 51

PART II. Revolution in Judea

4. Years of Turmoil............................ 61

5. Josiah and the Book of Deuteronomy.......... 85

6. Law in Deuteronomy 97

7. Deuteronomy's Revelation 109

8. The People and the Land 135

9. The Heritage of Deuteronomy................ 147

SECOND INTERLUDE: The End of Monarchy ... 163

PART III. Revolution in Babylonia

10. Priests, Prophets, and Scribes in Exile 169

11. The Holiness Code. 187

12. The Heritage of the Holiness Code 209

PART IV. The Last Revolution

13. The Torah. 221

FINAL THOUGHTS 241

Notes. 255

Bibliography 273

Index. 277

Illustrations

1. The kingdoms of Israel and Judah. 8
2. Victory stele of Esarhaddon 79

TABLES

1. Kings of Northern Israel to Omri. 11
2. Kings of Northern Israel from Omri to Jehu. 16
3. The House of Jehu 22
4. Rulers of Judea from Athaliah to Hezekiah. 52
5. The last Judean kings 65
6. Kings of Assyria 745–627 BCE 75

Acknowledgments

The idea for this book arose as a response to my students at the Jewish Theological Seminary where I was Rabbi-in-Residence from 2001 to 2008. I wanted them to see that the critical study of the Bible could lead to new spiritual understanding, and I hope that these many years later, they, as well as current rabbinical students and all those who seek to understand the origins of Western ethical formation, will find this book not only intellectually stimulating, but spiritually nourishing.

I left my position as Scholar-in-Residence to offer the time and focus necessary to finish work on *Mahzor Lev Shalem*, a High Holiday prayer book, and then devoted myself to *Siddur Lev Shalem*, a new translation and commentary of the Shabbat and Festival prayer book. All the while, however, the ideas for this book were calling to me. Several scholars played critical roles in finally moving this manuscript along, including Prof. Marc Zvi Brettler who encouraged me to take the manuscript out of my drawer and pursue publication. Prof. Stephen A. Geller read both an earlier and a later version; his pointed comments were always helpful and his assurances that the manuscript should see the light of day were very much appreciated. I owe a special debt to Dr. Adriane Leveen, whose extensive comments and queries helped me think through what needed more elaboration in telling this story.

Friends, too, played an important role. John Clayton read an early version and commented extensively. Elliot Cohen was the first person who encouraged me to write for publication, and I am forever grateful to him.

My family has been essential to my writing. My wife Merle read and edited several different versions of this manuscript. Her probing questions along with her excitement about the ideas I was trying to express were critical spurs for my writing. My daughter Lisa read and commented on an earlier version and created the map that appears in this book. Her anticipation for its publication never waned. Their encouragement and that of my son, Uri, was a constant companion as I worked.

The manuscript underwent a double review, by The Jewish Publication Society and the University of Nebraska Press. The staff at JPS have been enormously helpful and caring. The invaluable advice from JPS's director Rabbi Barry Schwartz moved this project forward. Joy Weinberg, JPS managing editor, is a meticulous and devoted editor; almost every page reflects her advice and her sure hand. Many thanks to the University of Nebraska Press for their work in seeing this book to publication. David Hornik's skilled and light hand was invaluable in editing the manuscript. My thanks to Jessica Freeman for her work in collating the index.

Introduction

The Hebrew Bible—twenty-four books—is the product of a near thousand-year history. That's part of the story the Bible tells about itself.

The Bible ascribes the authorship of its first five books—the Torah—to Moses, who may have lived sometime in the mid-thirteenth century BCE. The Bible also says that its penultimate books, Ezra and Nehemiah, were written by these two leaders of contingents of Jews who returned from exile in Babylonia in the fifth century BCE.

But only in the modern period—that is, since the seventeenth century—have we understood that the Five Books ascribed to Moses have a long history themselves. Indeed, if we study that history, reading between the lines of the biblical text along with modern archaeological discoveries, we find that the teachings regarding the proper worship of Israel's God represented in these books are the products of bitter struggles that took place over many centuries. From a historian's point of view, the outcome was not assured, for each stage in the development of biblical religion constituted a revolution—some won by military force, some by political machination, and some by sheer force of will.

The analysis of internal contradictions, differing locutions and styles, and not least, contending theologies that punctuate the Five Books have all contributed to a scholarly consensus that supports the conclusion that multiple epochs formed the text as it has come down to us. Though academic battles still rage over the assignment of specific passages to different hands, and over the dating of these disparate materials, the general outline of the theory that the Pentateuch is the product of different eras and perspectives has held up over the course of time.

Most popular works explicating the varying voices in the Five Books of Moses have concentrated on the narrative portions of the Bible. It is easy to show that the first chapter of Genesis tells quite a different story than the second and third chapters. In chapter 1, for example, the human is the last in the order of creation, whereas in chapter 2, Adam is created before animal life; in chapter 1, Adam and Eve are created simultaneously, while in chapter 2, Eve is created from Adam's rib after Adam experiences loneliness. Equally, the change in style is readily noticeable: the formal, almost abstract day-by-day description in the first chapter contrasts with the dramatic tales of the wily snake and the deceit and betrayal of Adam and Eve in the second and third chapters. Such contradictions and differences as these force the conclusion that different hands are at work in each of these chapters.

Though it is easy to demonstrate that different authorship is reflected in these chapters, dating them is a contentious and almost impossible task. Moreover, the precise authorial assignment of some other narrative portions of the Five Books has proved more controversial. Regarding those portions, the literary scholar and Bible translator Robert Alter wisely remarked that the editors of the Five Books have done such a fine job of creating a continuous narrative that we should think of the work as an omelet: once made, we can never really tease out all the individual elements with which it was constituted.

The case is somewhat different regarding the law codes in the Five Books. These codes are found in distinct places, generally as complete documents. One can easily show how one is dependent on another and thereby establish priority. And there is general scholarly agreement regarding the dating of at least one of the three codes, that in Deuteronomy. As a result, this book is able to place each of the codes it examines in its historical context. I read them alongside the biblical histories of Joshua, Judges, 1 and 2 Samuel, 1 and 2 Kings, and finally 1 and 2 Chronicles and the archaeological evidence that supports or contradicts these biblical historians.

What does it mean to read these biblical texts with the eyes of a historian? It is, first of all, to notice the contradictions between passages, the seams in the text where materials don't fit together quite right. It is to compare one account against another—for instance, the ways in which the books of Joshua and Judges tell different stories of the early settlement in the land of Canaan. Second, it is to read biblical texts, especially the "historical" books of the Bible, with a sense of suspicion. What is the provenance of the narrative, and what were the author's motives in writing it? Was this author contemporary with the events or writing about them long afterward? What seems like literary embellishment and what like factual reporting? Do we have any confirmation of the events from other than Israelite sources? What does the archaeological evidence tell us? What do we know of the surrounding cultures of this period? The results of this kind of reading can often tell a different story than the author intended us to hear.

As we read through the texts I examine in this work, I'll raise these questions. I will try to come to reasonable conclusions about what we can know about the period, based in part or in full on what we can glean from looking at the biblical report in the way I've just described. We need to realize that we are often dealing with events for which the biblical account is the sole source, and so all we can do is try to engage in careful detective work resulting in probable conclusions.

Some biblical scholars do not accept any biblical information as historical unless there is confirmation from outside sources: mention in archives of other nations or archaeological finds supporting the biblical claim. I believe this skepticism is overdrawn.[1] First of all, these outside sources themselves are subject to distortion. Foreign kings may claim more credit than is their due, and the records they leave behind need to be viewed with the same skeptical eye as the biblical account. Also, which extrabiblical accounts have survived or which we have luckily uncovered are largely matters of historical accident. Finally, so much would be missing, great holes in our understanding of the history of Israel in the biblical period, if we did not use the Bible as one of our sources of information. If we want to write a history of this time, we have little choice but to use the Bible as a source—only we must do so with great care.

ABOUT THIS BOOK

This work attempts to distill the results of current biblical scholarship to the study of biblical history and law. The history is an exciting story, the law is still a living source for contemporary Jews.

This book differs in its approach to the history of the text of the Five Books than most contemporary accounts, focusing not on analyses of the narrative portions but instead, uniquely, on the legal sections. Unlike the narrative portions, which underwent a final editing in order to tell a continuous story from the creation of the world to the moment when the people Israel are about to enter the Promised Land, the final editors of the Pentateuch did not attempt to create one single legal code. Rather, we find a series of laws in Exodus, a quite distinct law code in Deuteronomy, and a series of laws remarkably different in tone from these two in Leviticus and parts of Numbers. In these legal codes, which include criminal and civil law, domestic legislation as well as rules of governance, it is often easy to show the ways in which one code reworks the language of another. This evidence of priority leads to a historical understanding of cultural development.

(Excluded from our discussion are the priestly laws dealing with purity and sacrificial offerings. These laws are not paralleled in the other law codes, and so no comparative analysis can be made. Indeed, the dating of the priestly material continues to be a matter of scholarly controversy.)[2]

Each of these codes—the Covenant Code in Exodus, the law code in Deuteronomy, and the Holiness Code in Leviticus—is the product of revolutions that took place in biblical times, and this book describes the cultural and political background that defined each of these cataclysmic biblical moments. One of these revolutions was accomplished through a military coup, another was instituted after an assassination and a regency, and the third was a quiet revolution made by outsiders whose ideas proved persuasive. The first of these revolutions, spearheaded by prophets in Northern Israel, resulted in the promulgation of the Covenant Code found in Exodus, chapters 21–24. The second, in Judea, resulted in much of the book of Deuteronomy, a book authenticated by a prophetess. The third, the work of priests influenced by prophetic ideas, resulted in the work known as the Holiness Code, which occupies much of the latter half of the book of Leviticus beginning with chapter 17. Examining each of these works in terms of their contents and individual theological outlook, I reflect on, most importantly, what each contributes, in its own way, to our understanding of the meaning of postbiblical Jewish religious life.

From the historian's point of view, the outcome of these revolutions was not inevitable. Rather, each was the product of people who had decided beliefs in the God of Israel and the meaning of those beliefs for the life of their society. What constituted proper religious worship? How should the community be organized? What personal behaviors did God demand? Because these ideas were not simply matters of individual concern but theological visions intended as binding on the entire community of Israel, those who supported these beliefs embodied their ideas in law codes.

I, myself, believe that what these revolutions uncovered and brought to life has meaning beyond their time even to our present day, for they constituted a search for a fundamental understanding of the meaning of faith in God and the way of life that faith demands. The religious power of the ideas propagated by these revolutionaries can be experienced by anyone who enters into Jewish life today. Judaism is unthinkable without reference to these codes.

In popular thought prophets are conceived of as those who are opposed to the "establishment." But what has especially impressed me in the course of my research and writing is the relation of these codes to the prophets who spoke in each of these eras—that is, how much the establishment depended on them. Elijah and Elisha led the revolution that brought the House of Jehu to power and promulgated the Covenant Code. Huldah the prophetess authenticated the Josianic reforms of Deuteronomy. And the prophecies of Ezekiel and the Holiness Code have much in common. This is a different but important way to understand the prophetic inspiration that lies behind the Torah.

In the historical books of the Bible—Joshua, Judges, First and Second Samuel, First and Second Kings, and First and Second Chronicles—we hear about the opposition to the ideas and beliefs that came to be embodied in the Torah. These histories tell us that during the time from the settlement of the land until the Babylonian exile—a period of some seven hundred years—large segments of the Israelite population and many in the royal courts believed in multiple heavenly powers and in a variety of worship practices, which at their most extreme may have included either child sacrifice or a mock ceremony of child sacrifice, and a synthesis of Israelite belief in its God with the gods of the surrounding cultures. Later, the books of Ezra and Nehemiah describe opposition to the imposition of the instructions of Torah. Given the variety of beliefs the Israelite populace maintained, an outside observer might well have been surprised at the triumph of the ideas embodied in the Pentateuch, but, over time, the revolutions that brought these ideas to the fore prevailed and became the root of the Judaism we know today.

Each of the codes represents not only specific laws but unique perspectives on the meaning and purpose of the law. They were produced in certain moments in history, yet they propounded ideas that have meaning beyond their time.

This book offers both a delineation of each of these moments and a summary of how each of these distinct outlooks had lasting influence on Jewish thought. The ideas, understandings, and perspectives examined here may have grown to fruition in particular historical circumstances, but once delineated they had power beyond their own time, speaking to subsequent Jewish generations, even to our own. The code in Exodus calls itself the Book of the Covenant, and the idea that the people Israel stand in covenantal relationship with God has been a permanent underpinning of Jewish theology. Deuteronomy emphasizes the concept of mitzvoth—the idea that the Jewish people are addressed by God and commanded by God to behave in certain ways. The Holiness Code adds its own unique understanding to the meaning of religious behavior: God wishes each of us to behave in such a way that our very hearts are transformed. These religious ideas constitute fundamental Jewish understandings of the relation of the people Israel to God.

The greatness of the Five Books lies in part in its plurality: the inclusion of the varieties of approaches biblical Israel developed, with all their heterogeneity. This book recovers that sense of plurality and traces a measure of the timelessness of the ideas that the biblical revolutions realized. I believe that the ability of the Five Books to appeal to a variety of beliefs and theological perspectives—if you will, to affect a variety of human personalities—contributes to making the Torah timeless. With all this in mind, this work undertakes to present these codes, their history, their meaning, and their heritage.

Ultimately, I hope readers come to realize the difficulty biblical ideas encountered in their own time before they triumphed. If you will, there was no "inevitability" in their triumph—yet how lasting, how significant, are the ideas these revolutionary moments captured! These ideas uncovered spiritual realities that are just as powerful in speaking to our own generation as they were to their own age.

TERMINOLOGY

A word about some of the terminology in the book. The personal name of God is conveyed in the Bible with the Hebrew letters *yod-heh-vav-heh*. It is a name that may ultimately derive from the verb "to be," but its exact meaning is unclear. Even the verse in which the Bible itself seeks to define its meaning—in the moment when God first calls to Moses, and Moses asks, "Whom should I say sent me?" (Exod. 3:14)—is worded differently by different translators. Some render the response in the present tense, "I am that I am"; others frame it in the future, "I will be that which I will be"; and still others submit that this verse is not a description of God per se, but rather a description of God's relation with human beings: "I will be with you in the way I will be with you." Each translation is a valid interpretation—all of these are possibilities of the meaning of God's name—so how does one convey this open-endedness in English?

There is a continuous Jewish tradition that the proper name of God is unpronounceable and a substitute is to be used, as a way of preserving its ambiguity. Commonly, scholars use the English equivalent of the Hebrew letters and refer to the biblical God as YHVH. I, myself, find that rather than conveying the Hebrew, this acrostic—having some evocative association in Hebrew with the verb "to be" but meaningless as it is to the English reader—is off-putting, a way of distancing the biblical God from the God contemporaries might believe in. I prefer to use either the word God, so that the continuity of belief between us and the Bible is maintained, or the practiced Jewish substitute for the name of God, *Adonai*, which I think more readily conveys the fact that this word is a name.

A second note: Hebrew nomenclature refers to the Five Books of Moses as Torah, meaning "instruction." Within the Five Books, the word can refer to a specific legal instruction, as in "This is the Torah [the instruction regarding] the burnt offering" (Lev. 6:2) or "This is the Torah [the instruction regarding] the leper for the day of cleansing" (14:2). In contrast, the book of Deuteronomy uses the term Torah to refer to that book itself. But since the Five Books were compiled into a single text, the term Torah has come to be used for the totality, the Five Books as a whole, and I have similarly used the word Torah in that way.

Finally, all English translations are taken from The Jewish Publication Society's *Hebrew-English Tanakh*.[3] I have, though, changed its use of "Lord" for the personal name of God to "*Adonai*" for consistency with the other mentions of God's name in the body of this work. On a few occasions it was necessary to rewrite the sentence in order to convey a gender-neutral rendering of the text.

CONCLUSION

I write as someone who is deeply committed to Jewish religious life. This book represents my own attempt to understand the nature and meaning of my religious commitments, as well as the historical sources of those beliefs. Through the writing I have rediscovered the powerful nature of the ideas each of these revolutions propounded. How wise it was for the biblical editors to preserve each of them with all their contradictions, for each can instruct us in its own way. I find the pluralism that Torah demonstrates to be helpful in speaking to me at different moments, in different moods. Equally, I find that its willingness to include a plurality of perspectives is itself a template for celebrating the contemporary differences within the Jewish community.

I hope that you as a reader experience the story of the formation of Torah as a great adventure. It is so for me.

The Book of Revolutions

Like the origins of most ancient peoples, the origins of the people Israel are cloudy, though ancient authors tell stories of that time that make them seem clear and straightforward.

The Five Books of Moses narrate the genesis of the people Israel, from Abraham's coming into the land from the north, to the birth and subsequent travails of the next generations: the descent of Jacob and his children to Egypt, where the people Israel grew into a nation while enslaved, and their eventual escape into freedom. After wandering in the desert for forty years, they wait expectantly to enter the Promised Land. The book of Joshua takes up where the Five Books of Moses leave off: that eponymous hero crosses the Jordan and conquers the land in short order. In this telling, the native population is decimated, and the twelve tribes, descended from Jacob and constituting the people Israel, divide the land on both sides of the Jordan River between them, carefully apportioning it among their clans.

But other books of the Bible give hints of quite a divergent history. The book of Judges, which also entered the biblical canon, tells a differ-ent tale. Here we meet many of the tribes and clans said to constitute the people Israel living alongside other peoples and nationalities in the Land of Israel. Non-Israelites sometimes fight against these Israelites, sometimes join with them. For instance, Deborah, one of the early leaders called judges, rallies several tribes to defeat a Canaanite ruler living in the northern city of Hazor whose army is led by its general, Sisera. When Deborah sends out the call to battle the enemy, only a few tribes join with her; others stay away. Some tribes are missing from the list altogether, not mentioned as either joining in the fray or staying at home. Most interesting, it is Yael, the wife of Hever, "the

Kenite," who invites the defeated and fleeing Sisera into her tent. Kenites are a non-Israelite clan, which is why Sisera feels safe hiding there. Yael kills him while he is sleeping, and Deborah sings her praise in her victory song, one of the oldest Hebrew poems. In the song, she decries the various tribes who did not join with her in the alliance: those living across the Jordan like Reuben, and those living along the coast like Dan. She never mentions some of the tribes we associate with the people Israel, including the tribe of Judah, supposedly one of the leading tribes, and the tribe of Manasseh. (Regarding the latter, she names instead two clans listed elsewhere in the Bible as children of Manasseh, Machir and Gilead, the latter said to be a son of Machir.) So, while tribes we associate with the people Israel do not join the alliance, some native populations such as the Kenites who live among the people Israel do ally with them. The glue holding the people Israel together does not seem to be very strong, and indeed, there is room to believe, as some scholars do, that not all the clans that would later be considered a part of the people Israel were incorporated into the whole as yet; the people Israel may have only gradually developed into what later became the twelve tribes. Indeed, according to the opening chapters of Judges, one of Judah's major clans is that of Caleb, the son of Yefuneh the Kenizite, a derivative name of the Kenites.[1]

Similarly, sometime later, the second book of Samuel records that Bathsheba, whom King David seduces, is married to Uri the Hittite, an officer in David's army whose house in Jerusalem is in sight of David's palace. According to the Bible, Hittites are one of the native peoples living in the land before the entrance of the people Israel, and in this story, we are witness to this Hittite, a prominent member of David's army, married to an Israelite woman. Judges makes this phenomenon explicit: "The children of Israel settled amongst the Canaanites, the Hittites, the Amorites, the Perizim, the Hivim and the Jebusites and they took their daughters as wives and they gave their daughters to their sons" (Judg. 2:5–6). In this telling, the people Israel intermix with native peoples. In the same vein, the book of Exodus, speaking of the entrance into the land, warns against adopting the customs of the native population. God cautions: "I will not drive them out before you in a single year, lest the land become desolate and the wild beasts multiply to your hurt. I will drive them out little by little, until you have increased and possess the land" (Exod. 23:29–30).[2]

The two accounts, in Joshua and Judges, are thus contradictory in many ways. Joshua talks about the complete defeat of the northern alliance of Canaanite peoples centered on the city and fortress of Hazor; in this account, the Israelite invaders, united and marching as one, completely destroy the city upon entering the land (Josh. 11:10). But in the time of Deborah, perhaps a century later, Judges describes Deborah calling the tribes to gather and free themselves from the domination of the Hazor kingdom.[3] Archaeologists have tried to reconcile the inherent contradiction in this telling, with no common agreement among them.

It must be added that the archaeological evidence does not support the history described in the book of Joshua. The major cities of Canaan were not destroyed at one moment. The settlements archaeologists identify as early Israelite are small clannish dwellings; early Israelites did not build or occupy major cities.[4] As such, the book of Joshua seems to be a later mythologizing of origins in which a distinct and unified people Israel composed of twelve tribal clans of common ancestry conquer the land in one sweep.

What, then, is the origin of this people? In the face of limited literary and physical evidence, contemporary scholars have advanced divergent theories that have failed to elicit common agreement.

We do know that the people Israel arose in the Land of Israel at a time of collapse of the great empires of the Near East. The tribes and clans that composed the northern tribes calling themselves Israel and the southern tribe of Judah may have come together as a nation at the end of the second millennium BCE and the beginning of the first millennium BCE, an era exceptional in the Middle East in that no large empires or superpowers dominated the international scene. (Early biblical history in the Land of Israel, what is called the premonarchal tribal period, dates from approximately 1200 to 1000 BCE; the beginning of the Davidic monarchy may be dated shortly after the year 1000 BCE.) Because of the absence of major imperial powers, these small tribes settled the land as they fought battles and skirmishes with their regional neighbors without outside powers deciding the outcome or themselves holding sway.

Scholars remain uncertain as to exactly why the end of the second millennium BCE was marked by the decline of empires (some offer climate change resulting in drought and economic collapse as an explanation). Egypt, still a great power, confined itself to its own borders during this period, receding from its overlordship of the important land bridge to the north, modern Israel and Palestine, which it had long dominated. The Hittite Empire, which had occupied what is today Turkey and whose influence had often extended further south, totally collapsed, replaced by local principalities and city-states; the northeastern lands of Assyria and Babylonia were in turmoil. Amid this power vacuum, undisturbed by the wars and conquests of great empires, the tribes and clans later known as the kingdoms of Israel and Judah grew to maturity. These peoples settled in the hill country and mountains that form the central spine of the land, in the central plain and the southern Galilee as well as on the eastern side of the Jordan River. Archaeologists have uncovered rural clannish settlements that we identify as Israelite. At the same time, with no major powers to stop them, invading Phoenicians and Philistines came by sea and settled along the coast.

Scholars have propounded different theories of the origins of Israelite settlement. One theory popular in the mid-twentieth century proposed that in the middle of the second millennium, when Egypt ruled the Land of Israel, natives seeking freedom from Egyptian domination may have fled to the hill country, the spine of the Land of Israel; and as Egypt withdrew control at the end of the second millennium, they may have expanded their territory and consolidated into a common confederation.[5]

More recently, archaeologists and biblical scholars have demurred from this account. The Israeli scholar Israel Knohl, who has made significant contributions to our understanding of the Bible, has offered a more complex theory: there were multiple groups of settlers who later united and identified as the people Israel. Trying to make sense of a variety of biblical materials, Knohl argues that these included migrating peoples from the north—perhaps impelled by the collapse of the Hittite Empire. Abraham is said to come from the north, and the biblical story emphasizes that members of his family went back to his homeland to find marriage partners. There was then a historical memory of this migration.

A second group, Knohl says, was constituted by the native Canaanites, who formed a significant segment of the emergent people; the two groups frequently intermarried or otherwise joined together in alliance. These peoples worshiped a pantheon of gods referred to by the plural *Elohim*, and believed in a chief god, referred to as *El* or by the genitive *Baal*.[6] (In the Bible, God is frequently called *El* or *Elohim*, while Baal is usually considered a foreign god.)[7]

Knohl theorizes that after Egyptians overthrew the foreign Hyksos dynasty—scholars believe the Hyksos were a Semitic people in the sixteenth century BCE, a time that may be identified with the stories of the biblical patriarchs—some of these Hyksos settled in the Egyptian Delta, where they had made their homes before seizing power. Their sovereignty over Egypt and their later exile may be the memory behind the biblical story of Joseph. Two centuries later, the Pharaoh Akhenaton led a brief monotheistic revolution.[8] After his death, Egyptians restored their older religion, but some Egyptians who had supported this revolution—possibly the Semitic peoples who had settled in the Delta—fled to the Sinai and Arabian desert, where their Egyptian monotheism was reinforced by people who practiced aniconic worship: the stones that constituted the center of their worship were not dressed or sculpted in any way. Recent archaeological discoveries have uncovered remains of nomads with this practice in the Sinai desert. Additionally, Egyptian archives preserve mention of an Arabian people who worshiped a God they named Yod-Heh-Vav-Heh.[9] Knohl notes that the Bible reports that Moses fled from Egypt to Midian (the Arabian desert), where his father-in-law is said to be a priest and where he receives his initial revelation including learning the name of God, Yod-Heh-Vav-Heh. A biblical song may contain a memory of this history: "God is coming from Teman [i.e., at the edge of the Arabian desert; Teman is the Hebrew name for Yemen], The Holy One from Mount Paran" (Paran, similarly, may be identified with the Arabian desert).[10]

These Egyptian refugees who later migrated to Canaan from the Sinai and the Arabian desert constituted a third element in the formation of the people Israel: a group that brought with them a new theology that gradually replaced the storm god Baal and the pantheon called *Ha-Elohim* of the northern settlers and native Canaanites. Note that in one biblical account, the name of God is not revealed until the time of Moses, and the patriarchs do not know the Divinity by this name: "I appeared to Abraham, Isaac, and Jacob as El Shaddai, but I did not make Myself known to them by My name yod-heh-vav-heh" (Exod. 6:3). This is borne out by the fact that people are not given personal names with *yod* and *heh* before the time of Moses (the exception is Judah, the eponymous ancestor of the south); instead, when the divine name is included in their personal names it is the generic "el," notably Israel — "el" is the common Canaanite name for a god. Thus, Knohl theorizes, a late group of immigrants possibly constituting the tribe of Levi may have brought this new understanding of God to the peoples who had earlier settled the land. The Levites, being latecomers, had no share in the land. Instead, they became defenders of the faith they brought with them, taking upon themselves the role of priestly servants to this single Divinity.

Finally, we might note that Genesis contains a hint of an alternative origin of the worship of God. The Hebrew Bible includes fragments of ancient myths, older histories, and folktales that depart from the central biblical narrative. For example, consider: "And to Seth, in turn, a son was born, and he named him Enosh. It was then that humanity began to invoke God by name" (Gen. 4:26). The text ascribes the name of God, *Adonai*, as having been invoked before the existence of the people Israel—Enosh is the grandson of Adam and Eve, living several generations before the Flood—but this understanding directly contradicts the biblical insistence that the name of God was only revealed to Moses, and not even to the patriarchs. Thus, the Pentateuch itself presents us with divergent accounts of the history of the worship of *Adonai*.

FROM CLANS TO KINGDOMS

Origins are shrouded in semidarkness, and while one or another of these theories may seem persuasive, they are ultimately speculative. But the biblical story moves on in time, and if we are to accept its own account, for a brief moment at the beginning of the first millennium BCE these clans and tribes came together under a unified kingdom, first led by Saul of the tribe of Benjamin and then by a rival dynasty founded by the Judeans, David and his son Solomon. Archaeology casts doubt on the biblical claim of the vast reach and achievements of the Davidic kingdom, causing some historians to wonder if David and Solomon are historical figures at all. Yet references to the House of David in extrabiblical sources support the historical reality of these biblical figures. Unification of the tribes may have entailed the telling of tales of common origin, and many scholars place the source of some biblical narratives—patriarchal stories, the Exodus from Egypt—to this period.[11]

Even if we accept the biblical account of the reign of David and Solomon, this unified kingdom lasted during the rule of these two kings but then fell apart. The relationships uniting these peoples were not strong enough to take permanent hold, and so after this initial period of unification, the kingdom broke apart into Northern Israel, comprising the bulk of the tribes, and the single tribe of Judea, which was eventually joined by the small tribe of Benjamin.

Northern Israel occupied the central plains and areas on both sides of the Jordan River as well as the southern Galilee; Judea occupied the hill country around Hebron and Jerusalem, sometimes extending its reign further south into the Negev. Local Philistine and Phoenician

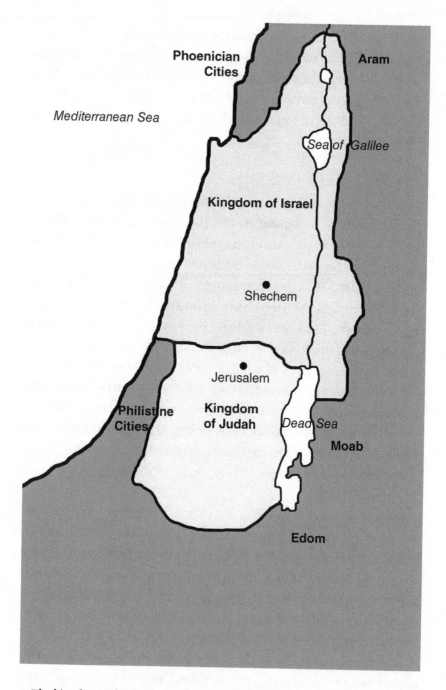

1. The kingdoms of Israel and Judah. Courtesy of Lisa Batya Feld.

city-states continued to occupy the coast. The two kingdoms, Northern Israel and Judea, though interrelated, were sometimes allies, sometimes warring enemies. We might well imagine what the relation of North and South would have looked like had the American Civil War ended with the South's permanently breaking away—the South would have preserved a sense of its distinctness even as it recognized its historical connection to the North; the two might have continued to contest each other for hegemony over North America. In like manner, though often rivals, Northern Israel and Judea retained a sense of kinship. The stories they'd fashioned during the time of the united monarchy, stories of origins, of patriarchs, of enslavement, and of desert wandering, were told and passed down on both sides of the new borders.

Archaeologists maintain that Judea's population was significantly smaller than the population of Northern Israel, perhaps only a tenth the size of its northern neighbor. (Interestingly, in the biblical calculation of the size of the tribes who left Egypt and traveled through the desert, Judah constitutes a little more than a tenth of the total.)[12] The lands in the north were always more fertile than the mountains of Jerusalem and Hebron; it is not accidental that major cities developed in the north but not in Judea. Although the Bible—edited at a later period when Northern Israel no longer existed—places Judea at the center of its attention, we can easily discern, by reading between the lines, that Judea during this period was always a minor player, frequently dominated by the North.[13]

Whatever expanse the tribe of Judah occupied in the time of David and Solomon's kingdom in the tenth century BCE was diminished in the ninth century BCE. In the Negev, south of Judea, the increasingly aggressive Idumeans (the tribes of Esau, Jacob's brother in the Bible) broke free of Judean domination and subsequently worked at expanding their frontiers, eating away at Judea's territory. Judea was also under constant threat to the west, on the Mediterranean coast, from Philistine city-states such as Ashkelon.[14]

The two kingdoms, Judea and Northern Israel, developed along different lines. Judea's royal dynasty came from the House of David; over its slightly more than four-hundred-year history, it was consistently ruled by a descendant of the House of David. Not so in Northern Israel. It retained a sense of confederation, and at different times kings traced their lineage to a variety of its constituent tribes. Dynasties were repeatedly overthrown, many almost immediately upon their founder's passing.

Jeroboam, a scion of the largest tribe, Ephraim, led the revolt against Solomon's son Rehoboam and established himself as the first ruler in Northern Israel. According to the biblical account, his son Nadab was almost immediately assassinated after his father's passing, Basha of the tribe of Issachar replacing him. After Basha's demise, his son Elah was assassinated by the head of the army, Zimri, who was in turn assassinated by Omri, the father of the first dynasty to last more than one generation. Omri's coup led to a protracted civil war with two army generals, Tibni and Omri, vying for power, both declaring themselves king. Eventually Omri was victorious, and although the Bible portrays the kings of the House of Omri in only negative terms, the triumph of his house ushered in a period of urbanization and economic prosperity that included his building a new capital in Samaria. The Bible doesn't mention Omri's tribal affiliation: perhaps this tribal anonymity, along with the establishment of a new capital, signaled his attempt to overcome tribal differences among the Northern clans. Archaeological evidence points to this dynasty as comprising the great consolidators and builders of the major cities of Northern Israel, and the remains of this period evidence increasingly sophisticated craftsmanship.[15]

Thus, during the ninth century BCE, Northern Israel was on its way to becoming a major regional power, and from this time on we increasingly have written records of other nations mentioning the kingdom. The marriage of Omri's son Ahab to the Phoenician princess Jezebel was a union of Northern Israel and the coastal city-state of Sidon, which had become a major sea power in the eastern Mediterranean. Goods produced by Northern Israel could now be trans-

TABLE 1. Kings of Northern Israel to Omri

Jeroboam I	928–907 BCE
Nadab	907–906
Basha	906–883
Elah	883–882
Zimri	882
Tibni	882–878
Omri	882–871

All dates are taken from Mordecai Cogan and Hayim Tadmor, *II Kings*.

ported overseas by the Phoenicians, and overseas goods imported into Israel—pottery from Crete, for instance, has been found in the hill country of Northern Israel. The union also ensured that Northern Israel could turn its attention to beating back threats on its northern border from the revived kingdom of Assyria. But the alliance, with its importation of foreign worship and imperial practices, brought down prophetic wrath, and the House of Omri was eventually overthrown by a revolution. Our first chapter will take up our story with the fall of the House of Omri and the prophetic role in its undoing. But we are getting ahead of ourselves.

It was Judea's sister state to the north, the newly prosperous Israelite kingdom, that would threaten Judea during the reigns of Basha and the House of Omri, even laying siege to Jerusalem. The Bible reports that Basha constructed ramparts outside of Jerusalem and was only deterred from capturing Jerusalem because of a sagacious and convenient Judean alliance with Aram, Israel's own northern enemy. During the reign of the House of Omri, Judea would become a vassal state and join in Northern Israel's wars, while Judea's prince would marry into Northern Israel's royal family, a sign of their subservient position: the prince who succeeded to Judea's throne married Ahab's sister Athaliah. So, though its dynasty was more stable than those of the North, Judea's dominion was much inferior. The book of Kings, written and edited considerably later, after Northern Israel had been defeated by Assyria and its population dispersed, offers hardly any acknowledgment of this reality.

In a later time, at the end of the eighth century BCE, the resurgent Assyrian Empire destroyed the Northern Kingdom. Some of its citizens, including priests and scribes, fled south to Judea. Thus, the northern and the southern traditions were eventually combined, and the Bible reflects this conjoined heritage, though since only Judea survived, it made itself the center of biblical history.

We will tell that part of our story later. For now, we focus our attention on a century after the breakaway from Solomon's son Rehoboam — that is, a century after the establishment of the two separate kingdoms. This is the narrative of the revolution that occurred in the North through prophetic leadership, which brought to power the dynastic line that ensured the exclusive worship of *Adonai* as the God of the people Israel.

It is at this moment, with the children of Ahab and Jezebel, and the fruits of the labor of the prophets Elijah and his acolyte Elisha, that our story begins.

Part I

Revolution in Northern Israel

1 Elijah's Victory

Jehu stood victorious, crowned the new king of Israel. His rise had been bloody, but he had been anointed by the prophet Elisha, successor to the famed Elijah. In front of his troops, he summarily killed Jehoram, king of Israel, and then had his troops assassinate Jehoram's visiting companion, his cousin Ahaziah, king of Judea. Jehoram had ridden out to see why his captain, Jehu, was coming toward the northern city where Jehoram was recovering from wounds inflicted on him in a battle against Aram (modern Syria). It was an ideal moment for a coup.

The biblical account depicts the scene in dramatic terms as taking place in the field of Naboth—the same field that Jehoram's mother, Jezebel, had seized after devising a criminal plot to kill its owner. Now, Jehoram and Jehu were meeting there for the last time. "Do you come in peace?" Jehoram asked. "How can I be at peace," replied Jehu, "when your mother carries out her countless harlotries and sorceries?" "This is treason!" Jehoram cried out to Ahaziah. Turning his chariot back to the city in flight, he was cut down by Jehu's spear; Jehu's troops then assassinated Ahaziah as well.

In the book of Kings, which narrates the history of the kingdoms of Judea and Israel, the stories connected with Elijah and his acolyte and successor Elisha are the most extensive of any of its stories of kings or prophets. Almost a quarter of the books of First and Second Kings concerns the exploits of these prophets and their confrontations with the reigning House of Omri, the great dynastic rulers of Israel in the first half of the ninth century BCE. The crowning of Jehu as king represents the culmination of Elijah and Elisha's prophetic ministries; the clash between kings and prophets during this era represents a critical turning point in the religion of Israel.

TABLE 2. Kings of Northern Israel from Omri to Jehu

The House of Omri

Omri	882–871 BCE
Ahab	873–852
Jehoram	851–842

The House of Jehu

Jehu	842–814

According to the book of Kings, Elijah's conflict with Omri's son Ahab and his wife Queen Jezebel is both a religious and a moral struggle. Ahab had desired Naboth's vineyard, which lay next to the palace. When Naboth refused to sell it, Jezebel used the courts and royal power to ensure that Naboth was falsely accused, convicted, and sentenced to death so that his field might revert to the monarch. Thus, in the biblical story, it is Ahab's wife, Jezebel, who advises the king and formulates the plot against Naboth. Interestingly then, the biblical author is careful to note that the person who counsels the king to commit the dastardly murder of Naboth is a foreigner who had brought "foreign gods" to Israel: foreign worship and unethical behavior are intimately linked in this story's telling. Elijah, the prophet of God, upbraids the king for this corruption of power and is, in turn, pursued by the king. The biblical depiction of the end of the House of Omri pictures that revolution as the overthrow of a morally and religiously degenerate regime; by placing the scene of the final defeat of this royal house in the field of Naboth, it creates a satisfying coda to this story.

Similarly, King Ahab's reign is the context for one of the Bible's epic religious battles: a sacrificial duel between Elijah and the priests of Baal on the hills of Carmel. After a long drought, the prophets of Baal pray for rain, but their prayers are unanswered. It is Elijah, who sacrifices and prays to the God of Israel, who brings salvation—the rains come. Yet, despite Elijah's seeming victory, he must run away. He describes himself as the only surviving remnant of God's servants;

Baal worship, purportedly imported by Ahab's wife Jezebel, remains a dominant religious element in Northern Israel during his lifetime. In the center of the Northern Kingdom, in Samaria, the new capital city that Omri had founded, Ahab built an altar to his wife's god, Baal;[1] Queen Jezebel was the daughter of the king of the Phoenician city of Sidon, and seemingly the local Phoenician gods have been imported into Israel. The Phoenicians, ruling in city-states along the coast, were important Mediterranean navigators who eventually founded Carthage,[2] an outpost in North Africa that would become powerful enough, in a later era, to challenge Rome. With the marriage of Ahab to Jezebel, the tribes of Israel who dwelt in the central spine of the land and the Phoenicians who occupied the port cities along the coast were now not only united by treaty and marriage but by common worship as well. Assimilating the gods of other peoples into the pantheon of divine beings was a common form of religious worship at this time. And the alliance made political sense: it protected Israel's western flank and cultivated an ally who would join forces against Israel's northern enemies, whether Aram or Assyria, which threatened its borders.[3] It also made economic sense in that the Phoenicians were a seafaring people, eventually setting up colonies and associations throughout the Mediterranean; imports and exports to and from Northern Israel passed through these Phoenician ports.

Elijah and his acolyte Elisha represented the forces that opposed the worship of gods other than the single God of Israel, and vigorously opposed the importation of a Phoenician god even though the severing of relations would have political and economic consequences. The two prophets stood for a new nationalism that would see the people Israel in distinct terms—insisting on a separation from its neighbors aimed at both a moral and religious regeneration.

Ahab died seemingly in battle, outliving Elijah, and was succeeded by his son, Ahaziah, who died within a year. His brother Jehoram ruled for a decade before Jehu spearheaded the revolution that overthrew him and the Queen Mother Jezebel, ending the House of Omri. As noted, the Bible's setting of the assassination scene in the field of Naboth emphasized the moral quality of the revolt and the fulfillment of the prophetic search for justice along with the single worship of the God of Israel. The Bible puts these very thoughts in Jehu's instruction to his troops: "Remember how you and I were riding side by side behind his father Ahab, when the Lord made this pronouncement"—that is, remember the prophecy that Ahab's house would be destroyed because of its immorality and religious syncretism.

Jezebel, Ahab's wife, was still alive and seemingly still a personage of influence—therefore, a powerful threat to the new regime. Queen Mothers were important in biblical times, as has been frequently the case in many cultures throughout the ages. Jehu sought her out in her redoubt on the Jezreel plain. As the book of Kings describes it, ever the imperious queen, "Jezebel...painted her eyes with kohl and dressed her hair, as she looked out the window." As Jehu victoriously entered the city's gate after having killed her son Ahaziah, Jezebel defiantly cried, "Are you at peace with yourself, Zimri [Zimri was the assassin of a previous Israelite king, who was defeated and killed within seven days of his having seized power by Omri, the founder of the dynasty now being overthrown], murderer of your lord?" The biblical historian then records, "[Jehu] looked up toward the window and said, 'Who is on my side? Who?' And two or three eunuchs leaned out toward him. 'Throw her down,' he said. They threw her down; and her blood spattered on the wall and on the horses, and they trampled her" (2 Kings 9:30–33). One can hear in the biblical passage the audience's appreciation of this violent death.

THE PROPHETS

As the Bible tells it, Jehu had been anointed as the appropriate avenger by the prophet Elisha (Elijah's apprentice), and so his revolution is seen not merely as a personal coup but a prophetic victory: a triumph in a religious war to restore the God of Israel as the center of worship over the foreign gods who had become popular objects of worship. Baal is a generic name for the god at the head of a pantheon of gods but not the more specific name of the god. In neighboring Tyre, the god who was worshiped was Melqart—identified in Hellenistic times with the Greek god Heracles[4]—and the worship of Melqart would later spread throughout the Mediterranean; perhaps this was the god whom Jezebel installed in Samaria. The Bible also mentions that the royal family promoted goddess worship; in Tyre and Sidon a goddess sometimes referred to as Astarte or her daughter was worshiped.[5] The biblical message that Jehu's victory represented a moral and religious rejuvenation of the kingdom after the degeneration under the House of Omri is apparent in Jehu's very name: Jehu is composed of the same letters as in God's name, *yod, heh,* and *vav.* In the mind of the biblical writer, Jehu's triumph was God's victory: the restoration of the central worship of the God of Israel and the installation of just and moral rule. It certainly set Israel on a course in which the Philistine pantheon would no longer be revered alongside or instead of the God of Israel.

In the ninth century BCE, Israel developed from a clannish agricultural society to one with major urban settlements. The Bible records the breakaway of Northern Israel from Judea as occurring fifty years earlier, following the reigns of David and Solomon, but it was during the reign of the House of Omri that Northern Israel achieved prosperity. Ahab ruled at the moment when Israel was transforming itself into an urbanized, prosperous society. His father, Omri, had founded the new capital of Samaria, uniting the Northern Israelite tribes in a common regime.[6] Archaeologists have confirmed the building projects in the era of the House of Omri, especially newly fortified and expanding cities. The book of Kings tells of the ivory palace and cities Ahab built and, significantly, archaeological discoveries support this aspect of the biblical account (1 Kings 22:39). Among the archaeological finds are beautifully carved ivories—the introduction of such fine craftsmanship far surpassing the crude ceramics that preceded this period—signaling newfound wealth. The story of the theft of Naboth's vineyard, told to exemplify the moral bankruptcy of Ahab's reign, also encapsulates the growth of royal power as well as the emergence of a wealthy leisure class, and the increasing chasm between the poor and the wealthy. The story illustrates the kind of corruption that history witnesses again and again in newly developing economies, especially those whose monarchs then accrue increasing power.

A few generations later the prophet Amos describes these conditions in Northern Israel by denouncing the women of the leisure class:

> Hear this word, you cows of Bashan
> On the hill of Samaria
> Who defraud the poor
> Who rob the needy;
> Who say to their husbands,
> "Bring, and let's carouse." (Amos 4:1–2)

> They lie on ivory beds,
> Lolling on their couches,
> Feasting on lambs from the flock
> And on calves from the stalls.
> They hum snatches of song
> To the tune of the lute—
> They account themselves musicians like David
> They drink from the wine bowls
> And anoint themselves with the choicest oils—
> But they are not concerned about the ruin of Joseph.
>   (Amos 6:4–6)

The impression we get from the biblical critique of Ahab and Jezebel is that conditions in their time—only a few decades earlier than that of Amos's declamation—were not all that different. Israel was a rising power, and the marriage of Ahab to Jezebel and the adoption of Phoenician gods sealed an alliance that had political, economic, and military motivations. The inclusion of the Phoenician god into the pantheon of Israel's divinities—whether as the head of the pantheon, Baal, or as a female consort—accorded with common economic and political interests. Cultural and religious syncretism could cement the mutually beneficial relationship.

In the minds of many, Baal and Israel's Divinity could easily have been thought of as one and the same, since in the ancient Near East, as well as in the ancient world generally, there was a tendency to identify and conflate the chief gods of a nation and the gods of other cultures. As we noted earlier, in a later time Alexander's conquests would lead to an identification of the Phoenician Melqart with the Greek Heracles. Native Canaanites, too, used the appellation "Baal" to describe the head of their pantheon. The story of Elijah and the priests of Baal demonstrates that the bulk of Israel's populace followed the priests of Baal. According to the Bible's account, Elijah and Elisha were swimming against the current, but Jehu's revolution and Elijah and Elisha's message sent Israel on a different route, distinguishing its God from those of other peoples. Rather than engaging in syncretism—seeing *Adonai* and Baal as one and the same, or both as members of a heavenly pantheon—the prophetic insistence on the exclusive worship of Israel's God differentiated *Adonai* from the surrounding heavenly beings, as if to say: we are a distinct people with a distinct God.

The prophets, beginning with Elijah, adopted this religious exclusivity with its attendant national sensibility, while simultaneously articulating a fervent sympathy for the developing underclass in an increasingly wealthy society; they understood that along with a demand for exclusive worship, the central concern of Israel's God was a moral one. To be sure, other nations also identified their gods with moral concern, but in the Israelite prophetic voice, this moral and religious focus was the single most important characteristic of the Divine. Nothing like this prophetic stance distinguished the other cultures of the time.

In their political outlook, prophets fall back on a premonarchal Israelite philosophy in which rulers derived their legitimacy from the common assent of tribal leaders. As we saw, when Deborah called for the tribes to engage in common defense, only some responded, while others chose to withhold their support of her leadership. At a somewhat later time, the Bible records that the prophet Samuel inveighed against the establishment of a monarchy. Israel was a confederation before it was a monarchy, and in the Northern Kingdom, unlike Judea to the south where the Davidic line continued for hundreds of years, monarchs and dynasties were repeatedly deposed. When Jezebel upbraided Jehu with the remark "son of Zimri," she was warning him that those who overturn monarchs can themselves be overturned. That, after all, had been the hundred-year history of Northern Israel. Jeroboam, an Ephraimite, was the breakaway founder of the Northern Israelite alliance but his son, Nadav, had hardly reigned two years when he was overthrown by Basha of the tribe of Issachar. His son Elah had hardly reigned two years when he was overthrown by a guardsman named Zimri. Zimri reigned for seven days before being overthrown by Omri.

Thus, monarchy in Northern Israel was an unstable notion, passing from one dynasty to another and from the scion of one tribe to another. That the monarch could be so easily displaced allowed for the development of the prophetic idea that monarchs could be judged by the degree to which the societal covenant had been upheld. Beginning with Elijah, the careers of the early recorded prophets whose messages have come down to us, Hosea and Amos, are centered on Northern Israel, not Judea; they speak to the changes taking place in that society and to the notion of a societal compact that the state embodied. Prophets in Northern Israel would challenge the legitimacy of monarchs and priesthoods.

TABLE 3. The House of Jehu

Jehu	842–814
Jehoahaz	817–800
Jehoash	800–784
Jeroboam II	789–748
Zechariah	748–747

The line of Jehu was the only Northern Israelite dynasty to continue for several generations: a dynastic rule of a hundred years. Jehu's great-grandson, Jeroboam II, would rule over what was in some ways the most splendid time in Israel, when its kingdom stretched from the Negev in the south to Damascus in the north. As the aforementioned quotation from Amos attests, the early part of this next century, the eighth century BCE, saw a continuation in Israel of the noted trends: increasing prosperity and urbanization, with a concomitant increase in the disparity between rich and poor.[7] Elijah and Elisha's successful revolution ensured that the prophetic voice would continue to be heard and revered even as some of the sins they decried—such as inattention to the needs of the urban poor—continued to be practiced.

JUDEA

During much of the rule of the House of Omri in Northern Israel, Judea was subservient to the North. The same was true during the later rule of the House of Jehu. To be sure, at the beginning, when Northern Israel itself was threatened at first by Aramean armies, and later by Assyrian forces, Judea was able to enjoy a measure of freedom.[8] Athaliah, Ahab's sister (there is some disagreement about the exact relation), ruled for six years in opposition to the revolution in the North, but that period soon ended. Hearing that her son had been murdered in the revolution's new order, Athaliah saw an opportunity to declare Judea's independence from Northern Israel—now controlled by Jehu, the person who had killed her nephew, her son, and her sister-in-law—and seize power, thus continuing the Israelite royal line of the House of Omri in Judea for six years after that dynasty had been wiped out in the North. Strikingly, like the rule of her brother Ahab, Athaliah's rule seems to have been especially tyrannical: the Bible asserts that she killed all the male princes of the kingdom. Joash, an infant, was somehow saved from this slaughter, and a countercoup installed him as king at age seven. In the intervening time, Athaliah, no doubt, had established the worship of foreign gods as official practice, a surmise we may glean from the report that her overthrow was orchestrated by priests, and Joash, perhaps reared by these priests, is remembered fondly for having renovated and restored the Temple in Jerusalem. Thus, the battle against Baal worship engaged both Northern Israel and Judea at the same historical moment.

Judea's independence was short-lived. The Bible tells that in the next generation, Amaziah, king of Judah, tried to break free of Israel's dominance during the reign of Jehu's grandson Jehoash in the early days of the eighth century, but Israel routed the Judeans, who fled. King Jehoash of Israel captured King Amaziah of Judah at Beth Shemesh. "He marched on Jerusalem and he made a breach of four hundred cubits in the wall of Jerusalem from the Ephraim Gate to the Corner Gate. He carried off all the gold and silver and all the vessels that there were in the House of the Lord and in the treasuries of the royal palace, as well as hostages; and he returned to Samaria" (2 Kings 14:12).

In other words, Judah was thoroughly defeated, once again becoming subservient to Northern Israel. Once the walls of its capital, Jerusalem, were ripped open, it could no longer defend itself or offer resistance, and it was forced to pay tribute to the North. Of course, the authors of Kings and Chronicles—surviving Judeans—were reluctant to convey the stark reality and would not say outright that Judah was, in fact, subservient to Northern Israel. But they did not hide some of the bare facts, perhaps because these realities were too well-known by their audience, and so they left us with enough hints to reconstruct this piece of the history of the two kingdoms: for a period of almost 150 years, with only some interruption, Judea was under the thumb of Northern Israelite rule.

HISTORICAL CONCLUSIONS

The main sources of the story narrated here—the two books, First and Second Kings (they are really one book divided because of length)—are as much works of literature as works of history. They present a point of view, not a neutral exploration of facts. We might well wonder if some of the biblical details of Jehu's revolution were enhanced by dramatic retelling. Did the final end of Ahab's dynasty really take place in the field of Naboth, or was this an ironic authorial expression punctuating the end of the Omri dynasty and the undoing of Ahab and Jezebel's progeny? Or perhaps the reverse: Did the final end come in the field of Naboth and an imaginative writer offers us a reason—a story with a moral—that could explain why it occurred there? Did Elisha send his servant to anoint Jehu in secret as the Bible records (2 Kings 9:1–14), or is this "secret" a way of according legitimacy to Jehu's seizure of power? The miraculous and magical tales with which the authors of Kings punctuate the prophetic careers of Elijah and Elisha—raising up the dead, rising to heaven in a fiery chariot—cause the historian to question the historicity not only of these events but of the entire story of these two prophets.

Yet we also need to acknowledge the archaeological confirmation of the dynasties that ruled during this period and of the growth of Northern Israel. Famously, the Moabite Stone, an inscription first discovered in 1868, mentions Omri and Ahab and the wars they fought; moreover, as noted earlier, archaeological excavations have uncovered extensive renovations and building dated to this period.[9] Assyrian inscriptions mention both Ahab and Jehu.[10] Some historians stop there and say that's all we can affirm about this period.[11]

Yet I believe the most persuasive argument for maintaining that the broad outline of events the Bible portrays is most likely historical is the internal evidence offered by these books. There is little doubt that the book of Kings was written—and edited and reedited—by Judeans. Throughout the work, Northern Israel is portrayed as sinful, while many kings of Judea are praised for their devotion to the Temple in Jerusalem and their upholding of religious worship centered on *Adonai*. So there is no reason for a subsequent author in Judea to glorify the House of Jehu unless one couldn't contravene certain well-known facts. Jehu overthrew Omri's dynasty—a dynasty that had grown so close to the Phoenicians that it imported some of its religious features—and the House of Jehu chose to glorify itself by identifying its victory with the restoration of Israel's national God, *Adonai*. Jehu may have used prophetic support to give his regime legitimacy, but included in that mantle of legitimacy was a nationalistic fight against the syncretism that had imported a Phoenician god or gods into Northern Israel. After excoriating Jehu's grandson, the Israelite king Jehoash, with the standard prose it uses to describe every king of Northern Israel, the book of Kings depicts Jehoash crying at the deathbed of the prophet Elisha (2 Kings 13:14). At least for the author of Kings, the loyalty of the House of Jehu to the prophetic purposes of Elijah and Elisha (Northern prophets) is unquestioned, and this from an author who wants to portray the kingdom of Northern Israel as sinful.

Kings portrays Elijah as imitating Moses. He is the only prophet who goes back to Sinai. He is transported there—a distance of forty days, we are told—by an angel. He stands in "the cavern" of the mountain and receives a revelation. The depiction is clearly a replication of Moses' vision on Mount Sinai; in effect, Elijah, a Northern prophet whose career is spent entirely in the North, is the new Moses. Though the southern Judean writer insists that Northern Israel was a sinful breakaway province, it could not be denied that a major revolution establishing the God of Israel had taken place in the North. That revolution was both political and religious and had such a profound effect that Judeans ultimately had to recognize they were inheritors of its outcome. Eventually, in the south, Elijah and Elisha came to be revered, recognized as the progenitors of the prophetic roles southern prophets later inherited. Elijah and Elisha, Amos and Hosea live on in our consciousness because southerners accepted the role these Northern prophets had played in shaping their own religious perspectives, even though by the time the book of Kings was written, the North had disappeared from history.

So the main outlines of the biblical account are entirely credible: as much as Jehu's revolution may have been a political victory, it was a religious revolution as well. And the Bible identifies that revolution as first of all a resistance to the syncretistic worship of Philistine gods alongside *Adonai*. Second, it understands that prophetic demand as tied both to the exclusive worship of *Adonai* and to a moral code. Elijah and Elisha not only worked to establish the single-minded worship of *Adonai* but also critiqued the corruption of justice on the part of monarchs and courtiers. The stories the book of Kings tells may be dramatic illustrations of these perspectives, imaginative literary constructions, but the revolution they depict was a matter of historical memory.

A NEW LAW CODE

That brings us to what I believe is one of the fruits of this revolution: the promulgation of the Covenant Code, the first biblical law code, found in Exodus 21–24.

One of my Jewish Theological Seminary professors, H. L. Ginsberg, convincingly argued that the Covenant Code is the work of Northern Israel, a view that has largely been adopted in biblical scholarship. Ginsberg was a shy, diminutive man and when I sat in his class, I had no idea how new and exciting his scholarship was. He mumbled his lectures, only looking down at his notes, never at the class, and today I regret reading the *New York Times* under my desk during his lectures. Only now, long after his passing, have I realized the significance of his contribution.

Especially crucial for Ginsburg's argument is that the religious calendar legislated in this legal portion of Exodus is that of Northern Israel. The laws of the pilgrimage festivals enunciated in Exodus 23 declare that the time of the ingathering of the year's produce—the final harvest—marks the end of the calendar cycle and the beginning of the new; in this accounting, the new year comes in the fall.[12] But Judea celebrated its new year in the spring, and indeed, in the final redaction of the book of Exodus, the author resident in Judea overturns the formulation in the Covenant Code and emphatically announces that the month in which the Exodus took place, the spring month, ought to be considered the beginning of the year (Exod. 12:1). That latter author elaborates in great detail the celebration of the Passover festival—a memorial of the Exodus— yet Exodus 23 knows nothing of a Passover festival, only a Festival of Matzot (the agricultural celebration of unleavened bread that is said to mark the Exodus).

There are other indications that the Covenant Code came from Northern Israel. We give the code this name because the code refers to itself as a covenant; it understands itself as an agreement between the people and God (Exod. 24). For the North, with its history of confederation, the notion of covenant between ruler and peoples was much more central than it was for Judea; the latter emphasized a monarchal view—if you will, a divine right of kings. In Judea, the covenant was understood to have been made between God and the Davidic line.

Other parts of the Bible demonstrate an origin in Northern Israel. The early prophets from Elijah and Elisha to Amos and Hosea were all Northern Israelites. Some of the narrative portions of the Bible also hint at a Northern Israelite origin. Jacob, renamed Israel, is the eponymous ancestor of the North. In Genesis, the location of his major revelation and of the main altar he builds is at Beth-El, the chief temple of the North, not Jerusalem. Similarly, many psalms refer to the people Israel by the name Joseph. Indeed, the longest and most complex narrative in Genesis centers on Joseph, who is father to Ephraim and Manasseh, the two chief tribes of Northern Israel. In the biblical story, Joseph takes leadership over his brothers and is given a double share of Jacob's inheritance—the symbol of the birthright. And the ancient audience could not have missed the political reference intrinsic to the story when all the brothers bow down to Joseph. Even if, on its surface, the narrative recounted a mythic past, the story would have made sense to its initial listeners because of its reflection of contemporary reality.[13]

During certain times in history, like the ninth and eighth centuries BCE in Northern Israel, cities grew, populations moved from farms and villages to urban centers, a developing economy attained sufficient resources to support a leisure class, and a national consciousness began to replace clan and tribal affiliations in importance. Such times frequently spurred the writing of national epics, the gathering of oral folk traditions, the weaving of these tales into an ordered narrative encapsulating a sense of national purpose. Similarly, the establishment of royal power often brought with it new administrative procedures, the appointment of judges, and the need for uniform law. What may have constituted case law at an earlier time—decisions of local courts or elders—could now become the subject of a uniform national code. The need for a common law can especially be associated with the rise of centralized rule, such as monarchy, and the development of urban culture. All this was true of this moment in Northern Israel's history.

Finally, there is a most significant reason for dating this code to this time: the exclusive worship of Israel's God is a central element of this code, and we are told it is at this time that this ideology comes to dominate Northern Israel. It is Jehu's revolution, associated as it is with the triumph of Israel's God, *Adonai*, which births this code and its religious demand (the specifics of which appear in the next chapter). To be sure, the code includes materials from earlier times; it is a collection of law, not simply a promulgation of a certain moment in history.[14] But its editing and its theology and its moral concern reflect the revolution wrought by the prophets Elijah and Elisha and the House of Jehu.

A word about what a code of law may have meant in the ancient Near East. Promulgation of a code may not have meant that it then became the law of the land. Instead, it may have simply involved the erection of monuments with inscriptions of the words of the code in public places, so that people could see the announced principles upon which the regime stood. Courts and local officials may have had their own traditions of behavior that were not fully in accordance with these directives. Certainly, many areas of law requiring adjudication were not covered by the Covenant Code, notably among them domestic law, relations between husband and wife. Yet the code's public prominence would have offered a religious and moral ideal that remained a challenge to local authorities.[15]

How was it that the Covenant Code reflects Northern Israelite ideas and ideals, yet ultimately was preserved as part of the heritage of

Judea? Through what process did the developments in the North seep through to Judea? Perhaps when it was essentially a vassal state, Judea adopted Northern Israel's code, and when Judea became independent, the force of the history of the preceding century was too great to completely overthrow this tradition. Perhaps the code was never formally adopted but remained an important model, a precedent of sorts, since ironically, when Northern Israel was destroyed, priests and scribes who fled before the Assyrian invaders brought the code south. Judea modified its inheritance from Northern Israel but never fully departed from it, and so it was preserved, though Judea would soon try to emend it with some of its own traditions. In the end, Judea took for itself the name Israel, and Judea's Divinity was worshiped as the God of Israel.

And so, when the Northern Kingdom of Israel disappeared from the historical stage, Judea survived to tell the biblical story from its own viewpoint. In our day, though, archaeology and literary scholarship help us read between the lines. Jews may be the descendants of the people of Judea, but they are known as the people Israel. In Northern Israel, a revolution spurred by prophets effected the exclusive worship of *Adonai*; and in carrying out this revolution, the House of Jehu promulgated the Covenant Code centered on this belief. The kingdom of Israel shaped the Jewish people's early religious legal history, as well as much of its narrative and self-understanding; and, as we will see, the Covenant Code, the creation of Northern Israel, set the pattern for all future biblical legal codes.

Having placed the code in its historical setting, we now proceed to analyze it.

2   The Covenant Code

In the book of Exodus, following the story of the Exodus from Egypt, we encounter an extensive law code, the revelation of which culminates in a dramatic ceremony. This is one of three general law codes included in the Pentateuch (the other two are found in Deuteronomy and Leviticus), and scholars agree that it is the oldest.[1]

The narrative as it unfolds in chapter 24 is clearly the work of many hands, a pastiche of several different versions of the story.[2] At times Moses is the central character, and he is pictured as ascending the mountain alone; at times "the seventy elders" join with Moses; at times the people as a whole are addressed. But central in this chapter is the idea that what is being celebrated is a covenant—a mutual agreement between God and the people Israel. Moses descends from the mountain and describes to the people the law that he has received, here called *mishpatim*/judicial ordinances, and they agree to obey it: "Everything of which God has spoken we will do" (24:7); and as a sign of the covenant, the blood of a sacrifice is sprinkled on the altar and on the people. Describing this moment, the Bible calls the agreed-upon code "the Book of the Covenant" (24:7) (in the ancient Near East, the word in Hebrew, translated as "Book," referred to any kind of writing).[3] Just as in this moment the Bible refers to these laws as *mishpatim*, so, too, at the very beginning of the enumeration of the laws, the Bible announces, "These are the laws/*mishpatim* which you shall put before them" (21:1), thus framing the content included in the Covenant Code.

The laws enumerated in Exodus 21–23 emulate the common legal traditions of the Near East, though seen through a more egalitarian Israelite lens and adding a distinct ethical and religious stamp to the common Near Eastern inheritance. Much of the content of this legislation, the civil code that constitutes the first half of this document, is clearly related to other ancient Near Eastern law codes archaeologists have uncovered, such as the Babylonian Code of Hammurabi as well as fragments of Hittite law. (The Hittite Empire, centered in southern Turkey, flourished during the latter part of the second millennium; the Bible mentions Hittites as one of the Canaanite peoples.) These law codes represent the common commercial and criminal legal understandings of their time and place. Many of the specific situations covered in the Covenant Code are similarly detailed in both of these non-Israelite sources. For instance, both the Covenant Code and the Code of Hammurabi deal with the different punishments or fines due in the case of injury to a slave or freeman. Similarly, both codes talk of the payment owed when a pregnant woman is injured and loses her baby. In this latter case—injury to a pregnant woman—almost the same wording appears in the Hittite codes and Exodus.[4]

The differences between the codes prove to be equally of interest. Unlike the Code of Hammurabi, Exodus's law does not emphasize class distinctions; rather, there is much more of a sense of the equal worth of every citizen. For example, the murderer of a slave receives the death penalty in the Covenant Code, while in Hammurabi's Code the killer may substitute a monetary payment. In light of this, one can say that the Covenant Code's formulation of "an eye for an eye" as a fundamental principle of law—murder must be punished by the death penalty, no matter who the injured party is—represented an important equalizing of all citizens in their representation before the bar of justice, though full equality was not completely achieved in this code. Crucially, unlike other Near Eastern codes of law, no special status or rights are given to nobles, communal leaders, or elites of any kind; they are treated like common citizens.

Another similarity between the Israelite code and its precedents is the style of legal rhetoric. The characteristic form of legal expression in the ancient Near East is casuistic law—that is, the law is phrased in "If... then..." clauses, for example, "If the defendant had done such and such, then his punishment is x"; sometimes a "but" is inserted— "but if the consequences were otherwise, then..."—in which case a different punishment is offered or acquittal is mandated. This was the characteristic legal rhetorical style employed throughout the ancient Near East, formulated so that judges deciding cases would know the different specifications under which the law applied. While the law itself does not identify its intended recipients, most likely it was the political and judicial elite, those who would have had to execute the law. Indeed, in one version of the covenantal ceremony described above, a governing elite—Moses, Aaron and his sons, and the seventy elders—go up the mountain to celebrate the revelation (Exod. 24:1,9), and we can imagine that the chief audience of this part of the code was the political and judicial elite, those who would have had to execute the law.

Until we get to the latter half of the Covenant Code, almost the entire subject matter, and certainly all those laws phrased in the formulaic "If... then...," may be dubbed secular, for their subject matter comprises torts, contracts, and criminal law. These are matters of concern for any ordered society: personal injury, theft, regulations of guardianship, and so on. The stated punishment, to be administered by the court system, is monetary payment or physical retribution. The first half of the code never calls for the involvement of a priesthood or specifies any religious ritual, such as sacrifice, as an atonement.

RELIGIOUS AND ETHICAL TEACHING

After this enumeration of common civil circumstances and penalties, suddenly the rhythm of the Covenant Code is interrupted, and we are no longer in the realm of judicial process but of personal and religious ethics.[5] At first, we have a series of apodictic statements denouncing certain idolatrous practices: witches and those who have intercourse with animals (might we presume that this is part of some religious ritual?) are to receive the death penalty (22:17); sacrifices are only to be offered to *Adonai* (22:18). Then the legislator turns to a wider audience that includes the entire populace and at first announces a law that is phrased like the earlier ones, with "If … then …" clauses: "You shall not ill-treat any widow or orphan. If you do mistreat them, I will heed their outcry as soon as they cry out to Me, and My anger shall blaze forth and I will put you to the sword, and your own wives shall become widows and your children orphans" (22:20–23). This is quite different from the previous formulaic legal clauses, both because the punishment is to come from God, not from any earthly authority, and because it is not a punishment targeting an individual person but rather encompasses and holds accountable an entire people. The legal formula we are so used to from the earlier section is now used to inculcate a moral injunction, enforced not by earthly authorities but by divine intervention.

In the same fashion, the very next law, while also an "If … then …" clause, departs both from the language and substance of what came earlier. "If you lend money to My people, to the poor among you, do not act toward them as a creditor; exact no interest from them. If you take your neighbor's garment in pledge, you must return it before the sun sets; it is the only available clothing—it is what covers the skin. In what else shall [your neighbor] sleep? Therefore, if that person cries out to Me, I will pay heed, for I am compassionate" (22:24–26). Here, too, the punishment will not come from a judicial process, especially so in the latter case, since it is nightfall and the poor person could not even in theory appeal to any court—the judges having gone home—but the punishment will come from God. By the same token, in the first case, regarding interest on a loan, though the two parties might agree about the arrangement, and therefore the situation might never come before the court, the practice is excoriated, nevertheless, since interest should never be charged: loans should be freely available; the poor should not be taken advantage of. While the earlier laws are judicially enforced, note that in regard to these ethical matters not subject to legal procedure, God is to be the ultimate guarantor of justice, because it is God who sees all and will exact punishment when the courts are unable to do so. While earlier in the code God is referred to in the third person, here God is clearly the speaker describing the nature of divinity in the first person: "I am compassionate."

These latter laws are preceded and followed by a series of simple sentences, beginning with the exhortation that "whoever sacrifices to a god other than *Adonai* shall be proscribed," and moving on to the affirmation that the people shall be a holy people and not eat torn animal flesh found in the field. The statements are categorial—"Do not . . ." They are instructional, direct, and delivered with absolute and single-minded authority, not with the more passive and abstract language of "If . . . then . . ." The code here has become a religious document, and this religious thrust is now inserted into the judicial system: an instruction to witnesses not to give false testimony and an instruction to judges not to follow the rulings of a majority when they know that they are wrong. These ethical and religious instructions are simultaneously directed to the entire people and to the political elite.

Interestingly, the injunction to be holy concerns an animal killed in the wild whose meat should not be eaten (22:30). Presumably, the killing and butchering of domestic animals took place ritually in the local sanctuary and the consumption of meat by any Israelite would have been limited to that which had been sanctified.[6] The stated consequence of eating or touching the meat of an animal that had been killed in the wild is that one becomes impure and must wash to cleanse oneself. Here too, though, this is an act with religious consequence: there is no priestly supervision, only individual responsibility. This understanding, that individuals have personal religious responsibility, will be a central feature of the later Holiness Code in Leviticus.

When the Covenant Code finally does return with an instruction phrased as a casuistic clause, it does so, once again, with a moral message, and so we are told: "If you encounter your enemy's ox or ass wandering, you must take it back to him. If you see the ass of your enemy lying under its burden and would refrain from raising it, you must nevertheless raise it with him" (23:4). Again, we are clearly not in the judicial realm, but on the road, amid everyday life, in the private decision-making of individual citizens. The law asks us to help even our enemies: their goods ought to be restored; and when people we encounter need an extra hand, they ought to be able to call on our sense of obligation to a common community, even if they are strangers or we normally see them as an enemy.

The code moves to its conclusion, delineating the holiday seasons, and then exhorts the people not to adopt local pagan gods as they come into the land. The land will be conquered only slowly—there is a recognition that peoples will be living side by side—and the ideal frontiers of the state are defined. There is a promise of a "divine messenger"/*malakh* who will lead the people into the land. They are being led to a land where they are to exclusively worship *Adonai*; indeed, the message that the people are to exclusively worship *Adonai* punctuates this section throughout.

We can well imagine that the code is an assemblage of materials collated by an authority bringing together earlier case law that had developed among the elders and the tribes and fusing these laws with the religious understanding that now became the articulated ideology of the Northern Kingdom. Thus, the code is a compendium of materials from disparate sources, but reflects the understandings that coalesced in this moment of time.

What distinguishes this law code, first of all, is its ethical bent. While other Near Eastern codes differentiate between nobles and freemen, the Covenant Code makes no such distinction. Even slaves are treated as persons, though there is some differentiation between their status in the law and that of freemen. The exhortations at the end of the code affirm the ethical behavior demanded of each individual, even when there can be no judicial enforcement. A distinction is made between the Israelite and the foreigner, especially in the slave law, but even one's "enemy" deserves kind behavior. Even the stranger—that is, the nonnative, or noncitizen—should not be oppressed. Secondly, the code is not simply a civil code regulating judicial processes and everyday behaviors of people: it is a code that demands the exclusive worship of the God of Israel. Civil and religious law are intertwined.

The Covenant Code is particularly insistent on the exclusivity of worship of the God of Israel: "Whoever sacrifices to a god other than the God of Israel shall be proscribed" (Exod. 22:19). "Nor should the name of any other god pass from your lips" (23:13). It accordingly ordains the proper service due God: it orders that the gifts to the sanctuary from the harvest not be delayed, and that the firstborn of humans and of animals be dedicated to God (22:29).[7] Further, it adds the element of personal holiness we have just remarked on: that the people themselves are to reflect God's holiness and are made impure by hunting animal flesh in the wild (22:30).

From a theological perspective, it should be noted that the code's insistence on the exclusive worship of God does not negate the reality of other divine beings. It is Israel's duty to worship its God, and no other, though other nations may worship their own god or gods. It is only *Adonai*, not any other divine being, that one should worship, though there is much evidence—archaeological and even inner biblical evidence—that Israelites believed in a variety of divine beings.[8] And as we noted, again and again in the code, there is an insistence that a chief characteristic of Israel's God is concern with the ethical, demanding of justice for all and the protection of the poor.

There is a ritual component to the code. The festival cycle should be observed; the timing is tied to the agricultural year, with the exception of the Festival of Matzot/unleavened bread, which is tied to the Exodus from Egypt. Each of the festivals is to be observed by gifts offered in the sanctuary. The gifts of first fruit should not include a kid cooked in its mother's milk (23:19),[9] perhaps a reference to a fertility rite practiced in the region and therefore another exhortation against foreign cultic practice, but one that, in itself, contains an ethical teaching. Interestingly, though, no priestly roles are mentioned.

The code emphasizes the maintenance of an ethical community, rhetorically expressed as proper care for the widow, the orphan, and the stranger (22:20–23) and by the decent treatment of those who need to borrow money (22:24–26). The standards of the court system itself are scrutinized—they must be fair and just. One should not swear falsely or take bribes or favor any party—even deserving ones (23:1,2,6,7,8). The code goes on to institute a unique provision for the poor and for animals: every seventh year, you should avoid planting your own seed, and let the poor and animals into your fields to harvest their needs (23:10–11). Similarly, work should cease every seventh day so that foreign workers, your servants, and your animals can rest (23:12). Some have argued that this is not yet the law of the Sabbath day, but rather an instruction to employers to count one day in seven as a rest day.[10] Significantly, this law is not given a theological foundation; it is not a celebration of Creation as it is in later biblical texts, but rather a means of creating a caring society in which workers of every sort are not turned into endlessly toiling slaves.

Finally, it is important to note that the parallel Code of Hammurabi is a law code given by a king to his people. In both its preface and epilogue, it extols the person of the king, Hammurabi. The Covenant Code is given by God; it extols no king or ruler as an author of law.[11]

As we can easily see, elements that the book of Kings emphasizes as critical to the prophetic message of Elijah and Elisha—the exclusive worship of the God of Israel, the insistence on ethical behavior, and the insistence that God rather than any earthly authority is the ultimate guarantor of justice—are critically important to this code.

THE COVENANT CODE AND THE REVOLUTION OF THE HOUSE OF JEHU

As the previous chapter demonstrates, this code is clearly the work of Northern Israel, and the political and economic conditions of the late ninth century BCE seem like the probable moment for the publication of this legislation. It is most reasonable to place the promulgation of the code in the time of the dynasty of Jehu. There is scholarly agreement that the code represents a time when the tribes are already settled in the land, and while it incorporates early material, it represents a fusion of different sources. It is unlikely that the code would have been promulgated in an earlier time, before the extensive urbanization that took place in the ninth century or before the unification of the tribes and clans. The House of Omri, the first stable dynasty, would hardly have legislated the exclusive worship of the God of Israel.[12] The biblical account of the ideological bent of the Jehu regime and the religious ideology underpinning the code are in accord. The Covenant Code is the party platform of the new regime.[13]

Deuteronomy, a code published later in Judea (see part 2), clearly bases itself on this code while rewriting sections and adding other new materials. It would not have done so unless this code had achieved some popular or official status earlier on. Since, as we will show later, Deuteronomy itself is the work of the seventh century BCE, this work must have achieved its official status much earlier.

So all the evidence points to this code as having been promulgated by the monarchy in Northern Israel and as having been assimilated by Judeans—either because Judea as a vassal state was forced to adopt it, or because Judeans chose to imitate their more powerful Northern brothers, or because Northerners streaming into Judea brought this code with them. The code reflects the religious and ethical principles fought for by the prophets Elijah and Elisha. Thus, the very revolution instigated by these two prophets in Northern Israel resulted in the first law code recorded in the Bible. And central to its authoritative role is the very idea of covenant, a critical political concept of Northern Israel.

The code itself ascribes its publication to Moses. Undoubtedly the code draws on earlier precedent going back to a tribal past. Indeed, the prophets themselves claim to be the conveyors of traditional Israelite religion, not innovators of a new faith. But as we have seen and will show again and again in this work, other kinds of worship—worship of God's consort, syncretic inclusion of other gods in a divine pantheon, for instance—could also claim to be part of ancient Israelite tradition. Indeed, these objects of divine worship were clearly popular—Elijah, after all, has to go into hiding, unsure of any following. What triumphed with the revolution of Jehu was a prophetic vision: Israel stood in relation to Israel's God, *Adonai*; the two were attached to each other, covenanted with each other. Israel's God demanded exclusive worship, the exercise of uncorrupted justice, and the formation of a society in which the least among them was cared for. In return, the people Israel would receive God's protective care. God will be "an enemy to your enemies" (23:22) and "God will bless your bread and your water and will remove sickness from your midst" (23:25). The code is a fusion of the culture of the Near East, the new reality of an increasingly wealthy Northern Israelite confederation, and prophetic ideals. This fusion creates a new national consciousness, a covenanted relation between Israel and its God. If the people Israel remain loyal to this covenant, God will protect them. God and Israel are related to each other, covenanted with each other. Indeed, the latter prophets in Northern Israel, Amos and Hosea, would describe the covenantal relationship as that of husband and wife, or parent and child, metaphors for the most intimate of relationships.

3 The Heritage of the Covenant Code

The revolution that the Covenant Code embodies impacted all subsequent biblical legal thinking—indeed, all later Jewish thought down to our own day. The exclusive worship of *Adonai* conjoined with injunctions for the moral and religious ordering of society became a template for all biblical and postbiblical codifications. And the concretization of Israel's values in law became a feature of other biblical revolutions as well as, later, Judaism. These are critical components of biblical understanding, and they are essential foundations of Jewish theology.

THE COVENANT CODE'S INFLUENCE ON SUBSEQUENT BIBLICAL AUTHORS

As I will show, Deuteronomy and the Holiness Code in Leviticus both revise and expand the themes first enunciated in the Covenant Code; equally, almost every sentence and phrase of this final section of the Covenant Code became significant for later Judaism. To give one example: Deuteronomy quotes, with only a single word change, Exodus's formulation of the need for justice. "Do not take bribes, for bribes blind the *clear-sighted* and upset the pleas of those who are in the right" (Exod. 23:8) becomes "Do not take bribes, for bribes blind the eyes of the *wise* and upset the pleas of those who are in the right" (Deut. 16:19b).

Sometimes Exodus, Deuteronomy, and Leviticus can seem like they are in dialogue with each other. Thus, Exodus exhorts against taking interest from a fellow Israelite, especially the poor: "If you lend money to My people, to the poor among them, as a creditor, exact no interest from them" (Exod. 22:24), which Leviticus then phrases in its own way: "If your kinsman, being in straits, comes under your authority and you hold him as though a resident alien, let him live by your side: do not exact from him advance or accrued interest" (Lev. 25:35–36a). In other words, if you charge interest to a fellow Israelite, you are treating the lender as if he or she were a stranger. Deuteronomy picks up this theme, expanding the notion of lending to include food as well as cash: "You shall not take interest on loans to your countrymen, whether money or food or anything else for which interest may be taken, but you can take interest from loans to foreigners" (Deut. 23:20–21a). Notice, too, how what is a critical but simple phrasing in Exodus, stating that the law applies only to fellow citizens, "If you lend money to My people, . . ." becomes a source of literary elaboration in the later texts. Thus, Deuteronomy, echoing Exodus, states the negative—not to charge interest "to your countrymen"—then emphasizes: "You can take interest from foreigners." Leviticus turns this thought into a metaphor, saying that if one of your fellow citizens needs a loan, they have become like "a resident alien," a status to which no peer should fall. We can well imagine the scribes of Deuteronomy and the priests of Leviticus having the text of the Covenant Code in front of them and shaping their own codes with this prior model in mind, mining each paragraph and each word for inspiration.

As we can easily see, both in its general theological stance and in its particulars, the Covenant Code put its strong stamp on all the later biblical revolutions (discussed in subsequent chapters). Themes that are first introduced with brief mention in the Covenant Code, such as the holiness of all Israel, the celebration of a sabbatical year, as well as the larger effort to shape societal law in light of prophetic themes of ethical behavior and exclusive worship of the God of Israel, become essential elements of later biblical legislation. The Covenant Code incorporated into a law code religious and prophetic values, a perspective that was adopted by these subsequent iterations of biblical law. And it set the people Israel in a direction that typified all of its later thinking: the understanding that law should embody the unique ethical and religious values that characterized this people. Moreover, later tradition furthered this idea and made law into the central instrument by which the critical values of this people were expressed.

Equally, one of the most important ways in which the Covenant Code informed subsequent Jewish thinking was the very notion of covenant, and it is this theological idea that I want to focus on. As we discussed earlier, one of the central moments of the code's promulgation is the conclusion in Exodus 24:1–11, where the people proclaim, "All that God has spoken we will do," as Moses reads aloud "the record of the covenant" (verse 4). The people are then symbolically sprinkled with blood, and after Moses reads the words of the code aloud, he announces, "This is the blood of the covenant which God has made with you regarding all that has been spoken" (verse 5). The law is a solemn agreement, a covenant, a pact, entered into directly and freely between the people and God. The people have made God their lord, much as other peoples may have made human rulers and monarchs their overlord. The covenantal summary toward the end of the code in Exodus 23 enunciates the sense of reciprocity between God and the people: "You shall serve the Lord your God and God will bless your bread and your water. And I will remove sickness from your midst. No woman in your land shall miscarry or be barren. I will let you enjoy the full count of your days" (Exod. 23:25–26).

The code formulates a relationship of mutuality between God and the people Israel, much as was known throughout the Near East between peoples and other tribes, or between a tribe, a clan, or a nation and a king or overlord. On the people Israel's side, the obligation incurred by the covenant is behavioral: a just society, an ethical life, an observance of religious ritual, the exclusive worship of *Adonai*. In return, God assures that the land and the people will be fecund, and the people will be protected. God is substituted for human agency as the ultimate ruler, and it is the recognition of this that births the covenant.

This concept—the mutuality of responsibility inscribed in a covenant—
shaped subsequent Jewish theology throughout the generations. The
covenant represents an obligation entered into by both sides: Israel
agrees to serve God through a life of worship and proper behavior
and God agrees to enter into relation with this people. This is the
way Rabbinic Judaism described the relation between God and the
people Israel. As much as the covenantal relationship obligates the
people Israel, the sages of the Talmud and Midrash see the idea of
covenant as a way of humanizing God, obligating God, as well. Thus
in interpreting God's forgiveness of the sin of the Golden Calf and
God's revelation to Moses of God's attributes of mercy, the Babylonian
Talmud remarks:

> The verse states, "And the Lord passed by before him, and pro-
> claimed, 'Adonai, Adonai! God, compassionate and gracious, slow
> to anger, abounding in kindness and faithfulness, extending
> kindness to the thousandth generation, forgiving iniquity, trans-
> gression and sin'" (Exod. 34:6). Rabbi Yohanan said: "Were it not
> explicitly written in the verse, it would be impossible to say this:
> it teaches that the Holy One wrapped the divine self in a prayer
> shawl like a prayer leader and showed Moses the order of the
> prayer. The Holy One said to him: Whenever the Jewish people
> sin, let them act before Me in accordance with this order, and I
> will forgive them."[1]

Because of an ambiguity in the biblical phrasing, one can easily
understand the subject of the opening words "and proclaimed" as
either Moses or God. The Talmud prefers to choose the latter opinion, and so it interprets the verse as God speaking and modeling
prayer for human beings. The Talmud goes on: "Rabbi Judah said: 'A
covenant was made regarding the thirteen attributes that they will
not return empty-handed, meaning that if one recites them, one will

certainly be answered, as it is written, "Behold I make a covenant"' (Exod. 34:10)."[2]

The Talmud is quite explicit in laying claim to the covenant as having obligated God as well as the people. If we repent and turn to God in prayer, God will certainly be forgiving, for that is what God has agreed to. Always, there is a mutuality—if we turn to God, God will respond, for God has obligated the divine self to stand in relation to this people when they, in turn, fulfill their obligation.

This talmudic idea was incorporated into Jewish liturgy. It finds itself in a central penitential prayer recited on every fast day: "God, you taught us how to recite the Thirteen Attributes of Your name, remember the promise implied in these Thirteen Attributes, which you first revealed to Moses. . . ."[3]

Other prayers capture the strength of this idea of covenant and demonstrate how it persisted as fundamental to Jewish self-understanding. For instance, a prayer that speaks of human vulnerability, recited on the evening of Yom Kippur, has the recurring refrain, "Look to the covenant, not to the prosecuting angel."[4] This medieval prayer pleading for forgiveness—like so many others—insists that the covenant between Israel and God is eternal and that God offers abiding protection to this people, guaranteeing an ongoing relationship: sin should not be considered as abrogating the covenant when we turn back to God.

The idea of covenant is so central to Jewish self-understanding that Jews, to this day, may refer to themselves as *b'nai b'rit*, members of the covenantal community.

CONTEMPORARY THEOLOGIES OF COVENANT

In our own time, the idea of covenant remains a central concern for many twentieth-century and contemporary theologians. The Orthodox thinker David Hartman entitles a volume enunciating his personal theology *A Living Covenant* and sees the idea of covenant as central to his outlook, though he offers a noteworthy understanding of the meaning of the covenant today. He argues that in entering into the covenant, both sides circumscribe their activities. God has agreed that human beings have responsibility for what occurs on earth, and so God, in turn, withdraws from history. It is the human responsibility to enter into history and create God's kingdom on earth, an understanding of responsibility that defines the Jewish people. In each generation, human agency is charged with bringing the world closer to the Creator God. It is the human who unites heaven and earth, for God has handed over to human beings the responsibility for culminating the process of creation by forming a just society, a life reaching toward God. The people Israel have a special place in this schema in that they uphold this idea of human obligation.

In Hartman's view, the law is not fixed but given over to human authority to make judgments as to what will fulfill this mission. That is the ongoing responsibility of covenant—to bring our society in closer accord with the justice and kindly love that characterize the Divine, to make the law fulfill its prophetic inspiration. God, in turn, promises that as the people Israel perform this function, God will continue to be in relation to them. This is a thoroughly modern interpretation of the covenant, yet its roots are clearly in the biblical tradition.

Hartman offers marriage as a metaphor for the relation between God and the people Israel. Marriage is a relation of closeness and intimacy and that is what the individual Jew may feel as he or she fulfills his or her responsibility to God.[5] Hartman writes: "Unlike the metaphors of God as king and father, the metaphors of God as the loving husband, the devoted teacher, do not require reward and punishment to play a significant role in the covenantal relationship . . . the integrity of both partners is recognized, and the human partner is enabled to feel personal dignity and to develop capabilities of responsibility."[6]

The notion of covenant is thus captured in its most intimate form, marriage—two people agreeing to live out their lives with each other, the two obligated to each other. God and Israel exist in this relationship. It is an adult relationship in which each recognizes what Hartman characterizes as each other's "integrity" and "personal dignity." And so, the theology of covenant that Northern Israel set in motion and for which the Northern Israel prophet, Hosea, first offered the image of husband and wife continues its long-lived history.

Describing the meaning of Judaism for liberal Jews today, the late Reform theologian Eugene Borowitz centered one of his last works on the notion of covenant, announcing this perspective in the very title of the work: *Renewing the Covenant: A Theology for the Postmodern Jew*. Borowitz argues that the ongoing relationship between God and the Jewish people continues, and that Jews in entering into a relationship with God need to understand that they are under obligation. How moderns comprehend that obligation may differ from their ancestors in particular ways, but the covenant obligates Jews to root their quest for God in the texts and traditions of the Jewish past and in relation to the entirety of the Jewish people today. The covenant is made with a people, and the notion of covenant forces us to go beyond individual spiritual quests and to see our relation with God as involving the people Israel as a whole, both horizontally—those who live alongside us, and vertically—the past and future of this people. A Jewish understanding of religion, according to Borowitz, does not simply involve a personal notion of salvation, an individual quest, but incorporates a sense of obligation, on the part of the people Israel and on the part of God. The covenant is an expression of the mutual love between God and the people Israel, and all relationships of love issue in obligation. It is for each of us to engage with the tradition and with our fellow Jews to arrive at an understanding of how we ought to stand before our God. The obligation is a collective responsibility to be both rooted in the tradition and in our own contemporary sense of the ethical.

Borowitz's theology maintains both an acceptance and critique of key elements of contemporary society. On the one hand, he affirms our society's individual decision-making, its assertion of personal autonomy; he recognizes that fact, and even blesses its gifts. On the other hand, he insists that Judaism is a collective enterprise marked by a common history and dedicated to perpetuating the future of this people. Insofar as we enter into Jewish life, we recognize the limits of individualism, give up a measure of our independence, and accept an obligation beyond ourselves to God and to this people. Indeed, he argues, extreme individualism fails to recognize the needs we humans have for community, for empathy, for common care. In vouchsafing larger commitments than individual fulfillment, Judaism conveys a message important for the larger society to hear.

This sensibility, both that we find blessings in the culture in which we live, but also critique it and set ourselves apart from it, is an underlying motif of the Covenant Code. As biblical scholarship has shown, the code was influenced by the common legal traditions of the ancient Near East, assimilating its language and some of its legal perspectives, but also departed from them, fashioning laws that expressed the unique values of this newborn community. That process of both utilizing elements of the surrounding culture and transforming those elements to create a specifically Jewish path was the ever-again task Jews took up in their history.

In a remarkable essay, the late historian Gerson Cohen calls this the blessing of Jewish assimilation. Jews, he argues, have continuously borrowed from the surrounding cultures and have used the new learning, the new attitudes, to fashion a creative and ever-renewing Judaism. The philosophical and poetical works of medieval Judaism, influenced as they were by Muslim culture, are just some of the examples he offers in support of this thesis.[7] Indeed, both Hartman and Borowitz, in pointing to the way Jews today may imbibe understandings from the general culture and, in turn, contribute ethical and social insights relevant to the larger society, stand in the crosshairs first viewed in the Covenant Code. The covenant implies that who we are today is not to be cast aside in favor of some ancient image of piety, but rather is to be brought into relation with the worship of the Divine and the ethical behavior with which God instructs us and desires that we and our society reflect.

Covenant as a central organizing principle of Jewish theology animates contemporary feminist thinkers as well. Theologian Rachel Adler, professor emerita at Hebrew Union College–Jewish Institute of Religion in Los Angeles, sees the idea of covenant as a means to reconstruct Jewish ritual and law. She argues that the ancient Jewish marriage ceremony with its focus on acquisition—the man taking a bride, the bride entering her husband's realm—violates our contemporary commitment to gender equality. She proposes a marriage ceremony based on the idea of covenant—*brit ahuvim*—a covenant of lovers. But in her understanding, it is not only the two partners who are party to the covenant; they are also covenanting with the people Israel, to establish a Jewish home, and with God, to live sacred lives. This inclusive sense of covenant obligating individuals to each other, to the larger community, and to God captures some of the sensibility animating the Covenant Code, which similarly emphasizes the ethical obligations of people to each other, to the community, and to God.[8]

The Covenant Code casts a long shadow.

THE LATER BIBLICAL STORY

The history of Israel moved on. Northern Israel did not last as a kingdom; it was conquered by Assyria and its inhabitants exiled from its land. The Judeans in the south were the ones who survived to write the history of this people and edit the books that became the biblical canon. The passages in Exodus 34, revising some wording regarding the dedication of the firstborn, and those in Exodus 12, emphasizing a different religious calendar and diverse aspects of the Passover celebration, reflect Judean amendments to the law. Indeed, that process of refining and reinterpreting is the beginning of the work that led to the promulgation of the two subsequent law codes: Deuteronomy and the Holiness Code in Leviticus. While the initial model for Judea's legislation may have come through Northern Israel's mediation of the common tradition of the ancient Near East, what happened now was increasingly an internal development, both a reassertion of older Judean practice and a refining of the Covenant Code to accord with theological insights and perspectives that developed in Judean prophetic, priestly, and royal circles.

Even while Judea would later reassert its native institutions, the Covenant Code influenced the formation of its law. By the time Judea regained its full independence, it had been subservient to the North for more than a century, and during this time the Covenant Code had become part of Judea's theological heritage. Judea was stamped by the religious legacy of Northern Israel, by the fruits of the revolution that Elijah and Elisha had set in motion. Ever after, the God of the Jewish people would be known as the God of Israel and the people referred to as the people Israel, despite the fact that both the religion and the people were preserved in Judea.

A century and a half after the dissemination of the Covenant Code, Judeans substituted a law code of their own: the book of Deuteronomy, promulgated in the reign of the Judean king Josiah. It transformed the Covenant Code and moved Jewish religiosity in directions that sometimes emphasized and intensified the intent of the Covenant Code, but in other cases, as we shall see, modified it and transformed its meaning. Deuteronomy reflects a different theology of covenant, a different relation between God and the people Israel. The dependence of the book of Deuteronomy on the Covenant Code can be readily traced, as can its innovative spirit. This is the next revolution to be described, the subject of the next section, but to get there we have to tell Judea's intervening history.

Our story now turns south, to Judea.

The House of Jehu had triumphed in Northern Israel, slaughtering all of Omri's dynastic descendants. Meanwhile, according to the biblical account, after Ahab's sister Athaliah, the Queen Mother of Judea, learned that Jehu's troops had also killed her son (who had joined with his cousin, Israel's King Jehoram, in battle), she seized power in Jerusalem. Fearing for her own life—her son, nephew, and sister-in-law had been killed in the first wave of battle, and Jehu, upon seizing the throne, had wiped out the entire Omri male line—Athaliah, in turn, killed off the entire male line of the House of David.

The biblical account relates that Athaliah brought with her the worship of Phoenician or Canaanite gods consistent with her family's practice, and set up an altar to Baal in a separate temple in Jerusalem. We are told that a dissident coterie of priests and royalists had seemingly saved an infant of the Davidic line from being assassinated like his brothers and cousins, spiriting him away so that Athaliah could not murder him. Six years later, when the baby, Joash (short for Jehoash; the full name includes the opening letters of the name of God and means "God has given"), turned seven years old, the High Priest Jehoiada declared the boy king, led an uprising that seized power from Athaliah, assassinated her, and destroyed the temple of Baal.[1]

During Joash's minority, royal rule devolved on this priestly cabal. And, having been raised and educated by these priests, when he reached maturity, Joash supported the priestly cause. In fact, the book of Kings describes an elaborate plan Joash devised to repair the Temple in Jerusalem and thus even outdo the priests in his devotion.

Kings praises Joash and his descendants as rulers who "did what was righteous in the eyes of *Adonai*." It isn't until the reign of Ahaz, almost a hundred years later, that the book of Kings has anything negative to say of this line of kings other than that they permitted local worship to continue.

TABLE 4. Rulers of Judea from Athaliah to Hezekiah

Athaliah	842–836
Joash	836–798
Amaziah	798–769
Azariah (Uzziah)*	785–733
Jotham**	758–743
Ahaz	743–727
Hezekiah	727–698

*Amaziah was wounded in battle and his son, Azariah, ruled alongside him for some of his reign.

**Jotham, the son of Uzziah, ruled as regent during his father's lifetime.

That's the story the narrator of the book of Kings tells. It's a story of domestic religious harmony instituted in Judea with the assassination of Athaliah and lasting for a century.

Not so the history of this period as told in the book of Chronicles—a book written much later than Kings, and which often uses Kings as one of its chief sources. At first, Chronicles parallels the book of Kings in telling the story of Joash's coming to power. Indeed, the language in the two accounts is virtually the same; only minor differences occur. But then the Chronicler drastically departs from this tale, describing how after the demise of the High Priest Jehoiada, Joash radically changed religious policy: "But after the death of Jehoiada, the officers of Judah came, bowing low to the king; and the king listened to them.

They forsook the House of *Adonai*, God of their fathers, to serve the sacred posts [*asherot*] and idols" (2 Chron. 24:17–18a).

If we are to believe the Chronicler, we can extrapolate that earlier Athaliah had not acted alone, that her policy of worshiping multiple divinities was popular with many. Indeed, the Chronicler now portrays representatives of the populace asking the king to allow for this multiple worship. The author of Kings may have wanted to represent Judea as being faithful in the single worship of *Adonai*, but the Chronicler chooses to tell a fuller tale.

What we might imagine, then, is a factional dispute. There were those who argued for religious purity—the single worship of *Adonai*—a view, as portrayed in Kings, espoused specifically by the High Priest and those associated with him in the Temple. Others, however—even other priests?—believed that multiple divine forces needed to be worshiped.

Similarly, the Chronicler tells us that in the next generation, Joash's son, Amaziah, led Judea in victory against its southern neighbor, Edom, and that Amaziah then installed an icon of the Edomite gods in the Temple in Jerusalem, "bowing and burning incense before them" (2 Chron. 25:14). The reasons for this are obscure. Might this be a statement regarding Edom's vassalage, the Edomite god being subject to *Adonai*? Or is this yet another example of religious syncretism, a peaceful settlement between two peoples allowing them to live side by side, their gods dwelling in the same temple? The reasoning may be hidden behind a historical veil that hangs over much of this period, but surely it represents an acknowledgment that multiple divine forces were worshiped within the Temple precincts, contra the assertions of the book of Kings.

Again, according to the Chronicler, royal power appears to have been unstable and factionalism seems to have dominated the politics of Jerusalem. Even the book of Kings admits that Joash was assassinated after being defeated in battle with Northern Israel. His son Amaziah was defeated once again by Northern Israel, and according to the Chronicler—but not the author of Kings—he, too, was assassinated. Succeeding Amaziah was his son Uzziah—whom, on the whole, the Chronicler praises, but then describes Uzziah's being stricken with leprosy while vying with the High Priest, insisting that the monarch could offer his own sacrifice in the Temple. Uzziah's son Jotham ruled as regent in place of his sick father and then succeeded him. The Chronicler then describes Jotham's son, Ahaz, saying of him that he

> followed the ways of the kings of Israel; he even made molten images for the Baals. He made offerings in the Valley of Ben-hinnom and burned his sons in fire, in the abhorrent fashion of the nations which the Lord had dispossessed before the Israelites. He sacrificed and made offerings at the shrines on the hills and under every leafy tree. *Adonai* his God delivered him over to the king of Aram, who defeated him and took many of his men captive, and brought them to Damascus. He was also delivered over to the king of Israel, who inflicted a great defeat on him. (2 Chron. 28:2–5)

Thus, while the book of Kings seeks to underscore the legitimacy of the House of David and offers us a long list of kings "who did what was right in the eyes of *Adonai,*" the Chronicler reveals a darker and more complex picture of these hundred years. Both books, though, end this period by describing the heterodox practices of the reign of Ahaz. (Kings also denounces Ahaz, although with a somewhat less elaborate list of sins.)

From our vantage point, the Chronicler's portrayal of these times appears more realistic. It seems less likely that for a hundred years proper worship was restored in Judea and then suddenly under Ahaz questionable practices were instituted. More likely this was a period of constant flux in which various factions continued to argue over what constituted proper religious practice. These theological battles would have centrally involved the Temple priests, who play crucial roles at critical moments in both histories. We can imagine these arguments as centering on whether Israel's God demanded exclusive worship or whether there were many heavenly powers to be propitiated. Was worship in the "high places" an acceptable part of traditional religious practice, or was divine worship to be confined exclusively to the Temple in Jerusalem?

Religious struggles were reflected in political battles. Factions fought each other for power. At different times different factions won out and were supported by royal favor, for although both Kings and Chronicles lay blame and praise at the foot of each king, it is hard to believe that kings acted alone. As the Chronicler reports, kings could be assassinated if they made decisions that offended powerful elites. Political factions, foreign alliances, were linked with religious outlooks, and the Jerusalem priesthood was certainly a player, though not always the most influential one, in determining outcomes.

These were times of political and religious ferment. Among the various factions were local priests serving in local temples who maintained their individual traditions. Popular folk religion differed from both prophetic and priestly norms. Even among the priesthood in Jerusalem, there may have been disagreement over what constituted proper worship and what required religious reform, for we know—and will shortly demonstrate—that even the Temple precincts included images paying homage to more than one heavenly force.

During this time of turmoil, we can well imagine that priests began to write down what they prescribed as ordained worship. In the book of Leviticus, we find phrases such as, "This is the Torah/teaching regarding the whole offering" (Lev. 6:1) and "This is the Torah/teaching regarding a person who has a scaly disease" (14:32)—individual teachings regarding aspects of worship and ritual purity. We would best envision individual scrolls, or individual tablets that describe an aspect of worship.[2] We are not yet at the moment of a compiled set of rules, but rather of many different tablets and scrolls. At this time, what constitutes divine worship is being debated and written traditions are probably only beginning to play an important role.

In the North this is a time of great prosperity. Although at first, during the reign of Jehu, Aram was able to defeat Northern Israel and seize some of its territory, over the next two generations the dynasty strengthened itself so that Jeroboam II reigned over the most extensive lands and the most prosperous period in Northern Israel. This is when the prophets Amos and Hosea excoriate the nobility for having created a society that ignores the needs of the poor, and those driven from the land. The book of Kings reluctantly credits Jeroboam II with having pushed the boundaries of the kingdom to its greatest extent, "from Lebo-Hamath to the sea of the Arabah" (2 Kings 14:25). Archaeologists identify Lebo-Hamath with Labweh in northern Lebanon near Baalbek, and the sea is the Dead Sea. Never before had Northern Israel occupied these extensive boundaries.[3]

During these hundred years from the reign of Athaliah to where our story picks up, Judea came under the influence of the religious culture of the North, which repeatedly subjugated—and even sacked—Judea. Possibly it was at this point, while the South was under the vassalage of the North, that Judea adopted the legal tradition centered in the North. Certainly, priests and scribes of the royal court were aware of the code that the North had adopted.

There is evidence that Judeans tried to edit the code in order to incorporate their own traditions. The book of Exodus records, "This month [that is, the month in which the Exodus took place] shall mark for you the beginning of the months; it shall be the first month of the year for you" (Exod. 12:2). The Exodus took place in the spring, in the modern month of Nissan. The North, however, celebrated the new year in the fall, as the Covenant Code itself asserts (23:16), so we are witness to a Judean assertion of its own calendar over against that of the North. Similarly, the ambiguous declaration in the Covenant Code, "You shall give me the first born of your sons" (22:28)—which may be either a call for the sacrifice or mock sacrifice of the firstborn or an assigning of a priestly role to them—is refined in 34:20: "You must redeem every first born among your sons." When "redemption" is mentioned in the Bible as a matter of law, it indicates a monetary payment.[4] In other words, the text calls for a monetary gift rather than the actual dedication of the firstborn. The Jerusalem priesthood was entirely hereditary, while in the North the priesthood may have included those who were dedicated to and schooled for that role. For example, Hannah's son Samuel, an Ephraimite—that is, a member of one of the chief tribes that later constituted the Northern Kingdom (1 Sam. 1:1)—served as an acolyte of Eli, the High Priest. In this light, redemption of the firstborn makes sense as a Judean emendation of a Northern practice. Thus, over time, the Northern code embedded in Exodus 22–24 appears to have been refined in Judea to accord more with both Judean traditions and movements of religious reform.

Jehu's revolution, which resulted in his dynasty's promulgation of the Covenant Code, took place in Northern Israel in 842 BCE; the story we are about to tell takes place in Judea a hundred years later, in approximately 735 BCE. After years of domestic turmoil and foreign wars, after having been defeated by a coalition of Aram and Northern Israel, Ahaz is king in Judea. What follows is a rollercoaster of religious reform and the reinstitution of worship of many divine forces— generations at war with each other.

Out of this ferment emerges a voice announcing the single-minded devotion to the God of Israel—the book of Deuteronomy.

Part II

Revolution in Judea

4 Years of Turmoil

Ahaz, king of Judea, saw his chance.[1]

Fifty years earlier, the army of Northern Israel had laid siege to Jerusalem, broken through its walls, exacted enormous tribute, and held Ahaz's great-grandfather captive; now, in 735 BCE, Northern Israel had joined with Aram, its neighbor, to once again lay siege to Jerusalem. It appeared the combined armies might be strong enough to capture the city as they had fifty years earlier. Tightening their stranglehold, the invaders killed one of Ahaz's sons and several courtiers who were leading troops in the field (2 Chron. 28:7). But Ahaz saw a way to break free of the threat. The era in the Middle East when the tribes and clans that composed Israel and Judea had formed national entities—the end of the second millennium and the beginning of the first millennium BCE—was exceptional. No large empires or superpowers had dominated the international scene. But now, after this period of imperial hiatus, the age of empire had returned. By the latter half of the ninth century BCE, the Assyrians, occupying some of what is now modern-day Iraq, had reunified their kingdom and created the governmental institutions that were to make them into the mightiest power of their time. From then on they posed a threat to their southern neighbors, Aram, Israel, and the Phoenician city states along the coast. With the ascension of Tiglath-pileser III to the throne in 745 BCE, the Assyrians were once again on the march, but during these early stages of his reign, Aram and Northern Israel combined to successfully resist Assyria, halting its march. Feeling empowered, they furthered their own efforts to dominate the region, invading Judea. Simultaneously, Edom in the south, which had long been subject to Judea, reclaimed much of the Negev. Thus, in 735, Jerusalem was once again under attack by a coalition of its neighbors who were at the very doors of the city (2 Kings 15:5; 2 Chron. 28:5–8).

But at this juncture, seeking salvation from the threatened slaughter, Ahaz grasped an opportunity to break free of Northern Israel's grip: he aligned himself with Assyria in the latter's war against Aram and Northern Israel. His move was politically astute. By entering into an alliance with this mighty empire, he judged, correctly, that Assyria could defeat his enemies and Judea might survive. Judea, aligned with Assyria, could free itself from Northern Israel's domination:

> Ahaz sent messengers to King Tiglath-pileser of Assyria to say, "I am your servant and your son; come and deliver me from the hands of the king of Aram and from the hands of the king of Israel, who are attacking me." Ahaz took the gold and silver that were on hand in the House of *Adonai* and in the treasuries of the royal palace and sent them as a gift to the king of Assyria. The king of Assyria responded to his request; the king of Assyria marched against Damascus [the capital of Aram] and captured it. (2 Kings 16:7–9)

Both the books of Kings and Chronicles understand that Ahaz's turn to Assyria was a necessary political alliance on Judea's part to fend off the encroachment of enemies on all sides — not only that of the northern alliance of Israel and Aram, but the loss of territory to the south, including Eilat, to a resurgent Edom.[2] Chronicles adds that the Philistines to the west had moved up from the coast and subjugated much of the coastal plain, including Beth Shemesh, to their rule.

Ahaz made an astute calculation in reaching out to Assyria for help and subjugating himself to this expanding empire. Northern Israel, which had aligned itself with Aram against Assyria, had overreached, and the siege ended. In the next two decades, Northern Israel lost increasing areas of its territory to Assyria and, shortly after Ahaz's death, was completely defeated, with much of its population carried away into exile. Judea survived.

Though Judea had freed itself from Northern dominance, it was now a client state of a powerful imperium: Assyria. The biblical historian relates that in 732, after the capture of Aram's capital, Damascus, by the Assyrians, Ahaz traveled there to greet his new ally, Tiglath-pileser, and pay tribute:

> Now when King Ahaz went to Damascus to greet Tiglath-pileser, King of Assyria, he saw the altar in Damascus; whereupon King Ahaz sent a model of the altar and a plan with all the details for its construction to Uriah, the priest. Uriah, the priest, built the altar according to the directions which the King had sent from Damascus. . . . As for the bronze altar which had stood before God, he moved it from the front of the House. (2 Kings 16:10–11,14)

Ahaz had traded one master for another, and, in throwing off the political and cultural hegemony of the North, adapted himself to the culture of the new Assyrian overlord. The copy of the baroque Assyrian altar, perhaps even including the decorating symbols and representations of Assyrian divinities, replaced the simple bronze one that had traditionally occupied the Temple courtyard. Seemingly, this was just one of many innovations, all of which were instituted "on account of the King of Assyria" (2 Kings 16:18).

It was not only the imitation of Assyrian culture and style that was now given free rein. Older practices that may have been suppressed in earlier reigns emerged in the open. The book of Kings praises Ahaz's father and grandfather for "doing what was right in the eyes of *Adonai*," but the biblical historian particularly notes that Ahaz copied the ancient practice of "passing his son through the fire."[3] This may be a stock phrase used to discredit the monarch rather than a true historical report, but other accusations are perfectly believable. The Chronicler remarks that the regime now encouraged the revival of necromancy, that is, approaches to the dead, and similarly, the prophet Isaiah, a contemporary witness, excoriates Judeans for the pact they have made with the dead. This accords with the archaeological evidence of ancient Judean burial practices—crypts supplied with food and jewelry. The querying of the dead might be condemned by some, but as attested by the scene in the book of Samuel in which the witch of Endor raises Samuel from the dead to inquire of him, Judeans did believe that the dead could be addressed and foretell the future (1 Sam. 28). And as I will elaborate later in this chapter, the symbols and worship of multiple divine forces—even if they were thought to be secondary to *Adonai*'s supreme power—had been adopted in Jerusalem, even in the Temple courtyard.

Ahaz's nationalistic victory that gained Judean freedom from Northern Israelite domination thus, simultaneously, led to the increase and revival of the worship of multiple divine beings and objects. During the 150-year period in which these polylatric (worship of many divine forces) and polytheurgic (rituals aimed at influencing the many divine forces) religious practices prevailed, a constant struggle between supporters of these practices and religious reformers ensued.[4] The latter sought a pure and single-minded worship of the God of Israel; the former wanted to return to the worship of the many intermediate divine and semidivine beings that had been the folk norm of ancient Judea; still others saw no difficulty in assimilating multiple gods, whether of native Canaanite or foreign origin, and other heavenly powers to the religion of Israel. Although in general the biblical literature that has come down to us represents the triumph of those who promulgated the single worship of the God of Israel, there is some evidence, even in the Bible, of more "heterodox" beliefs among the populace. In various places the Bible acknowledges multiple divine forces even as it asserts the ultimate power of *Adonai*. The book of Psalms makes reference to a "council of the gods/*adat el*" (Psalm 82:1), and Psalm 89:7 alludes to the existence of many divine beings: "For who in the skies can equal *Adonai*, can compare with *Adonai* among the divine beings/*bnei elohim*."

For some among the members of the Jerusalem priesthood, the exclusive worship of Israel's God was the sole object of reform. For others, like the literary prophets, the religious ideology of exclusive worship of *Adonai* was joined with a critique of political and social elites out of deep concern for justice and social equity. The struggle between contending religious forces — religious reformers insisting on the exclusive worship of the God of Israel versus those who worshiped multiple divine energies and beings — played out with one generation instituting reform and the next undoing its work. Prophets added economic and social issues to the mix. The wrestling for power between these forces defined these years. Thus, during the last almost century and a half of the First Temple period, power shifted back and forth between these factions until exile fundamentally changed the context of Israel's theological understanding.

TABLE 5. The last Judean kings

Ahaz	743–727 BCE
Hezekiah	727–698
Manasseh	698–642
Amon	641–640
Josiah	639–609
Zedekiah	596–586 (Jerusalem destroyed)

The biblical account traces this seesaw battle through the generations. Ahaz, as mentioned, authorized a variety of "heterodox" religious practices. Hezekiah, Ahaz's son and successor, took the kingdom on a radically different course, breaking the alliance with Assyria and instituting religious reform. Hezekiah's son and successor, Manasseh, who came to power when he was twelve, re-cemented the alliance with Assyria, and in his reign "heterodox" worship the reformers had sought to wipe out was practiced again. Manasseh's son and successor, Amon (is it accidental that his given name was that of an Egyptian god?), was assassinated after a reign of two years and his son, Josiah, age eight, was put on the throne. Josiah, the great reformer whose accomplishments we will shortly detail, fell in battle with the Egyptians. But his sons and successors undid his work of reform and reinstated polyatric and polytheurgic practices—including, we are told, child sacrifice.[5] At which point this almost 150-year chronology takes us down to the exile of Judea to Babylonia and the end of the First Temple monarchy.

The extreme differences in religious outlook and practice, the swings in religious practice between one royal generation and another over such a long period of time, indicate that there existed in Judea a fundamental split between reformers and those who combined belief in the God of Israel with practices that religious purists opposed. As alluded to earlier, although the books of Kings and Chronicles lay these policy differences at the feet of the different Judean monarchs, it cannot be the case that the distinct policies regarding religious practice instituted by these royal figures were merely the expression of their own personal preference. Rather, they must have represented the clash of differing opinions among both the elite and the populace within the nation: each side must have represented a sizable faction, and each could claim that it exemplified the "true" tradition of the Judean past.

One way these differing factions in the kingdom could make their voices heard was in the choice of successors. Kings had multiple sons from many wives, and so there were many possibilities as to who could succeed a dead monarch. Indeed, in Assyria, wars of succession were the norm in almost every generation. Reading between the lines, we can deduce from a variety of biblical hints that there existed a plurality of political institutions that influenced the choice of a new monarch in Judea. Along with the monarch, at various times "elders," the "people" (perhaps some representative group not explicitly named), and the Queen Mother, among others, are mentioned as determining the succession. Assassinations were not unheard of, and several times minors were chosen as successors, so that at the beginning of their reigns the country was served by regents and the new king could grow to maturity under the tutelage of the forces that had gained power. Thus, the radical political and religious swings under the reign of each new Judean monarch during the last century and a half of Judean history likely represent the triumph of contending political and social elites who had momentarily gained the upper hand. Only exile would put an end to these religious battles.

The author of the book of Kings accuses Northern Israel of engaging in the full litany of "heterodox" practices: "They rejected all the commandments of *Adonai* their God; . . . they made a sacred post [*asherah*] and they bowed down to all the host of heaven, and they worshipped Baal. They consigned their sons and daughters to the fire; they practiced augury and divination" (2 Kings 17:16–18a). What is translated here as "sacred post" is the worship of God's consort, and the "host of heaven" refers to a pantheon of divine beings.[6] The reference to Baal may imply a syncretism of local or foreign gods and *Adonai*, as might have been the case in Judea with Ahaz's installation of an Assyrian altar in the Temple in Jerusalem. One can understand that the Judean author of the book of Kings might traduce the North with a standard list of "detested" practices, but what is interesting is the author's subsequent addition: "Nor did Judah keep the commandments of *Adonai* their God; they followed the customs that Israel had practiced" (2 Kings 17:19). The writer of Kings must admit that the very beliefs and practices for which he excoriates the Northerners were practiced equally by Judeans; Judea was not any "purer."

One might even suspect that this Judean historian traduces the North with the sins of Judea, but that Northern Israel may well have had a purer sense of religious worship than the Judeans. After all, it was in the North that prophets had free rein. And it was the North that had published the Covenant Code with its insistence on the exclusive worship of *Adonai*. The Judean author might disparage the North, but it was his own home ground that nurtured the "sins" he excoriates.

THE REIGN OF HEZEKIAH AND THE INSTITUTION OF RELIGIOUS REFORM

Ahaz ruled for sixteen years. His son, Hezekiah, came to power toward the end of the eighth century BCE, just as Assyria was completing its conquest leading to the exile of Northern Israel, and so Hezekiah inherited a kingdom much transformed by the new political situation. Because of the conquests of Assyria and the encroachment of its neighbors, Judea's territory was the smallest it had ever been, and because of Hezekiah's own further loss of territory, by the end of his reign a quarter of a century later, Judea was probably no larger than the area immediately surrounding Jerusalem and the Hebron hills. Archaeological evidence supports the biblical story that during this period, Edom expanded into the lands of the Negev in the south; in the west, the Philistine states captured the entire coastal plain; and in the north, Assyria annexed the territory that had been occupied by Northern Israel and administered it by exiling the local population and transporting other peoples into the territory. Judea occupied the smallest territory in its history.

But the territorial and population diminution in Judea could also lead to a newfound unity. So it was at this moment of seeming national humiliation that the reformers gained the upper hand. Much as in the passages just quoted from the book of Kings, prophets like Isaiah argued that Northern Israel—so recently defeated and exiled by the Assyrians—had been conquered because of the religious apostasy of the people, and Judea, too, was now threatened because of its religious apostasy. What was needed was a purification of Judean religious life: not a return to older religious folk practices, but a commitment to the single-minded faith in the God of Israel. Added to the power of reform was the fact that more centralized control could be exercised from Jerusalem, particularly since most local shrines had now been destroyed or converted to the use of the foreign gods of their conquerors. Furthermore, the diminution of territory meant that all Judeans now lived within a day's walk to the Temple in Jerusalem, and so it could easily become the center of religious activity. Thus it was at this moment that, for the first time, the proper worship of God was limited to the Temple in Jerusalem and banned elsewhere. Both the books of Kings and Chronicles credit Hezekiah with the destruction of local altars in Judea, and the latter credits him with bringing the entire people together to celebrate the Passover in Jerusalem (2 Chron. 30).

As noted, Hezekiah's rule coincided with the destruction and exile of Northern Israel. According to the book of Kings, he came to power just slightly before Assyria's last assault on the North, when the latter had already been stripped of much of its land and sovereignty. Shortly afterward, Assyria completely annexed the North and a major portion of its population was carried off into exile. The so-called Ten Lost Tribes were dispersed, resettled elsewhere in the empire, and so disappear from history.

There is both biblical and extrabiblical evidence, however, that many Northerners, including priests and Levites, moved southward. These refugees brought with them their own traditions, which needed to be harmonized with those of Judea; equally, refugee priests needed to be integrated into the Jerusalem Temple. For now, as this remnant from Northern Israel joined with the population of Judea, it was the worship of the God of Israel that could unite them. Establishing a common religious frame may have been seen as a necessary domestic agenda, a fact confirmed by the very name "the God of Israel"—that is, the sobriquet of the northern tribes, Israel—which was now associated with the religious reform movement of Judea. As much as it was the Jerusalem Temple's priesthood who may have been agents of reform, Northern priests and scribes represented reforming elements as well, for they had chosen to join with Jerusalem rather than with their fellow Northerners exiled to Assyria. Indeed, as mentioned earlier, it may well be that Northern Israel had evolved a much more exclusive definition of religious worship and these refugees became the spur for reform.

All aspects of religious life needed to be sorted out. What was to be deemed the proper worship of God? Who could serve in the Temple? Who were legitimate priests? Hezekiah took this opportunity to institute reform. The biblical historian records:

It was he [Hezekiah] who abolished the high places,
And broke the sacred pillars
And cut down the pole of Asherah

And smashed the bronze serpent that Moses had made
— For until those days the Israelites were offering sacrifices to it —
It was called Nehushtan. . . . (2 Kings 18:4)

The "high places" were connected with local worship, religious ceremonies conducted on mountaintops, and the "sacred pillars" may have been associated with goddess worship; certainly "the pole of Asherah" was. Though the Bible does not say who was worshiped on the mountaintops, and it may have been the case that *Adonai* was, these sacred places had been outside the supervision of Jerusalem's priesthood and were now abolished. Given the mention of "sacred pillars" it may well be the case that such worship involved fertility rites, ceremonies that had meaning for an agricultural society.

Even within the Temple precincts, worship of divine forces alongside the God of Israel had seemed natural. The Bible here reports that sacrifices on the Temple grounds were offered to Nehushtan, a fiery serpent god. (In Numbers 21:9 Moses is mentioned as having saved the people from a plague by putting an image of a snake on a pole.) Similarly, this passage remarks on the representation of God's consort, a goddess named Asherah, also within the Temple precincts. The existence of both of these images on the Temple grounds, snake and goddess — at least one of which the biblical author freely admits as having ancient lineage tracing its origin to Moses himself — demonstrates how pervasive these "heterodox" traditions were in Judea.

Archaeologists have found four inscriptions in Judea to "YHVH and his Asherah" — that is, the God of Israel and another divine power, most likely the consort of God, demonstrating that the worship of multiple divine powers, and in this case a goddess joined with *Adonai*, was practiced in Judea; and, furthermore, that the biblical denunciation of such practices had a basis in the religious reality of ancient Israel and was not a matter of literary or prophetic imagination.[7] The book of Kings reports that the "high places" continued to exist throughout the kingdom of Judea from the time of Solomon's son and immediate successor, Rehoboam, onward. While the biblical author may see these as "heterodox practices" and the result of foreign influences, in fact, by the Bible's own account, they represented long-standing local practices that undercut the reformists' sense of the "pure" worship of the Divine. The crusade that destroyed the icons depicting multiple divine or semidivine forces in the Jerusalem Temple represented a severe break with traditions associated in Judea with its hoary past as well as with cultic practices that were seen as normative. Hezekiah's program of reform represented a new order, one probably connected with a nationalistic fervor that emphasized the difference between Judea, now inheriting the mantle of the entire people Israel, and the surrounding nations. Just as Jehu had combined nationalistic fervor with religious reform, that is, the sole worship of *Adonai* serving to separate the people Israel from its neighbors, now, too, religious reform was combined with nationalism. Sole trust in the God of Israel would issue in salvation. The people Israel was to be distinguished through its worship of God alone. Indeed, the Chronicler ascribes a speech to Hezekiah in which the king asserts that the religious practices of previous generations have led to the losses now occurring at the hands of the Assyrians and others (2 Chron. 29:8). The speech itself may be the Chronicler's invention, but the acts that it traduces are not. Those who worshiped multiple divine beings and engaged in a variety of worship practices were as rooted in the traditions of Israelite settlement as the reformers who claimed to be enunciating the true religion of Israel.

Certainly, the reform should also be seen as a triumph of prophetic ideology. The prophet Micah, who lived at the time, combined the vision of the destruction that Assyria wrought first in Northern Israel and later in Judea with a description of certain elements that were anathema to the religious reformers:

In that day—declares *Adonai*—
I will destroy the horses in your midst
And wreck your chariots.

I will destroy the cities of your land
And demolish all your fortresses.
I will destroy the sorcery you practice,
And you shall have no more soothsayers.
I will destroy your idols
And the sacred pillars in your midst;
And no more shall you bow down
To the work of your hands.
I will tear down the sacred posts [*asherekha*] in your midst
And destroy your cities. . . . (Micah 5:9–14)[8]

Thus Micah, a contemporary eyewitness of late eighth-century Judea, specifically mentions popular religious practices such as the physical representation of divinities, magic, what I have called theurgic rituals—practices aimed at influencing fate through the manipulation of various supernatural forces—as well as the worship of God's consort in the form of an *asherah*.

We might surmise that the reforms Hezekiah instituted were equally to be associated with a reordering, or at least a clear set of instructions, regarding the entire Temple schema: its sacrificial system, the arrangement of holidays, the proper service to be performed by priests and Levites, the system of tithes by which they were to be supported. In this regard, many scholars have presumed that parts of the priestly code, those laws now codified at the beginning of the book of Leviticus, may have been promulgated during Hezekiah's reform movement. These are all surmises that cannot be substantiated, but there is good reason to think that this may be the case.

The passages in Numbers delineating the role of the Levites and the tithes due them (18:21,26) may date from this period. Earlier there had been no such provision for the Levites, but the influx of Northern priests, who were probably now given Levitical status rather than full entitlement as priests, meant that a large population of priestly assistants had to be provided for. The Aaronide priests in Jerusalem retained their more elevated status and were designated to perform the sacrificial rituals, but the Levites were now designated "to do the work" of the sanctuary (verse 6). Additionally, with the destruction of the local temples that had been sprinkled throughout the Judean territory and with the occupation of those lands by Judea's neighbors, many of those local priests must have fled to Jerusalem. They, too, needed to be integrated into the Jerusalem Temple and needed to be provided for.

In this regard, it is instructive to trace the fate of one Levitical family: the members of the Asaph clan. In the book of Psalms, the twelve psalms attributed to Asaph continuously mention Ephraim and "the people of Joseph." Given that these are the names associated with Northern Israel, it is reasonable to presume that these psalms originate there and that the Asaph clan are a Northern Israelite priestly family.[9]

Tantalizingly, both the book of Kings and the prophet Isaiah refer to Joah the son of Asaph—possibly meaning a member of the Asaph clan—as the recorder for King Hezekiah, one of the three important court officials Hezekiah sends out to negotiate with the Assyrians attacking Jerusalem.[10] These are biblical hints suggesting that Northern Israelite priestly refugees were an important part of Hezekiah's administration and were instrumental in the reform; and that Hezekiah, while purifying Temple practice, also aimed at harmonizing the religious sensibilities of Northern Israelite refugees and native Judean reformers. Hezekiah named his son and successor Manasseh, the name of one of the chief tribes of Northern Israel and a unique name among the kings of Judea, perhaps yet another indication of how much the incorporation of the North into the life of the South was a part of Hezekiah's agenda. Yet the Chronicler steps in to assert the Judean lineage of the Asaph clan and declare that David appointed Asaph to be the musician in the temporary sanctuary that David had established in Jerusalem (1 Chron. 16:5–7). Given that the Asaph psalms are an important part of the collection of Psalms, it is reasonable to assume that the Asaph clan was an important Second Temple group, and understandable that later historians would want to trace the clan's lineage back to David's court rather than to Northern Israel, but the internal literary evidence from Psalms is convincing and contradicts this claim.[11] (Each biblical historian has a personal agenda, and it is for us to weigh which source has bent the facts for ideological reasons.)

The book of Kings remarks of Hezekiah that "he trusted only in *Adonai*, the God of Israel; there was none like him among all the kings of Judah after him, nor among those before him" (2 Kings 18:5). This is quite an encomium given that the author thereby grants him a greater status than David or Solomon, the founders of the dynasty. David's is the longest single narrative in the entire Bible, but the biblical account does not shy away from his excesses, his violence, and his sexual appetite, and while the latter days of Solomon's reign are celebrated in the Bible as a period of imperial glory, in the end it is described as a time of royal religious degeneration. Hezekiah, though, is praised for his religious reforms and is seen as the ideal monarch.

If we look again at the passage I quoted earlier regarding the reforms instituted by Hezekiah, we can see the interplay of religious reform and nationalism all in the name of tradition—religious reform and the attempt to achieve national independence flow together, for the passage describing his religious reform immediately characterizes Hezekiah's political agenda: "He clung to *Adonai*; he did not turn away from following Him, but kept the commandment that *Adonai* had given to Moses. And *Adonai* was always with him; he was successful wherever he turned. He rebelled against the king of Assyria and would not serve him. He overran Philistia as far as Gaza and its border areas, from watchtower to fortified town" (2 Kings 18:6–8).

This biblical account of Hezekiah's attempt to extend his territory probably occurred as domestic intrigues and battles for ascension to the throne momentarily diverted Assyria. We might infer from the book of Kings that, in the turmoil over succession after the Assyrian king Sargon II's death in 705, a circumstance we know about from Assyrian sources, Hezekiah took the opportunity of joining other subject communities in the revolt against the hegemony of Assyria. A biblical notice that Hezekiah received a delegation from Babylonia

(2 Kings 20:12), Assyria's neighbor and frequent rival, may be a reference to Hezekiah's plotting with Babylonia to throw off Assyrian suzerainty, since Babylonia in the east and Egypt in the west were the main organizers of the revolt against Assyria at this time.

TABLE 6. Kings of Assyria 745–627 BCE

745–727 BCE	Tiglath-pilser III
726–722	Shalmansar V
722	Fall of Northern Israel
722–705	Sargon II
705–681	Sennacherib
680–669	Esarhaddon
671	Assyria conquers Egypt
668–627	Assurbanipal II

Hezekiah's intrigue proved to be an almost fatal error for Judea. Sennacherib, who finally emerged as the successor to Sargon, subdued the local rebels and, marching westward in 701, placed Jerusalem under siege. For some reason—modern scholars have not been able to determine exactly why, and the Bible itself ascribes it to a miracle—Jerusalem was not ultimately conquered; Sennacherib moved his forces elsewhere. Sennacherib's army did succeed in once again stripping Judea of all its surrounding territory except for the small enclave of Jerusalem, and Hezekiah was forced to pay a huge tribute to Assyria. For the next sixty years, Judea remained an Assyrian vassal state. Sennacherib had not conquered Jerusalem, but as noted above, Hezekiah was ultimately left with just a small city-state encompassing only Jerusalem and its surrounding mountains.[12]

Embattled, besieged, Hezekiah became a vassal of Assyria—a fact about which the biblical historian remains silent but that we know from the Assyrian record and the archaeological evidence. We now have the Assyrian report in hand, and indeed Sennacherib, the king of Assyria, boasts:

> Hezekiah himself, whom the terror-inspiring splendor of my lordship had overwhelmed and whose irregular and elite troops which he had brought into Jerusalem, his royal residence, in order to strengthen it had deserted him, did send me, later to Nineveh, my lordly city, together with 30 talents of gold, 800 talents of silver, precious stones, and . . . all kinds of valuable treasures, his own daughters, concubines, male and female musicians. In order to deliver the tribute and to do obeisance as a slave he sent his personal messenger.[13]

The book of Kings records the victories of its hero, Hezekiah, but elides his defeats. Kings also sidesteps mention of what we know from historical evidence: while Jerusalem may have avoided capture, subsequently it was dominated by Assyria, reduced to the size of a tiny principality surrounded by the official provinces of the vast Assyrian empire. As Sennacherib boasts: "As to Hezekiah, the Jew . . . himself, I made [him] a prisoner in Jerusalem, his royal residence, like a bird in a cage. . . . His towns which I plundered I took away from his country and gave them to Mitinti, King of Ashdod, Padi, King of Ekron and Sillibel, King of Gaza."[14]

The Bible credits David and Solomon with expanding the territory of the people Israel, but despite the biblical encomium, Hezekiah proved to be no David or Solomon.

ASSYRIA AND THE REIGN OF MANASSEH

Manasseh, Hezekiah's son, was crowned as king at age twelve. The reign of a boy king meant first of all that a regency ruled the country until the king grew to maturity—defined as twenty years of age—under the tutelage of a faction of the court. Manasseh's reign would reverse his father's reforms, and so the selection of a boy king may also have meant that a faction opposed to Hezekiah's policies, which had proved disastrous, came to power in a coup—other claimants to the throne having been passed over. We should not discard the possibility that Assyria, itself, had a hand in the selection. After all, the Assyrians claimed Judea as a client state—remember that the Assyrian king called Hezekiah his servant.

Manasseh was to have a long reign—the book of Kings counts it as fifty-five years. While some modern scholars date his reign as ten years fewer than the biblical record, that's still quite a long run— and during that time he always remained Assyria's loyal servant. We should not be surprised at this loyalty, for Assyria's might was fully on display, not only in its capital, Nineveh, but in its provinces as well. Even today, the archaeological remains of that great empire may well impress any viewer.

I had some sense of that as I strolled through the halls of the British Museum. The visitor walking through those halls might well be impressed by the roomfuls of sculptures exhibited there, remnants of the many civilizations of the ancient Near East. Some of these artifacts are the most exquisite examples of the artistry of these lost empires; having been plundered by one of the great modern empires, they are now once again displayed in something close to their original splendor.

But, over and over, we, like the ancients who first beheld these artifacts, may be overcome not by the aesthetic capabilities and talented craftsmanship they exhibit, but by the awesome power they represent. Like the Egyptian pyramids and the sphinx, the less well-known remains of Assyrian culture can easily induce awe in a contemporary visitor. In their sheer massiveness—they are double and quadruple life-size—the statues of Assyrian eighth- and seventh-century pre-Common Era kings dwarf other statuary we are wont to see. Many are not beautiful sculptures (sometimes the plethora of sculptures of the same figures make them seem like they were turned out in factories rather than individually crafted by artists), but they are commanding figures. Observing that the same Assyrian rulers have their outsize image reproduced again and again, I could not help think that the purpose of this art was to convince the viewer of the superhuman qualities of the kings it represented. In contrast to depictions of Pharoahs in Egyptian art—which seem to convey a certain otherworldliness, hinting at the eternal life of these rulers, now dead but thought to be living gods—the massive Assyrian statuaries convey the power and dominance of the living kings of Assyria; they are masters of this world.

What was it like to visit Nineveh, Assyria's capital, perhaps as a foreign ambassador, and view the palaces of these kings? At the entrance to the palace a visitor would encounter outsize sculptures of growling lions; and then, approaching the inner chambers, these gigantic figures depicting the contemporary monarch. Along the palace walls were friezes of defeated peoples being brought before the king. In these scenes carved in alabaster, the king always dwarfed his smaller opponents. The outsize representations of the monarch, and the grandeur of the palace, served a political purpose. Even before you entered the throne room, you were overcome; you understood that disagreement with the power depicted here was useless. Not for naught did these rulers call themselves "King of Kings."

As illustrated by the British themselves, now displaying these mighty sculptures, empires pass from the scene, and the greatest moments of an empire can ironically become its last days. Time renders hollow the projected image of irresistible power. Esarhaddon was perhaps the mightiest of the Assyrian sovereigns, controlling what was certainly the most geographically extensive Assyrian Empire and ruling at the beginning of what would prove to be the last sixty years of this empire. After putting down an attempted coup in Babylonia, he went on to conquer the entire Fertile Crescent and then Egypt, thus finally subjugating Assyria's only rival power and extending Assyrian hegemony over the entire region from the Arabian Sea and the Persian Gulf in the east and south to the Caspian Sea in the north and the Mediterranean as far as Cyprus in the west. Reigning from 681 to 669 BCE, he controlled all of what are modern Iraq, Syria, Jordan, Lebanon, Israel, Palestine, Cyprus, and Egypt, as well as major parts of Turkey and Iran. The ancient peoples of all this vast territory were vassals of

2. Victory stele of Esarhaddon, 671 AC. Berlin, Pergamon Museum.
Photo by Miguel Hermoso Cuesta. Creative Commons.

his kingdom and, indeed, in his inscriptions, Esarhaddon (the name means "The god Assur has given a brother") almost justifiably called himself "King of the World."

As one might suspect, ruling such a vast empire could be a difficult enterprise; the monarch had to be on the alert against incipient revolts among subservient states, and be watchful for conspiracies among courtiers, even in the royal family itself. In fact, Esarhaddon had ascended to the throne only after having warred with his brothers — a civil war and international power game in which Babylonia attempted to play off one side against the other and lost. Although Esarhaddon succeeded in bequeathing his empire to his son, Assurbanipal II, who, in turn, ruled this vast realm, shortly after the latter's death the empire did come to an end, royal rivalries having split the kingdom. In revolting against Assyrian hegemony by playing one claimant off against another, Babylonia, Assyria's eastern neighbor and erstwhile subject, ended up not only achieving its own independence but conquering and subduing its former imperial master and establishing itself as the dominant Middle Eastern power.

According to the book of Chronicles (but not included in the historical survey of the earlier book of Kings), Manasseh, king of Judea, Esarhaddon's and Assurbanipal's contemporary, was taken in chains before the king of Assyria — and, if we believe this historian, Manasseh then personally viewed the magnificent palaces of the Assyrian king.[15]

As we have seen, Manasseh was not the first king of Judea to personally observe Assyrian glory. A half century earlier, his great-grandfather Ahaz had visited the Assyrian king Tiglath-pileser and asked him to intervene in Judea's war with the Aramaeans and the Northern Kingdom of Israel. As we noted, the book of Kings records that Ahaz, obviously impressed with what he saw, installed a copy of an Assyrian altar in the Temple in Jerusalem where it stood until Hezekiah removed it. Ahaz may only have seen the Assyrian king in temporary quarters marshaling his armies in the west, but if Manasseh visited the royal palace of Esarhaddon, we can be sure that he was even more affected as the palace was arranged to overwhelm any visitor.

It was not even necessary to witness in person the palatial artifacts glorifying the king, since expressions of Assyrian culture permeated the entire kingdom. For more than a hundred years, Assyria constituted the greatest power in this vast region, and in the wake of its conquests it built administrative buildings and temples throughout its empire. Pottery is the most ubiquitous archaeological remain documenting cultural dispersion, and Assyrian-style pottery dating to the seventh century BCE has been found throughout the Land of Israel and Palestine.[16] Clearly, Assyrian influence was not only political but cultural as well, much as American and European cultural influences, from merchandise to art forms, have permeated the globe. Conquest does not only involve armies, although the force of arms always lies in the background.

Manasseh came to maturity just before Esarhaddon ascended to power.[17] His reign coincided with the rule of Esarhaddon and his son Assurbanipal II, the two Assyrian kings whose dominions extended throughout the Middle East from Babylonia in the east to Egypt in the west. In light of the international situation and the defeats his father had suffered, it is not surprising that Manasseh's reign reversed his father's political decisions and religious policies. Manasseh remained loyal to Assyria throughout his long reign, even when late in his tenure that empire began to crumble.

And the alliance paid off for Judea. Archaeological evidence shows that having reversed the policies and reforms of his father, Manasseh managed to expand the area that Judea ruled. The Bible, however, not wanting to credit his pro-Assyrian and anti-reformist policy, does not mention this achievement, and certainly does not extol his understanding of the necessities of international politics. The biblical historian only gives credit to his father, Hezekiah, crowning him with praise and remembering him as the champion of reform, the savior of Jerusalem.

The book of Kings and the Chronicler excoriate Manasseh for undoing his father's reforms and for reinstituting the very practices that had been abolished: worship of astral deities and of Asherah, God's consort, and revival of the practice of "passing his son through the fire" (2 Kings 21:6; 2 Chron. 33:6). Indeed, the book of Kings ascribes the exile of Judea, fifty years after the death of Manasseh, to the sins of his reign (2 Kings 21:11–14, 23:26, 24:3). It may be that the extreme language in Kings accusing Manasseh of every possible "heterodox" worship is overdone, and many of the accusations of apostasy may simply repeat stock phrases. But there is no reason to doubt that what took place was a counterrevolution. Manasseh was twelve when he ascended his throne (the biblical age of mature adulthood is twenty), and others undoubtedly served as regents during his minority, so we might well imagine that his policy did not simply reflect his own particular wishes but was the product of a strong faction of the court who counseled and raised him through his adolescence. Indeed, Hezekiah was fifty-four when he died, and we may presume that he had many other children, adults who could have ascended to the throne. Perhaps Assyria dictated the choice of Manasseh; they could more easily control a boy king, and one might recall the note in the Assyrian archives that the Assyrians, in turning Hezekiah into a vassal, had taken his concubines and their children as prisoners.

Allied with Assyria, which had defeated not only Northern Israel but Judea's other neighbors, Manasseh, now reaching maturity, expanded Judea beyond Jerusalem and its environs, regaining much of the territory that had been lost under Hezekiah. Reinstitution of local religious practice followed on the heels of conquest. This was not only an accession to local wishes but also an acknowledgment that Hezekiah's reforms had obviously failed. Hezekiah's policies, including instituting the sole worship of the God of Israel, had not served to protect the people of Judea but had led to their defeat. The prophetic ideal—placing all one's trust in the God of Israel—had been discredited. (Interestingly, while we have some of the recorded prophesies of Isaiah and Micah from the days of Ahaz and Hezekiah, and those of Jeremiah from the time of Manasseh's successor, Josiah, we have no datable prophetic utterances from the days of Manasseh. Could it be that the prophetic message had been so discredited that its voice could only have credence again after the later fall of Assyria?)

Manasseh's long reign was probably made possible not only by his longevity but, critically, by his capacity to mediate international realpolitik; equally, the religious practices he revived may have ensured domestic tranquility as well. Manasseh never revolted against Assyria or attempted any reform of Israelite religion, but allowed popular eclectic religious practices to continue as they always had been performed. He did not trouble his overlords nor his own populace, though reformers may have waited in the wings for their day to come again.

One can imagine that all the while those who had advocated and endorsed the reforms of Hezekiah bided their time and waited for a new regime to take power. Probably the priests who believed that the Temple in Jerusalem should be the sole locus of divine worship were especially disconcerted. The book of Kings goes out of its way to mention that worship of "the hosts of heaven"—that is, astral worship within the Temple precincts—was reinstituted, and "a sculpted image of Asherah"—that is, God's consort—was installed in the Temple courtyards (2 Kings 21:5,7). Given the later literary evidence, we can well imagine that a group of priests, feeling in spiritual exile, began to theorize about what went wrong, why their revolution had not achieved popular support. They realized that reform would have to involve not only the Temple in Jerusalem and its priesthood but also those outside their circle, indeed all the people. They began to formulate a vision of proper religious worship that was not only centered on the priesthood but on the people at large. They saw prophets not as rivals but as visionaries who pointed the way to religious revival. These priests began to write down their vision of a return to an age of reform. It may well be that parts of the Holiness Code (which we will examine in part 3 of this work) were formulated in this period. (We'll put in abeyance a full description of their work, since the complete formulation of their ideas did not occur until the exile in Babylonia a hundred or so years later.) Others, those who had helped shape the reforms of Hezekiah and were now out of power, as well as displaced priests and court officials from Northern Israel now resident in Jerusalem, began to formulate their understanding of needed religious and constitutional reform. Dissident priests and those who supported their ideology dreamt of the time when, once again in power, they would complete the revolution begun in the days of Hezekiah—and even go beyond it. Out of power, they formulated the ideas and laid the literary groundwork for what would later be promulgated as the book of Deuteronomy.

And then their time came: Assyria collapsed, finally to be conquered by Babylonia. For a moment, the fear of superpower intervention receded. As Babylonia consolidated its position, the wish for independence and the dream of religious reform could reassert themselves.

5   Josiah and the Book of Deuteronomy

Manasseh's immediate successor, his son Amon, was assassinated in a palace coup shortly after his accession to the dynastic throne of David. He ruled only two years (and since the biblical author counts any part of the calendar year as a reigning year, he may have ruled for a year or less). The biblical historian relates that the plotters were themselves killed by the "populace," who then proclaimed Amon's son, the eight-year-old Josiah, king. So Josiah was essentially his grandfather Manasseh's successor. But not quite—intervening was an assassination of a royal along with a long regency while the child king matured.

The child king was the product of political and religious elements that had been held in check by Manasseh's long reign but that now burst forth with renewed energy. Just as Manasseh's own rule, begun when he was a child, was inaugurated by a counterrevolution, so too Josiah's rule constituted a second revolution. Those who now came to power represented the forces that had been suppressed in his grandfather's time. And Josiah's accession, birthed in violence, presaged the violence that would accompany the religious revolution of his reign.

The time was ripe for change. Manasseh had ruled during the era of Assyrian ascendancy and power. He had seen the great Assyrian king, Esarhaddon, march through the entire region, conquering Egypt and subjugating the whole of the Middle East to his rule. But Assyria had swallowed too much. Its own internal power struggles were not subdued, and wars of succession weakened the giant. The last ten years of Esarhaddon's successor, the Assyrian king Assurbanipal II (died 627 BCE), were evidently chaotic, and his death led to a series of nasty wars of succession. A revitalized Babylonia, Assyria's southern neighbor and erstwhile vassal, was on the rise: first it revolted against Assyrian overlordship, gaining independence; then it turned and captured its former master. As the two rivals Assyria and Babylonia fought for dominance, battling each other in the eastern part of the Fertile Crescent, the peoples of the west, those living along or slightly inland from the Mediterranean coast, experienced a spell of relative freedom, though they still had to keep an eye on Egypt to the south, a sleeping giant who could be reawakened with the fall of Assyria.

Josiah grew to maturity watching the Assyrian Empire come apart. Taking advantage of the developing power vacuum, his reign would break free of foreign domination, expand the area ruled by Judea — as his grandfather had begun to do — and institute wide-ranging religious reform. Archaeological evidence confirms that in the late period of Manasseh's rule and during Josiah's reign, the kingdom of Judea expanded to the north, south, and west. And the nationalistic pride inherent in the expansion of the kingdom, along with the end of the Assyrian Empire that had wreaked so much havoc on Judea and depopulated the north, led to the sense of a return to days of glory.

The young Josiah may have been chosen as his grandfather's successor precisely because of his youth. Much as the English boy king, Edward VI, raised by Protestant tutors, became fervently anti-Catholic, Josiah's religious policies may have been more the result of this tutelage by reformers than the personal conversion attributed to him by the biblical author.

The book of Chronicles relates that in the eighth year of Josiah's reign, "he began to seek after the God of David, his ancestor, and in the twelfth year of his reign [at twenty] he began to purify Judea and Jerusalem from the high places, the *asherot* and the carved and molten images" (2 Chron. 34:3). Thus Josiah was sixteen when the Chronicler ascribes to him a turning to God, and he was twenty (the mark of adulthood) when he began to implement that conviction, embarking on a program of religious reform, suggesting that there was some youthful conversion leading to the reforms that followed.

Not incidentally, the year of his maturity (627) is the year of death of the last great Assyrian king, Assurbanipal, which, as mentioned, threw Assyria into turmoil and culminated in its defeat by Babylonia.

The Chronicles are thought to have been written well into the exile, while the book of Kings was probably edited at the very beginning of the exile.[1] The narrator of Kings tells the same story as the Chronicler, but with a different chronology. According to Kings, the purge of "pagan" objects began with the finding of a scroll of the law in the Temple; the rediscovery of a lost Law of Moses is the impetus for reform. But the Chronicler seems to describe a more realistic scenario of the stages of reform. Here, the scroll is found after the undertaking of the renovation of the Temple — that is, after the new regime had started to promote its reformist program. The discovery of the scroll (which we will encounter shortly) was of a piece with what was already underway, and served to further fuel the implementation of the new ideology.

Both historians agree that upon officially assuming the helm at age twenty, Josiah zealously engaged in a thoroughgoing destruction of "idolatrous" practices. The book of Kings presents us with a picture of violent and ruthless reform. Since Kings was probably composed at the very beginning of exile, perhaps only fifty or so years after these events, it is the closest historical report of what took place that we are likely to get. Although some of the reforms it mentions are repetitions of stock phrases found throughout the book, there is much that is new in its description. Indeed, for some practices, this is our only source. On the whole, therefore, its account is believable, and only its chronology that it has reordered for ideological reasons should be questioned.

First of all, Kings tells us, the Temple itself was purified:

> The King then ordered Hilkiah, the High Priest, the deputy priests and the Keepers of the Threshold to remove from the Temple Hall all the objects made for Baal, Asherah, and all the host of heaven. He burned them outside of Jerusalem on the terraces of Kidron and had their ashes carried to Bethel. (2 Kings 23:4)

We might note the objects that were removed: ritual icons connected with Baal, who had been worshiped as the head of the Canaanite pantheon; stone pillars dedicated to Asherah, *Adonai's* consort; and objects dedicated to "the heavenly host," that is, images used in astral worship, as later we are told:

> He did away with the horses which the Kings of Judah had dedicated to the sun, at the entrance to the House of God. . . . He burned the chariots of the sun. (verse 11)

Every cultic object associated with "heterodox" practice is smashed, burned, destroyed. From the description of what was done away with, we also learn of what had constituted common religious practice in the Temple:

> He tore down the cubicles of the male prostitutes in the House of *Adonai*, at the place where women weave houses for Asherah. (verse 7)

This is the first we learn of female service within the Temple precincts specifically associated here with weavings presented to Asherah, God's consort. We also hear of "sacred males" or as translated here "male prostitutes," but without more detailed descriptions it is hard to know their ritual function.

Prophets had excoriated the practice of child sacrifice, and the site for that ritual, just outside the Temple walls in the valley below the mount, was defiled:

> He defiled the Topheth in the Ben Hinnom Valley so that no one could pass his son or daughter through fire to Moloch. (verse 10)

Notably, sacred places in the wider territory of Judea, including any that had been solely dedicated to *Adonai*, were also destroyed. Places that had not been used for sacrificial offerings but only for burning incense—places that might well have been dedicated to the God of Israel—were decimated equally with local shrines. The Temple in Jerusalem was designated as the only place in which divine worship could occur:

> He brought all the priests from the towns of Judah [to Jerusalem] and defiled the shrines where the priests had been making offerings—from Geba to Beer-sheba. . . . The priests of the shrines, however, did not ascend the altar of *Adonai* in Jerusalem, but they ate unleavened bread along with their kinsmen. (verses 8a,9)

Not only were the sacred places outside of Jerusalem in Judea destroyed; the purge was extended to areas within the former territory of Northern Israel. We might recall the aforementioned text that the ashes of the burnt ritual objects were brought to Beth-El ("He burned them outside of Jerusalem on the terraces of Kidron and had their ashes carried to Bethel"). Beth-El was the site of the main sanctuary of Northern Israel, and Josiah demonstrated Judea's central role by burying the ashes of the burnt icons there and thus defiling this sacred center of the North. Now that the Northern population had been exiled or had fled to Judea, Jerusalem was designated as the center of gravity for the entire people Israel:

> As for the altar in Bethel [and] the shrine made by Jeroboam son of Nebat who caused Israel to sin—that altar, too, and the shrine as well, he tore down. He burned down the shrine and beat it to dust and he burned the sacred post [*asherah*]. Josiah turned and saw the graves that were there on the hill; and he had the bones taken out of the graves and burned on the altar. Thus he defiled it. (verses 15,16a)

Clearly, the description of the purges does not present us with a picture of any half-hearted program. On the contrary, some of it, like the burning of the bones of the priests on their altars, seems to have been undertaken to ensure that "heterodox" practices or rival sanctuaries would never again rear their heads: altars were destroyed in a manner that guaranteed they were desecrated and could never be reconstituted.

From the extent of the purge, we can surmise the degree of "heterodox" practice that had permeated Temple worship. In the Temple itself, an *asherah* (most probably a representation of God's consort) stood in the courtyard and women wove fabric dedicated to this divinity. Monuments to lesser deities, the sun and other astral figures, surrounded the courtyard, and we can confidently surmise that if the chariot of the sun was displayed as a holy object, the sun itself had become an object of veneration. Sacred males—not priests, perhaps male prostitutes, or perhaps people serving in some way we can no longer discern—functioned in houses adjacent to the Temple. Ritual objects connected with actual or simulated child sacrifice had been erected in the valley just below the Temple Mount walls, and it takes no reading between the lines to assume that they were not simply museum pieces but were actively in use in sacred worship.[2]

As noted, modern archaeology has corroborated the literary evidence of the biblical books that popular Israelite religion was hardly a pure monotheistic faith. A case in point are the four inscriptions to the "Asherah of YHVH" mentioned earlier—most likely the female consort of Israel's God. Additionally, archaeologists have found thousands of smaller figurines depicting a goddess with her hands holding her breasts—most likely representations of this heavenly figure, seemingly portrayed as a mother figure providing milk for her children and most probably associated with prayers for or ceremonies of fertility. This ubiquitous find is but one example of the popularity of these religious practices: proof of the common Israelite worship of a variety of divinities. Similarly, numerous seals have been uncovered with images of sun disks and horses, indicating that the astral worship alluded to in the passage in Kings was a common practice. And, as mentioned, recent finds such as stacks of children's bones in huge Carthaginian cemeteries (Carthage looked to the coastal cities of what is now Lebanon as the home of its religious beliefs) indicate that child sacrifice was practiced by this Mediterranean power. This, in turn, should alert us that the biblical notices regarding child sacrifice are not to be taken as mere polemics without any basis in fact, but may well represent actual worship in ancient Israel and its neighbors, though whether Israel's neighbors, the Phoenicians located in Lebanon, the progenitors of the colony of Carthage, also practiced child sacrifice remains a matter of scholarly controversy.[3]

Whatever the case regarding the latter practice, William Dever, a prominent biblical scholar who supervised the archaeology of several sites in the Land of Israel and is the author of the tantalizingly titled book *Did God Have a Wife?*, sums up the physical evidence uncovered to date by saying, "Archaeological data provide for the first time a credible historical-cultural context" for the historicity of the account in Kings of the Josianic reform.[4]

Thus, the Josianic reform was a war against deep strains of popular religion, and if the biblical account is to be believed, it was bloody—the violent verbal language of Kings and Chronicles probably reflects something akin to a civil war, a puritan revolution. Religious objects and temples were smashed, and even those temples outside of Jerusalem dedicated to the one God of Israel were decimated. Gravesites and altars were defiled. Josiah's reign was ushered in by the assassination of his father, a regicide, and while Kings is at pains to separate the reformers from this act—the author of the book of Kings could hardly lay the blame for the assassination of a scion of the House of David at the reformers' hands—the description of the Josianic reform is certainly studded with violence. This reform was deeply ideological in character: all traces of polyatric and polytheurgic worship had to be wiped out; the exclusive worship of the one God of Israel had to be permanently ensconced. And to guarantee that "heterodox" practice did not rear its head, the Temple in Jerusalem and its reformist priesthood had to be given sole responsibility for divine worship.

Giving energy to this religious reform was a new spirit of nationalism that could emerge at this moment of international power vacuum, a nationalism in which Judea could now see itself as a regional power and as representing a reunified people Israel. Most probably the connection of nationalism with religious reform allowed for its popular adoption, despite the fact that "heterodox" practices were so much a part of the people's daily lives. Manasseh's reign with its reinstitution of "idolatrous" practices could now be associated with Judea's becoming a vassal state of Assyria, and reform could be seen not only as a religious act but as the throwing off of the chains of foreign domination. It was at this very moment that the people of Judea could see themselves as constituting the nation of Israel, a people apart, living as one in the Land of Israel, something not seen for hundreds of years, if ever. ". . . of all the peoples on earth, *Adonai*, your God, chose you to be His treasured people" (Deut. 7:6).

And so, the purge was part of a larger nationalist movement. The people Israel would now maintain their unity and their independence. Their differentiation as a people was signaled by the one God, *Adonai*, who stood in a special relation to this people.

The impetus for reform had been building for generations. The reformers did not claim that they were doing something "new"; rather, they professed to be reinstituting the Law of Moses. Their claim for legitimacy rested on the testimony of ancient times. It was provided for them by the scroll found hidden away in the recesses of the Temple—a scroll that represented the final will and testament of Israel's first great leader: Moses.

DISCOVERY OF THE BOOK OF DEUTERONOMY

By the biblical account, the center of the reform is a book. While the book may not have been the spur for the initial impulse to reform, it certainly served as the "constitutional" legitimization and realization of the reform. Both the author of the book of Kings and the Chronicler describe the finding of the "scroll of God's teaching" as a critical moment in the reformation.

Kings' description of the discovery and promulgation of the book is especially dramatic. King Josiah had ordered the repair of the Temple, and in the course of the renovation, priests stumbled upon this astonishing find. The High Priest Hilkiah reported the discovery, the book was read to the king, "and when the King heard the words of the *Sefer Hatorah*, the Book of Instruction, he rent his garments" (2 Kings 22:11). The king mourned the desecration that had occurred because the book's teachings had been lost and therefore not observed. The scroll was then brought to the prophetess Huldah for authentication, and she declared that this was indeed the teaching of Moses, Israel's first and foremost lawgiver. The discovery legitimized the wide-ranging reform that, according to the book of Kings, Josiah then instituted, for we are told that Josiah, upon hearing the words of the book, embarked on a course of national repentance:

> At the king's summons, all the elders of Judah and Jerusalem assembled before him. The king went up to the House of *Adonai*, together with all the men of Judah and all the inhabitants of Jerusalem, and the priests and prophets—all the people, young and old. And he read to them the entire text of the covenant scroll which had been found in the House of *Adonai*. The king stood by the pillar and solemnized the covenant before *Adonai*: that they would follow *Adonai* and observe God's commandments, injunctions, and laws with all their heart and soul; *that they would fulfill all the terms of this covenant as inscribed upon the scroll.* And all the people entered into the covenant. (2 Kings 23:1–3; emphasis added)

The book was a covenant, and all the people of Judea and Jerusalem accepted that covenant "with all their heart and soul." This common Near Eastern term expressed single devotion to an overlord, but equally evoked the *Shema*, the classic formulation of Jewish faith found in Deuteronomy, chapter 6—an example of the way in which the historian's rhetoric to describe this period and the language of Deuteronomy dovetail with one another.

The overwhelming majority of biblical scholars agree that the book found in the Temple was the book of Deuteronomy, in whole or in its majority. Unlike most of the other books of the Pentateuch (Exodus continues the story begun in Genesis, and Numbers takes up where Exodus leaves off), Deuteronomy is almost self-contained.[5] It is set in the last days of Moses, who delivers several sermons reviewing Israel's history from the Exodus through the wandering in the wilderness. These addresses surround a summary legal code that from its very opening has linguistic and programmatic connections with Josianic reforms. After recalling the revelation at Sinai and enumerating the Decalogue, Deuteronomy's subsequent hortatory passages are almost single-mindedly focused on the proper and exclusive worship of God. The biblical author constantly inveighs against the dangers of worshiping any divine forces other than the God of Israel. The single-mindedness of Deuteronomy is reflective of the single-mindedness of the Josianic reform. The opening sermons attributed to Moses (chapters 6–11) constantly warn that the nation will be led astray (e.g., "Take care not to be lured away and serve other gods" [Deut. 11:16]). These pessimistic exhortations reflect the realities of the ups and downs of reform in the final 150 years of the First Temple period.

Deuteronomy contains a veritable playbill for the religious reforms carried out at the time. Note how it echoes the violent language of Kings: "When *Adonai* your God brings you to the land that you are to invade and occupy, and He dislodges many nations before you . . . you shall tear down their altars, smash their sacred monuments, cut down their *asherot*, and consign their images to the fire" (Deut. 7:1,5).[6]

From the warnings in these introductory chapters to the law against straying from the "true" faith and the enumerated laws condemning various religious practices, Deuteronomy can easily be seen as offering a historical justification for the reform of Josiah's day.[7] The objects of worship that Deuteronomy condemns are those very items that Kings and Chronicles credit Josiah with destroying—and some of these are mentioned nowhere else in the Torah. Deuteronomy is also the only one of the Five Books that prohibits the institution of sacred males (again, a ritual function for which we have no explanation).

Their expulsion from the Temple is mentioned as a part of the Josianic reform but not of the reforms in other eras.

And, as we have seen, the biblical historians inform us in the books of Kings and Chronicles that the objects of worship that Josiah tore down had been associated with the Jerusalem cult perhaps from its origin, and that it was only during this reform that they were removed from the Temple. Among these objects, for example, was the chariot of the sun, which, having long been displayed in the Temple courtyard, would have been encountered by every pilgrim entering the Temple precincts. In other words, in earlier times worship of other supernatural powers such as the chariot of the sun was not seen as competitive with the worship of the God of Israel. But Moses' exhortations in the book of Deuteronomy constantly harp on the theme of exclusive worship of God and call for absolute loyalty—"to love *Adonai* your God with all your heart and soul and might" (Deut. 6:5, 10:12, repeated without the word *might*, 11:13)—and this exclusivity takes center stage in the Josianic reform. The reforms of his regime demand the single worship of God to the exclusion of all other divine beings.[8]

Critical for the Josianic reform is the centralization of worship in Jerusalem, and Deuteronomy is the only book of the Bible that maintains there should be a single central sanctuary: "You shall not act all as now act here, every man as he pleases. . . . You must bring *everything* that I command you to *the site* where *Adonai* your God will choose to establish His name" (Deut. 12:8,11; emphasis added). Following on the heels of Hezekiah's reforms, now too, in the reign of Josiah, all local temples and secondary altars in Judea and Israel were destroyed, whether or not they were dedicated to the God of Israel. The centralization of worship, a single site, ensured that local practices that might not accord with Jerusalem's orthodoxy would not reemerge. This rule contrasts with the law representing the hoarier tradition: "In *every place* where I cause my name to be mentioned I will come to you and bless you" (Exod. 20:21; emphasis added).

Along with the law of a central sanctuary, Deuteronomy propagates a law permitting the eating of meat that had not been first brought to the Temple—a law made necessary by the destruction of local sanctuaries. Until Josiah's reform and the centralization of worship, Israelites could bring their animals to their regional sanctuary, make an offering, and then eat the meat. This practice is held up as an ideal in Leviticus 17, which records that in the desert all meat from the flock was eaten only after a sacrificial offering had been made.

It was only at the time of Josiah's reform, which established a single sanctuary in the land (even as Judea's borders were expanded, including some of the area that had constituted Northern Israel), that distance from Jerusalem became a live issue. It had not been a problem of equal weight at the time of Hezekiah's centralization of worship eighty years earlier, when Judea had only been a small city-state. Now, Deuteronomy solved this problem by recasting the eating of animal flesh as a totally secular activity that did not require sacrifice. Only the pouring off of the blood onto the earth was given religious significance, but this act did not require a priest; anyone could perform it. Furthermore, instead of a dedicatory sacrifice consisting of a partial gift to the Divine being necessary for meat to be consumed by all, sacrifices burnt partially or completely on the altar of the temple in Jerusalem largely became a pure gift to God. Any remaining sacrificial meat could be consumed by priests but not by laypeople, who could eat meat through secular slaughter.[9]

Significantly, the book of Kings mentions that the Josianic reforms culminated in an unusual paschal celebration during which all the people assembled and heard a public reading of the scroll. Deuteronomy is the only book of the Pentateuch that calls for the entire people to gather in a single place to offer the paschal sacrifice—in Exodus, after all, the paschal offering is signally a home celebration, not a pilgrimage festival. Here again, Deuteronomy and the reforms of Josiah as described in the book of Kings are in full accord.

Having placed Deuteronomy in its historical context, we now turn to examine this law code in greater detail.

6 Law in Deuteronomy

The voice of Deuteronomy is distinct from the other books of the Pentateuch. Not only do some of its specific laws contradict other passages in the Five Books—centralization of worship and the celebration of the Passover are examples—but its themes are more focused and its tone is unique. While it may relate earlier traditions, it has recast these teachings in its own particular theological perspective. Its insistent exclusivist theological voice permeates almost every page.

Many of the laws in Deuteronomy are clearly related to the laws enumerated in the Covenant Code in Exodus, yet they have been reworked, frequently elaborated, explained, and emended to accord more closely with Deuteronomy's outlook and context. To take one example: in a remarkable passage about ethical conduct, the Covenant Code in Exodus prescribes that if one sees an animal belonging to an enemy prostrate under its load, one must stop and help: "If you see the ass of your *enemy* lying under its burden and would refrain from raising it, you must nevertheless raise it with him" (Exod. 23:5; emphasis added).

Exodus's concern is with the animal—the suffering animal must be helped by the passerby whether it belongs to friend or foe. Deuteronomy reworks the law: "Do not look upon your fellow's ass fallen on the road and ignore them, help him to raise it up" (Deut. 22:4).

The law is essentially the same, but the rewording enacts some intriguing and critical differences. The law in Exodus is phrased as casuistic law ("If . . . then . . ."), which is typical of almost the entire Covenant Code and characteristic of law in the ancient Near East. The law in Deuteronomy is phrased as a negative instruction, and in accordance with its approach to law as command, the imperative form is thus used. Exodus is quite explicit that help is to be directed to the animal and that it makes no difference whether the person one meets is enemy or friend. Deuteronomy limits the required help of the animal to a fellow citizen—the Hebrew literally means "brother"; the law is now about the ethics of neighborliness. This attitude, with its strong differentiation between Israelites and foreigners, accords with Deuteronomy's insistent nationalism. So one of Deuteronomy's agendas is to reorganize extant laws. It no longer takes as its primary reference the common culture of the Near East, but rather represents a rethinking of Israel's heritage—and is, therefore, an attempt to reinterpret Judea's own past in a contemporary light.

The notion of a book, a scroll, incorporating ancient teaching and having ultimate authority stands out in the description of this moment of reform—it is the finding of the "lost" scroll authenticated by Huldah, the prophetess, that legitimates the reform. Given the importance of the book, it is not surprising that Deuteronomy instructs that the king should have a copy of this teaching before him:

When he is seated on his royal throne, he shall have a copy of the Teaching written for him on a scroll by the Levitical priests. Let it remain with him and let him read in it all his life, so that he may learn to revere *Adonai*, his God, to observe faithfully every word of this Teaching as well as these laws. Thus, he will not act haughtily toward his fellows or deviate from the Instruction to the right or to the left, to the end that he and his descendants may reign long in the midst of Israel. (Deut. 17:18–20)

The book was "found" in the Temple and authenticated by a prophet. Now, every king was to immerse himself in its instruction to rule properly, so that from this time forward no king would lead the people astray as Manasseh had.

And it was specifically Deuteronomy that was now *the* teaching, *the* divine revelation. Notably, Deuteronomy does not mention any other law, any revelation other than the Decalogue and these final words of Moses. Though it had clearly reworked Exodus's law, it does not acknowledge the Covenant Code as a viable teaching, an authoritative instruction.

This process of rewriting older materials and representing them as originals was not uncommon in the Near East. The reformers may very well have thought that the version of the law that they now put forward was, in fact, the correct interpretation of the original covenant. Their reform was not an innovation but a work of restoration—Israel's true religion was being reinstituted.

Deuteronomy is a text impelled by Judea's own internal struggles at religious self-definition. "The Book," as it calls itself, is the most important survivor of the struggles over worship and the definition of Judean religion that took place in the last 150 years of the First Temple.

Importantly, it represents a convergence of the religious consciousness of priest and prophet. The scroll makes the Jerusalem Temple the single site of legitimate worship of the God of Israel, *Adonai*, thus supporting the Jerusalem priesthood, and it is also a work endorsed by prophets. While the book evinces a more national interest, much of Deuteronomy's legislation also expresses moral concern and institutes legislation for the protection of the vulnerable and for those displaced by increased urbanization. Not incidentally, the famous line "Justice, justice shall you pursue" is Deuteronomy's rhetoric. And its call for the protection of workers and the poor is heartfelt:

> When you make a loan of any sort to your compatriot, you must not enter the house to seize the pledge. You must remain outside, while the party to whom you made the loan brings the pledge out to you. If that party is needy, you shall not go to sleep in that pledge; you must return the pledge at sundown, that its owner may sleep in the cloth and bless you; and it will be to your merit before your God *Adonai*.
>
> You shall not abuse a needy and destitute laborer, whether a fellow Israelite or a stranger in one of the communities of your land. You must pay out the wages due on the same day, before

the sun sets, for the worker is needy and urgently depends on it; else a cry to *Adonai* will be issued against you and you will incur guilt. (Deut. 24:10–15)

Prophets had not only insisted on the exclusive worship of the God of Israel, a cause central to the concerns of Deuteronomy. They had also emphasized that Israel's God was deeply concerned for the poor and had demanded a social compact based on empathy and care for the poor and destitute, and Deuteronomy, much like those prophets, includes in its law and exhorts concern for the poor and the vulnerable.

The Deuteronomic Code itself has a certain theological and political progression. Following the extended preface, an exhortative speech by Moses, the enumerated laws begin with the punishment of apostasy and emphasize the proper and exclusive worship of God. There is a detailing of the punishments for prophets who may lead people astray, and for the citizens and even whole cities who stray from proper worship and belief. After this warning against pagan worship, the code enshrines the notion of a single site and a single altar at which to worship God. It then sets out the laws for secular slaughter, since animal flesh would be consumed without it being brought as a sacrifice, and so it ordains that the blood of the slaughtered animal be poured out on the ground, an act committed by a layperson, not a priest; later it will catalog the animals that may be eaten outside of the Temple. This opening dovetails perfectly with the Josianic program.

Other early parts of the Deuteronomic Code are "constitutional" in their concerns, delineating laws of governance and the religious disciplining of elites and citizens. Some of the institutions mentioned here, such as kingship and prophecy, are mentioned nowhere else in the Pentateuch. (It should be remembered that kings and prophets rose to prominence well after the initial period of tribal settlement. According to the biblical account, Samuel seems to serve an intermediate role of both priest and prophet: anointing and then chastising Saul, the first national king recognized as legitimate by the biblical author. Nathan, who upbraids David, appears as the first prophet in the court of the king and seemingly has no other role; the extended public role of prophets does not come into prominence biblically until the careers of Elijah and Elisha.) While these opening legal portions of Deuteronomy regulate kings and prophets, other parts regulate the judicial process as well, though the book contains few laws affecting priests.

It is instructive that the code emphasizes the injunction, "You shall appoint magistrates and officials for your tribes, in all the settlements that *Adonai* your God is giving you, and they shall govern the people with due justice. . . . Justice, justice shall you pursue" (Deut. 16:20). Bernard M. Levinson, a scholar who has placed this section of the legal code of Deuteronomy in its Josianic context, argues that the law that immediately follows Moses' opening speeches—the law of the individual engaged in idolatrous practice—is included, among other reasons, in order to teach that two witnesses are needed for conviction.[1] The passage is centrally concerned with court procedure, and it is meant to be an instructional manual for local judges. If so, it may be argued that one of the Josianic reforms was the setting up of a new local court system. Outlying areas had had their temples destroyed, and there was no longer a resident local priesthood, one of whose functions may have been judicial, so a new judicial order had to be instituted. Here in Deuteronomy we may be viewing the moment when the primary judiciary role passed from the priesthood to a royally appointed judiciary. This may explain why the code includes many domestic matters, such as laws pertaining to marriage and divorce, workers' rights, laws of usury, and agricultural regulations: formerly these matters had been regulated on the local level, but now new officials had to adjudicate them. From its very opening, the code asserts the equivalence of secular judges to priests in matters of criminal and civil judgment.

The exodus of priests from local communities may explain, as well, why Deuteronomy permits the assigning of rights in agricultural tithing to the poor, not only to priests and Levites. Additionally, Deuteronomy mandates that the tithes of the third and sixth years be brought to Jerusalem and be eaten there. These modifications of the law of tithing make sense if there is no longer a functioning local priesthood needing support, most of the priests having migrated to the Jerusalem Temple. In this vein, we might note Deuteronomy mandates that Levites, no matter where they have come from, are to serve in the central sanctuary. This regulation may have been necessitated by the priestly refugees from the North and the areas of Judea conquered by Assyria, who now flocked to Jerusalem and who, for the first time, might serve sacred functions in the Jerusalem Temple.

One unique item the code discusses is a rule regarding a dead body found between two cities; the impurity caused by responsibility for this murder must be expiated (Deut. 21:1–8).

We are told that the elders of each of the proximate cities are to recite a liturgical formula attesting to the fact that they and their fellow citizens were not responsible for this individual's death. Note that as opposed to other places in the Five Books where a sacrifice is required as expiation, here no sacrifice is to be brought; though a ritual killing of an animal is performed, no part of it is offered up to God. The ceremony centers on the elders making a verbal confession indicating that they are not responsible for this death. Though priests are to be present for this ritual, they play the role of observers, not essential participants. Note as well that a critical part of the ritual is a verbal formula, though Temple sacrifices had no fixed liturgy. In Deuteronomy we see the beginnings of confession and prayer achieving a formal ceremonial function.

Providing as it does for the regulation of all these elite structures of governance, king, prophet, judiciary, Levitical priests, and elders, the code may be said to be a new constitutional arrangement.

In that vein, it is interesting that this code includes laws of war not present elsewhere in the Pentateuch: who should be drafted into the army, how one should approach the enemy, the limits of the siege, the treatment of captive women. Though these ordinances may reflect earlier traditions—many scholars think they may reflect the conditions of early tribal settlement—they too are now given the status of "constitutional" law.

The Deuteronomic Code is centrally concerned with the issue of purity of species and emphasizes the maintenance of distinct boundaries. Plants should not be intermixed. Linen and wool should not be worn together. The inappropriateness of mixing elements is demonstrated by a law against an ox and a donkey being yoked together—the cruelty of such a practice is obvious, but the maintenance of all boundaries and the differentiation of species is also given legal and religious legitimacy. Similarly, genders are to be distinguished: women and men are not to wear each other's garments. Israel is to be clearly distinct from the nations that surround it. No neighboring Ammonite or Moabite may join the people in marriage or as a citizen; the purity of Israel is to be maintained. In a reimagining of the march in the desert, Deuteronomy ordains that the purity of the encampment traveling together must be protected: human feces must not remain exposed and those who experience nocturnal emissions should stay outside the camp. Skin diseases must not be allowed to run rampant; no one from Israel should be a male or female prostitute; no bastard—that is, someone born of a prohibited sexual relationship, not someone born out of wedlock—should be allowed into the community.

More than anywhere else in the Pentateuch, Deuteronomy insists that Israel is to be a people apart—God's people. In nature, we meet distinct species; Israel, too, must maintain its uniqueness—boundaries must be kept and enforced.[2] Always there is a sense of nationalism—a common people who must care for each other as they face less friendly outsiders. A sense of exclusion of "others" and the exclusiveness of the people Israel pervades. The law against usury found in Exodus is rephrased here to emphasize that its provision applies exclusively to fellow Israelites and not to foreign traders. As noted above, the law about helping load and unload the burden of a fallen donkey that in Exodus is applied even to helping "your enemy" is here limited to "your neighbor." Laws against intermarriage find their place in this book. With the destruction and exile of Northern Israel and the importation by the Assyrians of foreign peoples as replacements for the local population, the people of Judea see themselves as the surviving remnant of the people Israel and have become a more self-conscious, tight-knit community, preserving their unique identity.

But along with this fierce nationalistic sensibility, there is also a prophetic moral imperative. Those within the community of Israel must care for each other; the people Israel must form an ethical society; a true community need be created. Lost objects should be returned to their rightful owners, and help should be offered to a countryman who suffers a breakdown of his donkey on the road. The poor need be cared for: the grain left behind in the harvest is to be theirs, not yours. Laborers should be paid promptly on the day of their work; if a person offers his cloak for surety, return it at nightfall, for he needs it for sleeping. Slaves should not be forcibly returned to their masters. Let widows and the stranger harvest the leavings of your field.

In the Covenant Code in Exodus, the law of the sabbatical year is agricultural: the land is left to the poor every seventh year. But the Assyrian conquest had forced people off the land, Northern refugees had poured south, even many Judeans had fled to Jerusalem before the onslaught—and so there were now many poor urban dwellers in need of a different kind of support. The sabbatical gift to them became monetary: the remittance of their debts. The new regulation calling for the cancellation of debts in the sabbatical year assured that these urban poor were not to be sold off into slavery because of the inability to pay back loans.

As in the case of this law of the sabbatical year, many of the ethical laws in Deuteronomy contain elements that can easily be traced to the earlier Covenant Code in Exodus but that are now emended or expanded. Signally, regarding the law that the Hebrew slave go free after seven years, a declaration with which the Covenant Code begins, Deuteronomy adds a new provision: slaves are to be given gifts as they leave, presumably so that they have some money and goods with which to start off a new life and are not immediately forced to sell themselves into slavery again.

To sum up, the new code incorporates many older elements of law, yet emends them to reflect both the new social realities of the kingdom and the central reforms initiated under Hezekiah and Josiah. It incorporates the prophetic cries for justice and care of the poor as well as the theology common to both the Jerusalem priesthood and the prophets of the single worship of the Divine. It regulates key institutions of the kingdom and provides instruction for judicial authorities who were perhaps replacing local priests. It emphasizes an increasingly sharp and self-conscious distinction between Israel and its neighbors: a new nationalism.

But along with this, there is a heightened, internally directed, ethical consciousness—*within the community of Israel, the poor and the weak need be cared for*—reflecting the influence of the prophets who during the previous century advocated a concern for the urban poor and spoke to an urban society that now included people of wealth and leisure. Thus, Deuteronomy is an inheritor of a tradition of law in Israel, adding new legislation to meet the needs of its time, transforming some older laws, simply retaining still others, and critically, incorporating prophetic demands for purity of worship and social justice. Throughout, it sees itself as maintaining, not replacing, a tradition traced to Moses, the original lawgiver. Essentially it identifies these last words of Moses before the people Israel enter the land with the revelation at Mount Sinai, thus erasing any memory of an earlier code. Deuteronomy seemingly quotes Exodus in saying Moses went up the mountain to receive "the whole instruction—the law and rules . . . for them to observe in the land" (5:28) and then immediately introduces its own code saying, "This is the instruction—the laws and rules—that *Adonai*, your God, has commanded me to impart to you" (6:1). It is an erasure of memory that might make sense if we recall that the Covenant Code was the work of Northern Israel, while Deuteronomy was promulgated in Judea. The new nationalism, while representative of the entire people Israel, is the product of a triumphal Judea. Although later writers would refer to it as Deuteronomy, the second law, it does not see itself as second but as the only law.

Most of all, Deuteronomy's vision is that the loyal worship of God will ensure God's continued presence in Israel. That worship must be single-minded and not obscured by devotion to any lesser divinities. If Israel follows this code, then God will be with the people Israel; if not, they will suffer exile. Regarding the injunction to keep a spade in the military camp so that soldiers may bury their feces rather than leave them in the open air, Deuteronomy remarks that the reason for this concern about pollution is that God may continue to dwell among the people. This is an evocation of an earlier time, but that image of God marching with the camp, of the people living in such a way that God might remain among them, is ultimately the driving image of Deuteronomy. In some sense, like the wandering generation described as hearing the words of this book, every generation in Israel, like that desert generation, travels together in one camp. It is obedience to God's voice, to God's teaching, that will make possible the presence of God in the midst of this peo-ple—as was the case in the desert. It is the distancing from pollution, especially pollution resulting from idolatrous practice, that will create a place for God to dwell, as God once dwelled amid God's people.

In this way Deuteronomy knits a tight weave of ideology and prac-tice. While the mark of its time is indelible, we need not think of all its incorporated laws as originating in the reigns of Hezekiah and Josiah. Some of these laws may have been part of a Judean heritage; indeed, some biblical scholars have argued that many of these ordinances, such as the law against pollution of the camp we just mentioned, may be traced back to early tribal times. Rather, we should think of this moment as one in which there was an attempt to promulgate a new constitution, one that incorporated traditional elements and spoke in the voice of the hoary past to the changed conditions of the present.

AFTERMATH

As the denouement of the story shows, this latest reform effort, as bloody as it was, as institutionalized as it was, was not sufficient to uproot heteronomous practices that were as ancient as Deuteronomy's own claimed origin. In 609 Josiah died at the age of thirty-nine, killed by the army of Egypt's Pharaoh, Necho II, who was marching north in an alliance with the remainders of the Assyrian Empire, attempting to fend off the new threat from Babylonia.[3] Seemingly, Josiah was trying to defend Judea's old alliance with Babylonia and sought to block Egypt's march, but the play of international politics once again proved dangerous for the Judeans. With Josiah's defeat, Judea's moment of independence proved to be just a short interregnum as it now became a vassal of Egypt. Josiah's son, Jehoahaz, reigned only three months before the Egyptian overlords replaced him with another son, Eliakim.[4]

Reform was dead, and these last days of the kings of Judea were notable for a return to eclectic religious practices and the dissolution of reform. Jeremiah, for instance, reports that child sacrifice was reinstituted in the Valley of Hinnom, in full view of the Temple precincts. It was only after the destruction of the Temple and the people's exile to Babylonia in 587–86 BCE that the vision of pure monotheistic worship triumphed, perhaps because those who were comfortable with syncretistic worship easily assimilated their own practice with Babylonian religious culture and were forever lost to Jewish history, or because the people now saw their exile as a validation of the prophetic message and so adopted the reformist vision of the proper worship of the Divine. Only those who differentiated themselves by the exclusive worship of the God of Israel survived.

But in their exile, these Judeans took with them the memory of a time that now could be seen as golden, a time when they had been ruled by a book. Edited after the destruction of the Temple, the book of Kings sees the reign of Josiah as an ideal. The book found in the Temple that had been so central to that reform was understood as the link to the glory days of Josiah, and it became the model for the time of return. That book was the expression of God's will for the creation of a righteous society; the day of its realization would come again.

Thus, the book of Deuteronomy was venerated by the exiles, perhaps most centrally by the elite former royal scribes. It was these latter, the archivists of the royal chronicles, who wrote a history of Israel. So we note that the historical books of the Bible from Joshua through Second Kings, which record the early history of Israel and the story of the kingdoms of Judea and Northern Israel, are written from a Deuteronomic perspective. Each reign, whether that of the Davidic kings or the kings of Israel, is judged by the degree of its success or failure to worship God properly—the author(s) carefully describing what efforts were made to remove idols and desist from foreign cultic practice. Most especially, the failure to remove the altars in "high places" is condemned, and this becomes the single standard of judgment for each king's reign.

The first biblical revolution, inspired by Elijah and Elisha, had established a code as its core. This covenant between the people Israel and God reflected a consciousness of the special relationship this people had with God, and instituted a religious and secular order that strove to uphold some of the ethical principles emphasized by the prophets. The Josianic revolution built on these themes and placed at the heart of its reform a book that represented its reinterpretation of the covenantal law. This code emphasized the worship of God alone and sharpened the distinction between Israel and the surrounding nations, including delineating further the ethical qualities that were to distinguish God's people. Josiah may have been killed in battle, but the book his reign had promulgated survived, as did the memory of his reform. The author of the book of Kings, writing in exile, remarks regarding Josiah: "There was no king like him before who turned back to *Adonai* with all his heart and soul and might, in full accord with the Teaching of Moses; nor did any like him arise after him" (2 Kings 23:25).

The book was the manifesto of the Josianic revolution, and if the revolution didn't succeed in the short term, it profoundly affected the Judaism that lived on. But before we examine its heritage there is still more to say about the unique ideology of this book.

7   Deuteronomy's Revelation

Placing the book of Deuteronomy within its historical setting enables us to see the central themes and metaphors of this book in perspective. What is most interesting is the way prophetic ideas and received traditions are given new life in different historical conditions.

The overwhelming fact for those living in Judea and Northern Israel in the eighth and seventh centuries BCE was the increasing expanse and might of the Assyrian Empire. Judeans watched as the Assyrians captured more and more of the territory of Northern Israel, finally totally defeating it and exiling its population, and then surrounding the very walls of Jerusalem—a siege from which the Judeans were miraculously saved but during which most of Judea's territory was lost. A little short of a hundred years later, they watched this mighty empire crumble. The language and rhetoric of Deuteronomy responds to this consciousness of imperial might and imperial defeat.

In 1955 a British excavation uncovered the throne room of Esarhaddon, the Assyrian king who had ruled over its vastest empire. Next to his seat of power were remains of written tablets: treaties that vassal states had signed with Esarhaddon in 672 BCE containing oaths taken by these states stating that, upon the demise of the king, they would do nothing to hinder the accession of Esarhaddon's son Assurbanipal to the throne. (Even the son's name, which means "The god Assur has given an heir," indicates how much the issue of succession was on the mind of the royal family.)

As archaeologists and linguistic scholars deciphered the tablets 2,500 years after they were written, new and striking realizations emerged. The tablets not only illuminated the power struggles and royal life of the time; they soon transformed scholarly understanding of the culture out of which the Bible grew—for the language of these treaties is entirely reminiscent of parts of the book of Deuteronomy.

First to be remarked on is that the book of Deuteronomy follows the form of these treaties: an opening prose statement, a listing of obligations, and a conclusion describing the blessings and curses that will follow on compliance or violation. This last item, the Assyrian treaties' list of curses, illustrates some of the striking rhetorical affinities with the book of Deuteronomy. For instance, among other particulars in a long catalog incorporated in Esarhaddon's treaties, curses listed toward the conclusion call for the "locusts to devour the harvest" and ask that the gods "make your wives lie in the lap of your enemy before your eyes; may your sons not possess your house." They further delineate the most terrible fate if the oath in the treaty is violated: "May your pregnant mother and her daughter eat the flesh of your sons."[1] Toward the end of the book, Deuteronomy expounds the curses that will befall Israel for violating the covenant with God, and included in the list is the plague of locusts that will descend on Israel (28:38). Similarly, we are told that "if you pay the bride-price for a wife, another man shall enjoy her, and if you build a house, you shall not enjoy it" (28:30). Deuteronomy goes on to warn that if you do not observe "the words of this teaching that are written in this book," then "you shall eat your own issue, the flesh of your sons and daughters" (28:53). Both Esarhaddon's treaty and Deuteronomy contain dozens more such curses, many of which are similar in both documents.

Esarhaddon's treaty opens by calling for the vassal's loyalty to the crown prince: "You swear that you will love Assurbanipal, the crown prince, son of Essarhaddon, King of Assyria, your lord, as you do yourselves," which is entirely reminiscent of the Bible's exhortation that the people Israel love their God "with all their soul, with all their heart and with all their might" (Deut. 6:4, 11:13). Just as Esarhaddon demands exclusive loyalty, so too does the God of Israel. Deuteronomy, then, is a covenant treaty made between Israel and God that has all the characteristics of an ancient international treaty made between vassal nations and their powerful overlord. Deuteronomy utilizes the understandings of its time to reframe the prophetic demands of the exclusive worship of *Adonai* and the loyalty Israel must exercise.

Esarhaddon kept the treaties with his vassals right next to the throne, and in the same vein, an addendum to the book of Deuteronomy insists that a copy of this book be kept next to the ark, God's footstool, in the Temple. Just as Esarhaddon kept his most treasured treaties close to him in the throne room, the treaty of Israel with its God is kept in God's throne room, the Holy of Holies.

Moshe Weinfeld, one of the most respected twentieth-century scholars of Deuteronomy, has pointed out that the form the Assyrian treaties take departs from previous examples in that there is no pretense of mutuality, of covenanting between two parties who respect each other; rather, the vassals agree to the terms Assyria has imposed. This is quite different from earlier Near Eastern treaties; in Hittite treaties, for instance, much like modern contracts, the parties talk of the consideration they have received from one another. Similarly, ancient Near Eastern stories of divinities reflect this more mutual conception of society: in ancient Mesopotamia, the chief god rules as head of a pantheon—he need consult, take other gods, other forces, into account.[2] The Assyrian king stands apart—he does not consult, he rules, he demands loyalty, he commands, he moves whole populations from one area of Mesopotamia to another.

Assyria did not invent the notion of kingship. Kings had existed in the Middle East for at least two millennia, if not more. But Assyria accentuated the notion of *king* in a somewhat different way than previous monarchies. The Assyrian king called himself "King of Kings,"[3] sometimes "King of the World." Other monarchs may have used these terms—archaeologists have uncovered tablets in which the king of Ugarit, who reigned hundreds of years earlier, is referred to as "King of the World"—but those empires had died before Israel rose to power. The expanse of the Assyrian Empire, its power, wealth, and glory, ensured that these terms were seen not as empty epithets but as visual actualities. The king of Assyria did not have to view himself as one king among many on earth, but rather could bask in being the supreme ruler to whom all the known world owed obeisance, for his rule extended over all the surrounding countries and none could successfully contend with his power. As noted earlier, this outsize vision of the Assyrian king was reflected in art, where he was depicted as dwarfing all other humans.

What seems most remarkable is that Judea, a subject people amid this vast empire, dreamed that its God was greater than the greatest of powers on earth, and it used the available cultural images to depict the power of its true ruler. Its image of God and of God's demands was a counter to the earthly power it was experiencing. In Deuteronomy it is God, not the earthly ruler, who commands loyalty.

KING OF KINGS AND LORD OF LORDS

A few years before Assyria rose to its dominant position of power, shortly before it conquered and exiled Northern Israel and undertook the siege of Jerusalem, in 733—Isaiah of Jerusalem dates the moment and tells us it was in the year that King Ahaz's grandfather Uzziah died—the prophet had a mystical vision:

> I beheld my Lord seated on a high and lofty throne; and the train of His robe filled the Temple hall. Burning snakes stood in attendance on Him. Each of them had six wings: with two he covered his face, with two he covered his legs and with two he would fly. And one would call to the other, "Holy, holy, holy! *Adonai* Lord of Hosts! His presence fills all the earth!" (Isa. 6:1–3)

Isaiah's vision is of a magnificent, powerful, and fiery king. It is quite different from earlier visions of God, where the Divine appears as friend, as pure fire, as a mysterious voice, or as riding on a thundering cloud. Here God is depicted in a throne room, surrounded by courtiers who are themselves fiery and terrifying powers but are fully worshipful of God, ready to do God's bidding—in the vision, one flies and picks up a coal from the altar and touches Isaiah's lips with it as Isaiah declares, "My eyes have beheld the King, *Adonai* of hosts" (verse 5).[4]

In Isaiah's vision, God does not rule in concert, does not consult with a pantheon, but dwarfs every other divine or angelic being as well as all earthly life. The vision is of God as a powerful king. Compare this throne vision of Isaiah with the prophecy of Hosea, for instance, who speaks of the relationship of God and Israel using the metaphor of lovers and of husbands and wives in marriage—quite a different image than that of royal authority.

Isaiah, like the book of Deuteronomy, is influenced by Assyria's immense power and cultural hegemony. In an imperial reality, monarchs are seen as having absolute power and could be imagined as ruling the entire known world. When Deuteronomic rhetoric appropriated for God the language and images reserved by Assyria for its living king, it was utilizing the contemporary cultural moment to articulate in the parlance of its times what the prophets had consistently maintained: the exclusive worship of the God of Israel.

Deuteronomy recognizes the existence of other forces and powers in the universe aside from the God of Israel, but asserts that Israel is to single-mindedly worship this one God.[5] Just as the Assyrian king could recognize that there were other powers—Egypt, for instance—but could still appropriately be titled King of Kings, for he had conquered Egypt, so too Israel could recognize a myriad of divine and semidivine forces but know that exclusive loyalty was due the God of Israel. Ultimately, the God of Israel could subdue those other forces and therefore deserved the sole worship of the people Israel. It was this demand for exclusive loyalty that energized, in Josiah's reign, a violent puritanical reform in which the symbols of any other divine or semidivine power were destroyed.

To be sure, earlier Northern prophets spoke of God's supreme power, consistently maintaining that the God of Israel was supreme over all other divine beings and that Israel owed its God exclusive loyalty. Amos, for instance, speaking perhaps fifty years before Isaiah, says that the

God of Israel is the one "who formed the mountains, and created the wind, . . . who turns the darkness into daybreak, and treads upon the high places of the earth. His name is *Adonai*, the God of Hosts" (Amos 4:13). Isaiah's vision, though, may be seen as inaugurating the moment when the metaphors of supreme and unimpeachable imperial power ascribed to the rulers of the great empires are used as metaphors for the God of Israel.

Evidently, the reality of Assyrian imperial power and then its abrupt loss of power made the prophetic demand for exclusive loyalty to the God of Israel credible: God would never be defeated, God's power would never crumble. This demand of exclusive loyalty central to the Deuteronomic revolution led almost inexorably, from that time onward, to a monotheistic revolution, and to the conception subsequently attached to Deuteronomy as its preface: "It has been clearly demonstrated to you that *Adonai* alone is God; there is none beside Him" (Deut. 4:35).

Only God is King of the World. All earthly powers, whether foreign or traditionally worshiped among the people Israel, are subject to God alone. The Assyrian king may have demanded the absolute loyalty of his subjects, but the people Israel owed such loyalty only to the God of Israel. As one translation of the *Shema*—the verse that many see as the ultimate Jewish declaration of faith—has it:

Hear O Israel, *Adonai* is our God, *Adonai* alone. (Deut. 6:4)

With its language shaped by the contemporary culture, Deuteronomy has transferred the object of loyalty from earthly powers to God. And so the passage continues:

You shall love *Adonai*, your God, with all your heart, with all your soul and with all your might. (verse 5)

Love in this biblical passage has the meaning of fealty, loyalty. Instead of the absolute loyalty demanded by the earthly ruler, Deuteronomy insists that complete loyalty is due God alone, and that the commands to be followed are those of the ultimate ruler, *Adonai*.

EARTHLY KINGS AND THE HEAVENLY RULER

Deuteronomy, the only one of the Five Books of Moses to mention kingship, places limitations on the extent of power to be exercised by the earthy ruler. Thus, while it recognizes monarchy as politically legitimate—a view that in the rest of the Bible is sometimes given divine sanction but at other moments is questioned—it severely limits the authority of Israel's own earthly rule:

> If, after you have entered the land that *Adonai* your God has given you, and occupied it and settled in it, you decide, "I will set a king over me, as do all the nations about me," you shall be free to set a king over yourself, one chosen by *Adonai* your God. Be sure to set as king over yourself one of your own people; you must not set a foreigner over you, one who is not your kinsman. Moreover, he shall not keep many horses or send people back to Egypt to add to his horses, since *Adonai* has warned you, "You must not go back that way again." And he shall not have many wives, lest his heart go astray; nor shall he amass silver and gold to excess.
>
> When he is seated on his royal throne, he shall have a copy of this Teaching written for him on a scroll by the Levitical priests. Let it remain with him and let him read in it all his life, so that he may learn to revere *Adonai* his God, to observe faithfully every word of this Teaching as well as these laws. Thus he will not act haughtily toward his fellows or deviate from the commands to the right or to the left, to the end that he and his descendants may reign long in the midst of Israel. (Deut. 17:14–20)

Three things might be noted about this passage from Deuteronomy. First, kingship is understood to be a foreign import—it is what all the other nations do, but it is not the originally sanctioned form of governance for Israel. Secondly, the author evinces special alarm regarding the return to Egypt. One of the reasons for circumscribing the rule of the king is that kingly rule may represent backsliding, setting up a society of slaves ruled by taskmasters. Kings, embodying notions of hierarchy and absolute power, may bring into question the very raison d'être of the people Israel—to remember that God freed you from Egypt and to behave accordingly. Lastly, it is God and God's teaching that is supreme, not the earthly power. The king is not the initiator of the law (whose preservation is here handed over to the priests), but the king is subservient to it and must keep it always beside him, to be ruled by it. The king can be judged by the standards set by the law.

In other parts of the Bible we can find hints of attitudes regarding the Davidic dynasty quite different than Deuteronomy's stance regarding earthly kings. Psalm 2, for instance, preserves an ideology of kingship that identifies the earthly king with the divine will. God says of the king, "You are my son, this day, I have given birth to you" (verse 7)—an expressed ideology much akin to the way other nations described their king as the son of God. Similarly Psalm 110 speaks of the king sitting at the right hand of God and goes on to say, "In majestic holiness, from the womb, from the dawn, yours was the dew of youth. You are a priest forever, a rightful king by my decree" (verse 4). Such excessive rhetoric describing the king could equally have been used by any of the nations surrounding Judea and Northern Israel.[6]

Deuteronomic ideology cuts earthly kingship down to human size. In this understanding, the king is neither the earthly representative of the gods promulgating the divine law as he is in Assyria, nor the very embodiment of the chief god as he is in Egypt. Indeed, he is not given any religious function or office. Rather, his role is secular: to administer the political aspects of the realm—governance, domestic tranquility, and external security—even though internal biblical evidence indicates that in both Israel and Judea, kings had wider roles and earlier had even performed priestly functions.[7] The law is not given by the king as, for instance, the Code of Hammurabi insists; rather, the king is subject to the law. Woe to the king who oversteps these bounds;

he would soon learn that *Adonai* alone reigns supreme. God is the ultimate ruler, not any earthly king, not the Assyrian monarch, nor the scion of the House of David, and God ultimately secures justice. Indeed, some have suggested that the name Israel derives from *yisrah el* — "El/God shall be our ruler/our king."[8]

The critique of the monarchy implied in the quoted passage from Deuteronomy, the expression of the danger of an overly ambitious monarch, follows on the heels of the reign of Josiah's grandfather, Manasseh, whom the reformers witnessed undoing the work of Hezekiah and thus corrupting Israel's "true" religion. The distrust created by the long history of Judean kings zigzagging between the singular worship of the God of Israel and the promotion of worship of multiple divine beings is here reflected in the limits put on kingship. The Davidic dynasty could not be entrusted with the preservation of Israel's pristine faith, and so is stripped of the priestly roles these kings once had.

God is the ideal ruler: reasonable, just, sympathetic to God's people. But most of all, God is the ultimate dispenser of destruction and victory, of life and death, of goodness and difficulty. What you should have learned from all your experience in Egypt and in your wanderings is that "*Adonai*, your God, is in your midst, a great, awesome God" (Deut. 7:21). You do not need to worry:

> Should you say to yourselves, "These nations are more numerous than we; how can we dispossess them?," you need have no fear of them. You have but to bear in mind what *Adonai* our God did to Pharaoh and all the Egyptians. . . . Thus will *Adonai* your God do to all the peoples you now fear. (7:17–19)

The affirmation of loyalty to God is a denial of the superiority of Egypt and Assyria and is a declaration of independence on Judea's part. Not for naught does Josiah's name translate as "God [Yah] will make him victorious."

Earlier, Isaiah, writing as Assyria threatened Jerusalem, captured this theological mood in which God is mightier than any earthly power:

But when *Adonai* has carried out all His purpose on Mount Zion and in Jerusalem, He will punish the majestic pride and overbearing arrogance of the king of Assyria. For he thought, "By the might of my hand have I wrought it, by my skill, for I am clever: I have erased the borders of peoples; I have plundered their treasures and exiled their vast populations. I was able to seize, like a nest, the wealth of peoples; as one gathers abandoned eggs, so I gathered all the earth: nothing so much as flapped a wing or opened a mouth to peep." Does an ax boast over him who hews with it, or a saw magnify itself above him who wields it? As though the rod raised him who lifts it, as though the staff lifted the man! (Isa. 10:12–16)

For all its power and might, even Assyria will learn the message of God's supreme rule. And indeed, Assyria fell.

Nationalism and theology are intertwined here. Israel can throw off the yoke of foreign domination because its God is the true ruler of all the earth. Neither the Assyrian king nor the Egyptian Pharaoh is the king of the world or the mediator of the will of heaven: the God of Israel is the Lord of Lords. In this regard, Deuteronomy represents a triumph of prophetic ideas: all— kings, peoples, empires—are subject to God's judgment.

COMMANDS

Kings command. Deuteronomy is steeped in notions of God's power and overlordship, so it comes as no surprise that, more than any other stratum of the Torah, Deuteronomy formulates the notion of law in terms of obedience to God's commands. Cognate forms of the word *command* appear more frequently here than in any other book of the Bible.[9] Law is seen as the command of God, or more precisely, the command of God spoken by Moses as God's representative.

The law that Judea had inherited from Northern Israel had been promulgated as a covenant, and its setting and content reflects the earlier Near Eastern culture. The covenant is mutual, freely entered into by the people. Deuteronomy may have been inspired by the Covenant Code, and it continues to call itself a covenant, but it reflects the new tone of an imperial Assyria and its form more closely resembles Assyrian vassal treaties. It was from the Assyrian regime that Israel learned that kings were not consensual rulers but commanding presences. The Assyrian king insisted that he was the sole authority and everyone else was to be in awe of him; his word, his demands, were to be obeyed, absolutely. In Deuteronomy, God is portrayed in this commanding role. Indeed, Deuteronomy understands that to be God's people is to be commanded, and God's commands demand greater obeisance than what is due any earthly king, for God's law cannot be anything but just and wise. God is the supreme ruler, more powerful than any earthly ruler can possibly be. The law, therefore, is commanded and Israel is to obey it fully. The only element of mutuality is Israel's agreement to obey all of God's commands.

The book of Deuteronomy emphasizes God's command to such an extent that many of the repeated expressions that include the word *command*—for example, "all the commandments that I command you" or "the commandments which I give you this day"—are unique to this book. These particular phrases convey Deuteronomy's sense that there is a corpus—a complete and final list—of commands that God has given that are fixed and unchangeable.[10] God has decreed these laws and commandments and demanded the people's obedience, and in return God gives the people Israel its land—life in the land is contingent on obedience.

Deuteronomic laws are the most sacred obligations one must undertake, for they are spoken by the ultimate monarch:

You shall faithfully observe all the Commandments that I enjoin upon you today, that you may thrive and increase and be able to possess the land that *Adonai* promised on oath to your fathers. Remember the long way that *Adonai* your God has made you travel in the wilderness these past forty years, in order to test you by hardships to learn what was in your hearts: whether you would keep the divine commandments or not. God subjected you to the hardship of hunger and then gave you manna to eat, which neither you nor your fathers had ever known, in order to teach you that human beings do not live on bread alone, but that they may live on anything that *Adonai* decrees. . . . Bear in mind that *Adonai* your God disciplines you just as a parent disciplines his child. Therefore, keep the commandment of *Adonai* your God: walk in God's ways and show reverence. (8:1–3,5–6)

Deuteronomy's Moses teaches Israel to be in awe of God, to revere God, and to obey God's instruction. Indeed, obedience to the commandments is the true test of loyalty to God. Jewish history is now understood in the light of the observance of this code. Travails, which may be seen as a contradiction of this promise, serve either to test the people's loyalty or else to provide a means of instruction. (It was, after all, during the reign of Hezekiah, the institutor of major religious reform, that Judea was stripped of most of its territory and Jerusalem was only narrowly saved from siege; the newly found book needed to acknowledge this reality, so these events, too, might be seen as a test.)

The people Israel are to "observe" the commands. As we will elaborate shortly, the word *observe* occurs numerous times in Moses' introduction to the law—the speech recorded in Deuteronomy, chapters 6 to 11—and at the end of the book, Moses sums up this message by insisting that these commands are not to be added to or subtracted from. They are to be fully observed, for blessing will come of this, "if only you obey and faithfully observe the commandments of *Adonai* your God that I enjoin upon you this day and do not deviate to the right or to the left from any of the commandments that I enjoin upon you this day" (Deut. 28:13b–14a).

Commands are given to be obeyed. The supreme king—to whom the earthly king owes fealty as well—does not want any subject exercising independent judgment, but rather expects the subject to carry out the king's words exactly. Servants of the ruler are not expected to have a will of their own. This is the precise charge Moses gives to the people in the book of Deuteronomy, and one of the key ways in which Jewish law would come to be understood by many.

It is important to keep Moshe Weinfeld's aforementioned insight in mind. Unlike the Covenant Code in Exodus, there is no mutuality in Deuteronomy's covenant. As in the treaties that Esarhaddon imposed on vassal states, there is no pretense of mutuality. The supreme power does not negotiate but commands.

Deuteronomy does acknowledge, indeed emphasizes, that there is a received tradition regarding the direct revelation of the Decalogue, but it simultaneously insists that its law code has the same status as this original covenant. It says of itself that it is a final covenant made with Israel at the end of the forty years' march through the desert, a covenant made on the Plains of Moab—that is, as the Land of Israel is in sight. The Deuteronomic speeches of Moses are exhortations aimed at justifying and preserving loyalty to the law—a law that goes beyond the Decalogue. The people Israel is to keep faith with God not only by preserving the purity of its worship but by obeying "all the commandments" that God has given. Moses not only enshrines the two tablets of the Decalogue given at the beginning of the wandering but sums up his teaching at the end of his life, before the people are to enter the land without him. The people Israel's stay in the land they are about to enter is dependent on this last covenant. It is this later report of the Sinaitic revelation, delineating the specifics of the civil law and of ritual observance—but not of the priestly functions—that occupies the bulk of the book of Deuteronomy and that Deuteronomy places alongside the revelation on Sinai.

Much as the Decalogue is the word of God spoken at the beginning of the desert march, at Sinai/Horeb, all of the law and exhortations found in Deuteronomy are the words of God spoken at the end of the desert march, on the Plains of Moab. Of course, the Decalogue has a special status as a revelation to the entire people, while the second covenant at the Plains of Moab represents the word of God that Moses alone heard and then transmitted to the people. Nevertheless, there is a constant attempt in the book of Deuteronomy to obscure this difference between the revelation at Sinai and the law given at the end of Moses' career. Thus, when at the end of the recitation of the law code Moses announces, "Observe all the instruction that I enjoin upon you *this day*" (27:1), it has the same ring to it as the statement with which Deuteronomy prefaces the giving of the Decalogue: "And all these words that I command you *this day* shall be upon your heart" (6:4). As the people are about to enter the land, Moses tells them to inscribe the words that he has just uttered on tablets of stone, "and inscribe upon them all the words of this Teaching" (27:3), just as the Decalogue had been inscribed on tablets of stone. The status of the latter law code, Deuteronomy, and of the Decalogue are conflated.

THE VOICE OF GOD

Deuteronomy—the Greek name literally means "second law"—is conscious that it is a second telling, a retelling of the meaning of the people Israel's founding revelation.

Seeking validation, reform movements frequently see themselves as representing a mythic past, not as establishing something new. Rather than viewing themselves as revolutionaries, they characterize themselves as reformists, as traditionalists restoring a pristine past. Their justification reaches beyond the direct historical past to a more ancient, seemingly idyllic time, a time often closer to the origins of a nation, when the true nature of this people and its mission was clearer, when the people's lives may have been simpler and its values in sharper focus. Deuteronomy, consisting entirely of speeches ascribed to Moses, begins with a recapitulation of the revelation of the Decalogue in the Sinai desert at the mountain known by its Northern Israelite name Horeb. By telling the story in Moses' voice, it lays claim to being a true representation of the most ancient and validated tradition.

Though the book builds on what has come before it, it radicalizes what had been understood earlier. Most especially, Deuteronomy shifts the very understanding of revelation itself, the way in which God stands in relation to humanity and Israel. Deuteronomy retells the story of the primary revelation from the perspective of its puritan theology. Its description of the theophany at Sinai borrows whole phrases from Exodus but gives them a new overlay of meaning. To make its point regarding the need for purity of worship, it clarifies that the revelation on Sinai is of the God who cannot be seen, the God of whom no image can be made. In many ways, an unseen monarch is more awe-inspiring than one who is visible.

We have seen how Deuteronomy synthesized the language of its time to validate prophetic understandings, but in this regard it does not adopt a prophetic theology but a priestly one. Prophets are visionaries. Priests argued that no one could see God and live. Even the High Priest could not view God directly in the Holy of Holies, for a haze of incense, a cloud, obscured God's presence.

In Exodus we are given a variety of accounts regarding the revelation at Sinai. One passage depicts Moses and the elders gazing upon the Divine. In this most concrete of biblical depictions, Moses, Aaron, and the elders of Israel went up the mountain "and they saw the God of Israel: under God's feet there was the likeness of a pavement of sapphire, like the very sky for purity. Yet God did not raise a hand against the leaders of the Israelites; they beheld God, and they ate and drank" (Exod. 24:10–11). This biblical vision depicts God as inviting selected people to join the Divine; they look up and see God, visit with God. The description in Exodus thus accords with certain prophetic visionary experiences, such as that of Isaiah, described earlier, who sees God seated on God's high throne (Isa. 6:1); or the more graphic image of God drawn by the later exilic prophet Ezekiel: "And on top of the image of a throne was the image of a human form. From what appeared as his loins up, I saw a gleam of amber—what looked like a fire encased in a frame" (Ezek. 1:27). These texts seem unembarrassed by a literal reading—prophetic experience is visionary—though some later Jewish commentators would try to modify these visionary experiences by reinterpreting them as metaphorical, not actual pictures of the divine host—nothing more than figurative verbal imagery conveying a sense of God's presence.

In Exodus the passages introducing the revelation at Sinai are not univocal, though they seem to imply a physical apparition of God similar to the prophetic visions described above: "*Adonai* came down upon Mount Sinai, on the top of the mountain, and *Adonai* called Moses to the top of the mountain and Moses went up" (Exod. 20:20). God's movement, "coming down," conveys a physical image of the Divine, and though it is not explicitly stated, it would seem that at least Moses has entered into the full presence of God who has come down from the heavens to the top of the mountain. In a later passage we are informed, "The Lord would speak to Moses face to face as one person speaks to another" (33:23).

But other passages in Exodus offer a very different thesis. In a later passage, Moses is alone on Sinai and asks to see God's face—"Let me behold your Presence" (33:18)—and God gives two different, seemingly contradictory, responses. On the one hand, Moses is at first mysteriously told, "I will make all my goodness pass before you, and I will proclaim before you the name *Adonai*, and the grace that I grant and the compassion that I show" (Exod. 33:19). But the next verse (20) adds, "You cannot see my face, for no person can see Me and live." Exodus presents us with multiple theologies, and scholars have frequently assumed that individual writers were at work shaping these differing passages. For example, in contrast to the internal argument just quoted, a priestly writer insists that Moses stood outside the sanctuary in the desert when God entered there, for even Moses could not see God: "The cloud covered the Tent of Meeting, and the Presence of the Lord filled the Tabernacle. Moses could not enter the Tent of Meeting because the cloud had settled upon it and the Presence of the Lord filled the Tabernacle" (40:34–35).[11]

Deuteronomy is fully imbued with this priestly theology, and it is remarkable to see how it reinterprets passages from Exodus so that they comply with this outlook. The introductory chapter to Deuteronomy borrows from some of the more explicit passages in Exodus—for instance, it deliberately uses the physical imagery introduced there describing the people Israel's meeting with God, "Face to face God spoke with you on the mountain from amidst the fire" (Deut. 5:4)—but turns this image on its head. Deuteronomy, playing with passages describing Moses speaking to God face-to-face, here asserts that not only Moses but the entire people saw God face-to-face—the "you" here refers to the entirety of the people Israel—and then tells us that this phrase is to be interpreted as the voice of God, not God's physical form. The phrase "face to face" does not allude to a physical apparition of God, but rather to the hearing of God speaking. "*Adonai* spoke those words—those and no more—to your whole congregation at the mountain, with a mighty voice out of the fire and the dense clouds" (verse 19). The people saw only a cloud and lightning; they could not see an image of God. It is what they heard that is critical. In adopting this playful, almost mocking rhetorical stance, borrowing visual language from Exodus and transforming its meaning, the Deuteronomic author asserts that the reader of course understands that no one can see God: Isn't it clearly true that at the greatest moment of God's manifestation, all one could possibly do is hear words, not see anything? The implication for the Deuteronomist is clear: therefore, the making of any image of God is blasphemous.

An introductory chapter of Deuteronomy captures the meaning of this theology perfectly. To be sure, some scholars believe that these earlier chapters were appended later than the main body of the book. Even so, it is certainly the case that these passages' message captures the theological thrust of the main body of Deuteronomy. If this is the work of a later author, that author is but spelling out the full implication of Deuteronomy's rhetoric that we've just seen enunciated: "God spoke to you out of the fire; you heard the sound of words but perceived no shape—nothing but a voice" (4:12). Therefore, Deuteronomy continues:

For your own sake, be most careful — *since you saw no shape when Adonai your God spoke to you at Horeb out of the fire* — not to act wickedly and make for yourselves a sculptured image in any likeness whatever:

the form of a man or a woman,

the form of any beast on earth,

the form of any winged bird that flies in the sky,

the form of anything that creeps on the ground,

the form of any fish that is in the waters below the earth.

And when you look up to the sky and behold the sun and the moon and the stars, the whole heavenly host, you must not be lured into bowing down to them or serving them. (4:15–19; emphasis added)

To worship any image, whether of natural objects or of imagined astral beings, is a violation of the experience at Sinai. The unseen God who spoke to you then could not be seen and therefore should not be depicted through imagery.

It is in this spirit that the scene with the elders in Exodus is rewritten. Rather than the Exodus account describing Moses and the elders seeing God, Deuteronomy records, "You came up to me, all your tribal heads and elders, and said, 'Our God *Adonai* has just shown us a majestic Presence, and we have heard God's voice out of the fire; we have seen this day that humankind may live though addressed by God. Let us not die, then, for this fearsome fire will consume us; if we hear the voice of our God *Adonai* any longer, we shall die. For what mortal ever heard the voice of the living God speak out of the fire, as we did, and lived?" (Deut. 5:20–22). Thus, just as God's revelation to the people is carefully interpreted as an auditory experience, not a visual one, so too Deuteronomy recasts "God's majestic Presence" as a voice speaking to the leaders. Note the sly reinterpretation that has taken place in this passage. No biblical passage or person had ever argued that one should not *hear* God's voice lest one die — what had been argued is that no one can *see* God and live — yet here the very line of God's response to

Moses in Exodus, "No person can see me and live" (33:20), is quoted as if it applied to speech.

Immediately following the description of the theophany on Sinai, the famous passage, the *Shema*, "Hear O Israel, *Adonai* is our God, *Adonai* alone" (Deut. 6:4), articulates many of the characteristic messages of Deuteronomy. It begins with "Hear": what we have to do in relation to God is listen, listen in a twofold sense. Being with God is a hearing, not a seeing. We can't see God, but we can hear God's voice, listen to what God wants. That easily flows into the second meaning of "listen" — "to obey," an overtone of the word "listen" that is used with this meaning several times in the book. Israel is instructed to be loyal, to attend to what God has said, to listen to God and not to any other divinity or foreign ruler. The one voice that is all-important is God's voice; the instructions that God gives must be constantly in one's mind. The voice speaks words that are teachings and commands that need be studied and observed. The succeeding verses in this chapter become a riff on these themes: one must constantly remind oneself of these words, talk about them, teach them, pass them on from one generation to another, write them down, affix them to one's doorpost, wear them on one's person. The word of God is all that we can "see" of God, so it is to be constantly with us.

Throughout these introductory chapters, rhetorical devices emphasize the way in which speaking and hearing are central to Deuteronomy's notion of revelation, and underscore how "speaking" and "hearing" supplant "seeing." In the speech of Moses following the revelation of the Decalogue, the word *voice* (*kol*) is repeated seven times (Deut. 5:19–26). Similarly, in the passages surrounding the Decalogue, in Moses' introduction and in his summation afterward, Israel is told to "hear" (*sh'ma*) the word of God seven times (the section 5:19–6:3).

Interestingly, the book itself is a collection of speeches — Moses' last words. The effect of Deuteronomy's emphasis on hearing God's voice is that the word itself becomes all-important, its message effected through the power of rhetoric and language. Deuteronomy's prose style is prose poetry, speeches designed with rhythmic meter, repetition, and chiastic structure. It is almost as if it offers perfected rhetoric as proof of the authority of its message, much as later Islam would claim divine authorship of the Koran because of its poetic excellence. What we have of the Divine are words, speech, commands. To keep God's word, to observe God's commands, represents the service that Israel owes God in return for God's presence, for God's having watched over them, for God's having spoken with them. Further, this substitution of voice for image means that "observing"—that is, obeying—God's word takes on more significance than the ecstatic visionary experience of God or the being with God. God is made known through God's words being heeded.

The theological weave of Deuteronomy is tight-knit. Immediately following Moses' description of the giving of the Decalogue are two sermons. The first, as just pointed out, continues the sevenfold repetition of the word *voice*; the second repeats forms of the word *command* seven times, exhorting the people to obey the commandments in the land that they are about to enter. In Deuteronomy's understanding, what remains of the contact with God after the experience of revelation is to listen to the voice, to obey the commandments.

Deuteronomy, then, understands God's revelation as being primarily about instruction, the teaching of commandments. To obey God's commands is to hear God's voice in one's own life, and that is as close as one can come to God. The proper service of God is to be a faithful people—"to listen" and "to hear," which leads to their consequence: "to obey."

To listen and to obey, and like God, to speak. Speech takes on a new significance for the human as well. While the priestly portions of the Bible do not include any prayers as part of divine worship—the modern biblical scholar Israel Knohl remarks that the sacrifices mandated in Leviticus were seemingly offered in silence since no liturgy is included in the formulation of the order of service—yet several times Deuteronomy requires prayers to be said.[12] In these passages prayer has a role in expiation and cleansing, something that Leviticus exclusively credits to the role of sacrifice and priestly ritual. In Deuteronomy, God reaches the human through speech and through acts of salvation in history, and the human reaches toward God in speech and through religious and ethical acts.

In the end, the unseen God is a more commanding presence than any being who can be visualized, but, in turn, God can be addressed.

INHERITANCE

A central concern of the treaties of the Assyrian king Esarhaddon is succession.

For the Assyrians, the orderly transition of kingship was a constant matter of concern. Esarhaddon had gained the throne after a civil war between him and his brothers. Now he is worried: if, after his death, there is a power struggle for succession, just as there was when he acceded to the throne, in the chaos resulting from wars between rival claimants to it, individual subject states will try to break free and the empire will fall apart. He therefore insists that the vassal states promise to support the orderly succession of his son Assurbanipal and not side with any other claimant. Esarhaddon further demands that the vassal states pledge total loyalty: they shall "love" his son. The treaties that promise loyalty to his son upon his death are the very treaties that Esarhaddon keeps in his throne room. He holds court with these documents, which attest to a promise of orderly succession, right at his side. (A revolt, involving rival claimants to the throne, did break out upon his death, and though it was quickly put down, the validity of his fears is demonstrated by the later collapse of the Assyrian Empire in civil wars prompted by rival claimants shortly after the death of Esarhaddon's son Assurbanipal. The throne room itself was sacked in 612 BCE, a little more than fifty years after Esarhaddon's death.)

Interestingly, Deuteronomy, too, is centrally concerned with the issue of the succession of generations. Future generations of God's people need to be equally bound to the covenant as the founding generation who experienced the Exodus from Egypt, that they not revolt against the God of Israel who took them out of the Land of Egypt.

The literary device of setting Deuteronomy at the end of Moses' life allows him to address a new generation, a second generation, an inheriting generation: not the generation of the Exodus but their children, the ones who are about to enter the land, who will live beyond his own time. The preservation of the memory of God's acts and the safeguarding of the pure worship of the true God of Israel across the generations are the central concerns of these last words of Moses. The language of exhortation on the Plains of Moab is addressed to the people who will live on after him, but what he says readily applies to all future Jewish generations who also will be inheritors and who must be taught and instructed in the ways of their ancestors. The words spoken to the generation of the desert, "You shall teach your children," are meant to ring out across the chasms of time. Thus, the device of setting the book on the Plains of Moab, making it the record of the last words of Moses before the people enter the land, fits well with the historical situation in which the book was promulgated: a people listening to a new instruction, the law promulgated by Josiah said to be the last words of Moses delivered to them across generations.

The Josianic revolution is interpreted and experienced not as a novel innovation but as the recovery of a lost memory: Josiah, in instituting his reform, insists that he is only returning to the ancestral religious faith that has been corrupted through the generations. The book of Kings, recording the events surrounding the promulgation of Deuteronomy, reports that Hilkiah the High Priest has found a lost and unknown scroll of God's teaching in the Temple. King Josiah hears the words and rends his clothes, "for great indeed must be the wrath of *Adonai* that has been kindled against us, because our fathers did not obey the words of this scroll to do all that has been prescribed for us" (2 Kings 22:13). Josiah's declaration focuses on the failure of memory, the break in transmission. The rediscovered book is an old teaching that has been forgotten. The vision of the true God has been lost. The people have strayed from what has been enjoined as Israel's mission for all time: the pure worship of the God of Israel.

Deuteronomy is written from this point of view: the central problem the book poses is how to ensure the proper transmission of the nation's faith. In its long introduction and at its end, Deuteronomy is concerned with how to preserve the memory of the Exodus and the Mosaic teaching for future generations. Placing this concern in the mouth of Moses at the moment when he has to contemplate the transfer of power, at the time of his own death, as he speaks to a new audience—not the generation who went out of Egypt, but their children who are to enter the land—focuses the reader on the problem of what is to happen with his message in a future time.

Deuteronomy insists that future generations must constantly recall the wonders of the Exodus, the revelation on Sinai, and the grace of God's care while the Israelites wandered in the desert. In Deuteronomy it is these forty years and only this time that holds pride of place. Over and over, aspects of this experience are mentioned and emphasized, but other historical events, other times, hardly matter to this author. There is barely an allusion to the patriarchal generation, just a mention here and there that Israel was saved "for the sake of the promise to your ancestors" (10:11). These ancestors are hardly mentioned by name and no event in their lives is narrated or alluded to. Similarly, whereas the Pentateuch begins by depicting God as the God of all creation and describing the first week, the first family, and the ancestry of the people Israel, in Deuteronomy the people are exhorted to sustain the vision of God they have experienced in the Exodus, at Sinai, and in the wandering in the desert. Not only are other stories and mythological tales ignored, but the vision of God's concern for the people at the time of the Exodus and the wandering in the desert is elaborated and becomes more miraculous in the retelling. God did not only feed the people with the incomparable manna, but they had no need for new clothes or sandals during the forty years of wandering, for "the clothes upon you did not wear out, nor did your feet swell these forty years" (8:4). If anything was problematic in the conditions the people experienced, it was a test by God "to learn what was in your hearts: whether you would keep His commandments or not" (8:2). It may be no accident that the prophet Jeremiah, who lived in the reign of Josiah, has the same understanding and also describes God's care in the desert and Israel's relationship with God as an ideal time when each is present for the other: "I accounted to your favor the devotion of your youth, your love as a bride—how you followed me in the wilderness in a land not sown. Israel was holy to *Adonai*, the first fruits of God's harvest" (Jer. 2:2–3).

The great danger for future generations will be their not remembering this special relationship. But while Deuteronomy does agree that the time in the desert was special—the people uniquely experienced God's care—unlike Jeremiah, Deuteronomy also argues that even the desert generation that experienced this care quickly strayed from proper worship of the Divine. God may have been in an unparalleled relationship with this people, but the people did not reciprocate in the same way. Deuteronomy is always conscious of the danger of apostasy.

In the Pentateuch, the verb *to teach* occurs exclusively in Deuteronomy. This should alert us to how much the question of intergenerational transmission, of ensuring that the commandments are passed on from one era to the next, is critical in this book. The faith of Israel and the proper worship of God are valid and compelling in every generation; given by God, the teachings, like God, are eternal, not ephemeral. Therefore, the issue of instructing a future generation in God's law is a repeated theme of the book. In the *Shema* (Deut. 6:4–9), the instruction to "love *Adonai*, your God" is immediately followed by the exhortation regarding intergenerational transmission: "And you shall teach them unto your children, by speaking of them when you sit at home and walk on your way" (verse 7). In Deuteronomy, love of God—that is, loyalty to God (love of God and reverence for God are practically interchangeable terms in Deuteronomy)—is intimately connected to the ability to sustain memory and the proper relationship with God, cross-generationally. Deuteronomy is self-consciously a teaching that comes after: after the Exodus, after God's primal revelation. Though later generations may not have been party to these experiences, the memory of them, the teachings regarding these moments, can make them present in their lives:

> And this is the Instruction—the laws and the rules—that *Adonai* your God has commanded to impart to you . . . so that you, your children, and your children's children may revere *Adonai*, your God and follow, as long as you live, all the divine laws and commandments that I enjoin upon you. . . .
>
> When in time to come, your children ask you, "What mean the decrees, laws and rules that *Adonai* your God has enjoined upon you?" You shall say to your children, "We were slaves to Pharaoh in Egypt and *Adonai* freed us from Egypt with a mighty hand." (Deut. 6:1–2,20–21)

In Exodus there is a similar passage in which we are told children may ask, "What does this mean?" (13:14). There, however, the phrase refers to a specific ceremony, the redemption of the firstborn, which has a very specific connection to being freed from slavery, since the plague of the firstborn was the final liberating moment. Here again Deuteronomy transforms rhetoric found in Exodus, so that now the memorialization of the Exodus extends not only to the ceremony of redeeming the firstborn but to the entire corpus of law it enunciates. In so doing, what is incumbent on later generations is not just a symbolic act of remembrance but observance of this entire Deuteronomic Code, all of which is a memorial of the Exodus.

Deuteronomy is a book of instruction for those "who come after." Its commands are the means of keeping faith with the originating experience of this people. The way to God, the supreme sovereign, is through obedience to God's word. Devotion to God stands above that due any earthly ruler, for God is the Master of all Masters (10:17). Deuteronomy, the constitution of the Josianic revolution, is the masterful combination of prophetic and priestly theology in a time of resurgence of empires.

8 The People and the Land

In order to prevent further revolts, Assyrians removed native populations from conquered territories and settled them elsewhere, dispersed throughout the empire. The imperial assumption was that conquered populations removed to a foreign land would continue to provide the manpower necessary to ensure the economic base of the empire but that, separated from their native lands, these refugees would no longer revolt against Assyrian authority. Implementing this policy after the conquest of Northern Israel, the northern tribes were exiled to Assyria—dispersed, and seemingly lost from history, they were later known as the "ten lost tribes"—and, in their place, other populations were moved into their lands. The archaeological evidence shows that following Assyria's final conquest of Samaria and the destruction of Northern Israel wrought by Sennacherib in 720, though much of the area was decimated, many cities in the north were rebuilt; the pottery remains are Assyrian, replacing the native pottery. These artifacts support the biblical account of the exile of the northern tribes and the introduction of foreign peoples in their lands, including eastern neighbors, who now squatted on lands west of the Jordan River.

Judeans, no longer surrounded by the related peoples of Northern Israel and with northern refugees now fleeing to Jerusalem, had to define who was to be considered part of the community and who was a foreigner. Thus, at this moment, the idea of distinguishing native and foreigner becomes a critical issue of self-definition and sense of brotherhood for the people Israel. Deuteronomy's exclusivist attitude toward foreigners reflects the new conditions in the Land of Israel in the seventh century BCE.

Earlier we remarked on how Deuteronomy forbids intermarriage between an Israelite and members of the nations roundabout, though intermarriage is not noted at earlier moments (to take just one familiar example, the biblical author finds nothing remarkable in Bathsheba being married to Uri the Hittite, a non-Israelite senior officer in David's army). The stance was not without controversy. Indeed, the book of Ruth may have been written in opposition to Deuteronomy's forbidding marriage to Ammonites and Moabites: Ruth is a Moabite and is said to be a progenitor of the Davidic dynasty.[1]

Along with Israel's separateness, Deuteronomy emphasizes Israel's chosenness. Bible scholar Moshe Weinfeld points out that in Assyrian treaties with vassal states, a favored vassal state is referred to as a *segulah*/treasure. In Deuteronomy, Israel is referred to in exactly this way: as God's treasure. It is not surprising then to find that in Deuteronomy, God's choice of Israel as God's people is described as a royal bestowal of favor. God chooses Israel to be God's intimate, not because of anything the people Israel have done, but out of divine largesse, and with this bestowal of favor comes the responsibility both of acting in a way that reflects well on the grantor and of serving the supreme ruler with appreciation for the great privilege afforded therein.

> For you are a people consecrated to *Adonai* your God: of all the peoples on earth *Adonai* chose you to be God's treasured people. It is not because you are the most numerous of peoples that *Adonai* grew attached to you and chose you—indeed you are the smallest of peoples; but it was because *Adonai* favored you and kept the oath made to your fathers that *Adonai* freed you with a mighty hand, rescued you from the house of bondage, from the power of Pharaoh, king of Egypt. . . . Therefore, observe faithfully the commandments, the laws and the rules, which I charge you today. (Deut. 7:6–8,11)

Israel is called *kadosh*, holy—that is, set aside, dedicated to God's service. God's special quality is holiness, and the people chosen by God share in this divine quality, just as the people who are closest to the person of the king share in a measure of royal privilege and authority. The holiness of the people is an expression of the fact that they are special, distinguished. They can be trusted as attendants of *Adonai* and share in God's glory.

Here, once again, we find Deuteronomy reinterpreting the Covenant Code of Exodus. The latter, too, calls for the people Israel to be holy: "And you shall be holy people to Me: you must not eat flesh torn by beasts in the field; you shall cast it to the dogs" (Exod. 22:30). In Exodus, holiness retains a priestly connotation, which is where the term originates. There, holiness defines what is unfit for consumption: the meat torn from animals in the wild conveys impurity. We are not told why. Perhaps it was because this meat was deemed unfit for sacrifice; Israelites who consumed it were partaking of that which was not fit for God, therefore unholy.

Deuteronomy inherits the injunction to maintain holiness but gives it new meaning, a meaning derived from a secular realm: to be holy is to be a part of God's court, to be one of God's guardians.

The court must be filled with loyal followers. They must worship only *Adonai*. Those who come closest to the person of the king must be of the pure-bred elite nobility, of proven loyalty. If one is disloyal, one must be severely punished. It is in Deuteronomy that we find the law of the recalcitrant city—the wiping out of entire urban populations that have betrayed the worship of the God of Israel.

Similarly, the purity of Israel as it lives its life in the land must be guarded. Only certain peoples may enter the community, and the single-minded worship of God must be maintained throughout Israel. This purity, of worship and of blood, is seen as the contemporary parallel to the injunction regarding the purity of the camp as the people traveled in the desert.

And so, this small nation-state that survived the Assyrian onslaught will achieve a glory beyond that of even the most powerful of nations:

> You have affirmed this day that *Adonai* is your God, in whose ways you will walk, whose laws and commandments and rules you will observe, and whom you will obey. And *Adonai* has affirmed this day that you are, as promised, God's treasured people who shall observe all the divine commandments, and that [God] will set you in fame and renown and glory, high above all the nations that [God] has made; and that you shall be, as promised, a holy people to your God, *Adonai*. (26:17–19)

It is all of a piece. Of all the Five Books, Deuteronomy emphasizes the exclusive worship of God, the supremacy of God. God has chosen Israel as God's special people and God will protect them, give them glory, so long as they remain loyal in their exclusive worship and obey God's commands. Monarchs offer protection, and God, the ultimate sovereign, will secure Israel against all enemies, all other kingdoms. Monarchs ennoble their courtiers; likewise, the people Israel will become famous, a people of renown. In return God demands loyalty, which, in Deuteronomy, is the primary meaning of the word *love*. God's mighty arm freed Israel from Egypt and God will remain protective of Israel if Israel obeys God's word. And when Israel obeys God's law, the society this people creates will be the envy of the peoples of the world. Just as God is supreme, Israel will be seen as cherished.

Deuteronomy begins its history with the Exodus from Egypt and continuously harks back to the Exodus, for what God did for the people Israel in Egypt demonstrates that powerful earthly kingdoms can be overthrown, for God is the ultimate source of political power. Thus, Moses says to the people emerging from the desert and about to face the nations settled roundabout:

> Should you say to yourselves, "These nations are more numerous than we; how can we dispossess them?" You need have no fear of

them. You have but to bear in mind what *Adonai* your God did to Pharaoh and all the Egyptians: the wondrous acts that you saw with your own eyes, the signs and portents, the mighty hand, and the outstretched arm by which *Adonai* your God liberated you. Thus will *Adonai* your God do to all the peoples you now fear. (7:17–21)

The hearers of this passage at the time of Josiah could easily apply this political view to contemporary events. Superpowers may rage at your door; have no fear. If you do what is right in the eyes of God then you will surely be protected.

We know that they heard it in this way because we have the evidence of the prophet Jeremiah who lived and preached at this time. He berates his listeners for turning to the superpowers of the day: "What then is the good of your going to Egypt to drink the waters of the Nile? And what is the good of your going to Assyria to drink the waters of the Euphrates?" (Jer. 2:18). Then he draws an exact parallel between the events of the Exodus and the vision of Israel's salvation at this time: "Assuredly, a time is coming—declares *Adonai* —when it shall no more be said, 'As *Adonai* lives who brought the Israelites out of the land of Egypt,' but rather, 'As *Adonai* lives who brought the Israelites out of the northland, and out of all the lands to which *Adonai* had banished them'" (Jer. 16:14–15).

Deuteronomy may have assigned its speech to Moses—the nation's liberator and great leader addressing the generation wandering in the desert—but Josiah's contemporaries would have heard it as ongoing admonition regarding Israel's politics. Deuteronomy's political perspective is a representation of the reformist understanding of the demands of international politics. If Israel remains loyal to God, then neither Assyria nor Egypt will subdue it. Judea ought not surrender its independence.

The biblical theologian took the realities of contemporary culture and politics and turned them on their head. In the favored position that other nations had placed their own earthly ruler, Israel placed God instead. Rather than a noble court, the people Israel are God's courtiers, God's noble entourage. Israel will survive if it but serves God's will, heeds God's commandments, and remains pure, for the nation is God's treasured servant, a people apart.

THE LAND

As noted earlier, archaeological evidence seems to show that for most of its history, the kingdom of Judea was a relatively small, mostly rural country, largely confined to the hill country, the areas around Jerusalem and Hebron. At an early time in its history, Judea was able to expand and establish a foothold in the wilderness to the south—though some of this territory was controlled by the Northern Israelite tribes in Transjordan—but for the latter part of its history, Edomite assertion of independence and expansion through the southern region usurped Judea's hegemony in this area. By contrast, it was Northern Israel that developed large urban centers and a powerful, wealthy upper class. It was Northern Israel that became a vital international player, at times expanding its territory through alliances and war.

After the defeat and exile of Northern Israel, Jerusalem was saved a comparable fate. For a while Judea may even have tried to expand its territory, but after revolting against Assyria, King Hezekiah was left with the smallest territory Judea had ever occupied—Jerusalem and its environs.

Conditions changed during the reign of his successor, Manasseh. Although, as mentioned, the northern lands were repopulated with foreigners, much remained desolate after the Assyrian conquest, the newly arrived immigrants represented a much smaller proportion of the previous population, and as Assyria declined in power in the latter part of Manasseh's reign, the international power vacuum allowed for Judea's physical expansion. Archaeological evidence points to Judea's expansion to the south into the Negev and to the west toward the coastal plain. In addition, some of the land of Northern Israel may have come under the sway of Manasseh's rule, especially those areas most proximate to Jerusalem. Archaeologists now doubt that the biblical accounts of the glory of Solomon's reign and the expanse of the Davidic Empire, some three hundred years earlier, were as great as the Bible narrates; the vast territory claimed for these reigns may have been a literary imagining of a glorious past. If so, it is only in the reigns of Manasseh and his grandson Josiah that this Davidic dream comes closest to fruition for Judea.[2] For a brief period of time, Josiah's kingdom could think of itself as a strong regional power.

Since the territorial expansion of Judea was a new phenomenon, we should not be surprised that land holds a special pride of place in the book of Deuteronomy and that the book's delineation of the expanse Israel is to occupy when it enters the land is biblically maximal. "Every spot on which your foot treads shall be yours; your territory shall extend from the wilderness to the Lebanon and from the river—the Euphrates—to the Western Sea" (Deut. 11:24). "The wilderness" is the southern, Negev desert; "the Lebanon" is the mountain range to the north; "the Euphrates" is to the northwest, the northern part of modern-day Syria; and "the Western Sea" is the Mediterranean. Though in all their ancient history, neither Northern Israel nor Judea ever occupied such an expanse, for a moment, in Josiah's reign, this dream seemed plausible.

The land is described in the most eloquent terms and is seen as a special gift from God:

> For *Adonai* your God is bringing you into a good land,
> A land with streams and springs and fountains issuing from
>   plain and hill;
> A land of wheat and barley, of vines, figs and pomegranates,
> A land of olive trees and honey;
> A land where you may eat food without stint, where you will
>   lack nothing;
> A land whose rocks are iron and from whose hills you can
>   mine copper.
> When you have eaten your fill, give thanks to *Adonai* your God
> For the good land which God has given you. (Deut. 8:7–10)

The rhetorical elements of these verses are not incidental. The word *land* is repeated seven times, and the seventh summarizes all that has gone before and calls it good. The land provides everything one needs or wants, similar to God's gift of manna in the desert, the miraculous food that kept Israel alive during forty years of wandering. In the desert Israel experienced God's care directly, harvesting its daily sustenance from the ground. Now Israel can reexperience God's presence in the land—God's own land—that provides Israel's nurture. The fulfilling life lived on the land symbolizes the continuing measure of God's care for the people Israel.

But what Deuteronomy gives with one hand, it takes away with the other. There is a consciousness that the land will not necessarily be a permanent possession, that it is given to the people Israel only insofar as they obey God's commands. This is unlike some earlier parts of the Pentateuch that see God's gift of the land as permanent. To give but one example, in Genesis Abraham is promised that God will grant the land to him and to his descendants "forever": "Raise your eyes and look out from where you are, to the north and south, to the east and west, for I give all that you see to you and your offspring forever" (Gen. 13:14b–15). And there is evidence that the people of Judea believed that their land could never be taken away from them. Jeremiah, a witness to this era, reports: "The prophets are saying to them [the people of Judea], 'You shall not see the sword, famine shall not come upon you, but I will give you unfailing security in this place'" (Jer. 14:13).

The land is God's special treasure and so God keeps watch over it. But that watchfulness means that God is also conscious of how the land might be abused. The people benefiting from the land might violate God's commands and be expelled from it, as God once did to Adam and Eve dwelling in Eden:

For the land that you are about to enter and possess is not like the land of Egypt from which you have come. There the grain you sowed had to be watered by your own labors like a vegetable garden; but the land you are about to cross into and possess, a land of hills and valleys, soaks up its water from the rains of heaven. It is a land which your God *Adonai* looks after, on which your God *Adonai* always keeps an eye, from year's beginning to year's end. (Deut. 11:10–12)

The Land of Israel differs from both Egypt and eastern Mesopotamia. Egypt is fed by the Nile, which rises every year. To be sure, in some years the flow is more abundant than others, and thus Egypt undergoes prosperity and poverty like other nations, but the Nile always rises. It is an eternal source of Egypt's fecundity; farmers water the nearby land through canals running off the Nile. Similarly, eastern Mesopotamia is nourished by the confluence of the Euphrates and the Tigris: their flow, fed by melting snow in the mountains beyond, is so massive that inhabitants of these realms can depend on a constant source of water. Great ancient civilizations succeeded one another along the banks of these rivers, and some of the earliest records of human habitation and urbanization can be found there.

But the Land of Israel is largely served by underwater aquifers that bubble to the surface in unpredictable ways. Snow and rain in the northern mountains can manifest in the flow of water in the desert, but who knows where or when—it may take as much as a year for these waters to bubble up in the south. In the plains, heavy rains in one year might be followed by drought conditions in the next. (We might recall that Joseph's brothers come down to Egypt because of famine in the land.) Therefore, Moses warns that the fecundity of the land is conditional and that uncertainty is built into the very nature of the land that the Israelites are about to enter. Water itself will be an unpredictable present from God, dependent on Israel's loyalty and obedience. It is a daily gift like the manna, a constant reminder of God's blessing or curse.

Moses' speech after the recitation of the Decalogue and before the introduction of any specific laws (the specification of commands begins in chapter 12) is bracketed with the *Shema*/ "Hear O Israel" in chapter 6 and its parallel in chapter 11. In its finale, the speech makes the land the instrument of God's judgment. If you are loyal, then "I will grant the rain for your land in season. . . . You shall gather in your new grain and wine and oil . . . and you shall eat your fill" (Deut. 11:14,15b). But if you are disloyal: "Take care not to be lured away to serve other gods and bow to them. For *Adonai*'s anger will flare up against you, shutting up the skies so that there will be no rain and the ground will not yield its produce; and you will soon perish from the good land that *Adonai* is assigning to you" (11:16–17).

Thus, in the thinking of Deuteronomy, the Land of Israel is especially fit for God's people precisely because existence in the land is always contingent. The very lack of predictability of life in the land ought to make this people especially conscious of God. And God's commandments form the conditions of the covenant between Israel and God. God's responsiveness to God's people, the continued sustenance of the people by its land, is totally dependent on the degree to which the people observe God's commands, central to which is the demand that the people not worship other gods.

That the land itself is the instrument of God's reward and punishment is equally found in the rhetoric of the prophet Jeremiah at this time. He warns:

> I look at the earth,
> It is unformed and void;
> At the skies,
> And their light is gone.
> I look at the mountains,
> They are quaking
> And all the hills are rocking.
> I look: no man is left,
> And the birds of the sky have fled.
> I look: the farm land is desert, and the towns are in ruin. . . .
> For thus said *Adonai*,
> The whole land shall be desolate,
> But I will not make an end of it.
> For this the earth mourns. . . . (Jer. 4:22–26a,27–28a)

The contingency of the gift takes on an extreme dimension in both Jeremiah and the book of Deuteronomy. In the appendix to Deuteronomy, after Moses' enumeration of the blessings and curses, Moses concludes his detailing of the law with the threat of exile as God's ultimate punishment for violation of the commandments. Not only can there be difficult times and drought, but the land can be taken away entirely: "You shall be torn from the land that you are about to enter and possess. *Adonai* will scatter you among all the people from one end of the earth to the other" (Deut. 28:63c–64a).[3]

Exile indeed followed soon after the promulgation of the book, and it was the book of Deuteronomy that provided the most acceptable theory of what had happened. King Josiah's death was followed by a reinstitution of practices that had long been attacked by prophetic circles, and so reform proved to be only a short interlude in Judea's history. The prophet Jeremiah testifies to this backsliding in the last days of the kingdom, berating the resumption of child sacrifice as the external threats to Judea intensified (chapter 19).

It was easy for the later book of Kings to portray the exile as resulting from the people's constant apostasy. This theory of Jewish history paralleled prophetic messages, and the exiles writing the historical books of the Bible incorporated this schema in their understanding of the entire sweep of the history of the First Temple period. As Judea's historians saw it, Deuteronomy's theology of the contingency of residence in the land was validated by history.

Jeremiah records that the people believed that those living in Jerusalem could never be finally defeated and exiled from their land, since they were living on God's land, in God's city, and worshiping in God's Temple. Where would God go if all this were lost? But Jeremiah constantly warns that the land itself is no protection, that God may abandon Jerusalem: "And I will cast you out of My presence as I cast out your brother, the whole brood of Ephraim" (Jer. 7:15).

Jeremiah and Deuteronomy offer the same message concerning the contingent residence in the land. Generations of Judeans, living after the Assyrian siege had been lifted in the time of Hezekiah, and after the destruction of Northern Israel, may have felt that just as Jerusalem was seemingly miraculously spared the fate of Samaria, Judea would permanently be spared destruction. Deuteronomy's theology engages this argument and adopts a prophetic stance: God is supreme and can take away what has been given as a gift. Indeed, its theology would be validated by the exile of Judea to Babylon.

And so Jeremiah announces: "Assuredly, thus said *Adonai* Tzevaot: Because you would not listen to My words, I am going to send for all the peoples of the north—declares *Adonai*—and for My servant, King Nebuchadnezzar of Babylon and bring them against this land and its inhabitants. . . . This whole land shall be a desolate ruin" (25:8–9,11). It is therefore not surprising that when exile does occur, the book of Kings portrays Babylonia as being the instrument of God carrying out God's decree, just as Jeremiah declares that the Babylonian king is God's instrument, *God's servant*.[4] Earthly kings are but puppets in God's historical plan.

God is the ultimate monarch. What is given by God can be taken away. The land is a conditional gift. But if it can be taken away, it can also be given back again. Thus, as much as this is a theology that explains the exile, it is also a theology that can promise restoration. If Israel returns to its God, all earthly kings can be defeated and one king, God, can rule again over the chosen in the land that is God's special place. History had proved the first element in this theology true—apostasy had led to exile—and so the second could be easily envisioned. The post-Exilic prophetic vision looks to the time when God will be installed as king in Jerusalem once again, and "All who survive of all those nations that came up against Jerusalem shall make a pilgrimage year by year to bow low to the King Lord of Hosts" (Zech. 14:16), "for on that day, *Adonai* shall be king over all the earth" (Zech. 14:9). Contingency issues in a historical theology that both predicts exile and offers the consolation of restoration. Contingency, after all, is the human condition.

9   The Heritage of Deuteronomy

As we have seen, Deuteronomy emphasizes many of the same propositions and arguments that prophets initially preached: the insistence on the exclusive worship of Israel's God, *Adonai*; the call for justice and concern for the poor and powerless; the assertion that ethical behavior is as defining of the religious life as ritual acts. In this regard, Deuteronomy brings to the fore an incisive set of theological understandings and laws that reflect the constantly insistent theme of *Adonai*'s ultimate power and moral essence.

Each of the law codes of the Torah emphasizes the exclusive worship of *Adonai*, the God of Israel. The Covenant Code, for instance, explicitly ordains that the people Israel shall not worship the gods of other nations: "You shall not bow down to their gods in worship or follow their practices, but shall tear them down and smash their pillars to bits" (Exod. 23:24). But a possible interpretation of that statement is that other nations rightfully worship other divinities who perhaps have their own independent power. In contrast, Deuteronomy insists on the superiority of *Adonai* over any other divinity, and the uniqueness of Israel's God; ideas that lead the way to a pure monotheistic belief. Historical circumstance may have engendered these deeper understandings, but once having been uncovered, the power of those ideas impelled aspects of Jewish thought from that time forward.

The idea that God was above all earthly powers; that God was the Supreme Power, the Master of all Masters; and that the people Israel were God's treasured people carried this people through its history of exile. Deuteronomy itself eschews the use of the word *King* in regard to God, instead calling God *Adonai Ha-adonim*, the Master of all Masters, meaning the ultimate ruling authority who exercises power for moral purposes: "For *Adonai* your God is the God of gods, and the Master of all Masters, the great, the mighty, and the awesome God who shows no favor, and takes no bribe, but upholds the cause of the fatherless and the widow, and befriends the stranger, providing food and clothing" (10:17–18).

It was easy to identify the transcendent and commanding sovereign pictured in Deuteronomy with the notion of kingship, for the rulers of great empires like the Greeks, the Persians, and the Romans exercised absolute authority. Thus subsequently, that latter metaphor took hold as a way of expressing Deuteronomy's insistence on God's absolute transcendence. Later Jewish sages, for instance, ordained that every blessing had to contain the name of God, and that to be considered a true blessing, it needed to include the identification of God as sovereign using the term *Melekh Ha-olam,* "King of the World" (sometimes translated as "Sovereign of the World"). Thus, every formal moment of prayer needed to include the recognition that *Adonai* is the ultimate ruler.

These motifs—that God is transcendent, that ultimate loyalty is owed solely to the one God, and that the awe and respect in which earthly kings were held should be reserved exclusively for God—are illustrated by the popular medieval poem *"Melekh Elyon*/The King on High,"* written to be recited on the High Holidays and found in prayer books to this day. Each stanza contrasts God as King with earthly kings. It refers to God as "the King on High," and to earthly rulers as "mortal kings." Customarily, the ark (containing the Torah scrolls) is opened when the stanzas describing God are pronounced, but is closed when the stanzas referring to earthly rulers are recited.

The poem appears to have been written in the sixth or seventh century by one of the greatest early poets, Elazar Hakalir, and then rewritten several times in the late Middle Ages so that several versions exist. Here, translated into English, are the first two stanzas of a medieval version of this poem:

The King on High
Mighty, above all,
Doing as He says.
Fortress and Shield,
Raised on high, and raising up all,
Seating kings on their thrones,
Will rule forever.

The mortal king
Disgraced and despoiled,
Hiding his mistakes,
Confused and weak,
Constantly sinning,
Tested in everything he does,
Plundering his own treasure,
How then can he rule?[1]

God is the true king. Earthly monarchs are "confused and weak, constantly sinning."

Imagine what it was like to recite this poem throughout the late Middle Ages as kings became increasingly more powerful and used their authority for personal glory. These kings saw Jewish communities as nothing more than sources of revenue, but Jews could see God as the ultimate authority and defender of their just cause. Jews, praying in their synagogue, could affirm their own dignity and assert that the kings who ruled over them were mistaken fools who would be judged by their Maker. It is no wonder that some scholars think that many later prayer books omit most of the verses describing earthly kings in negative terms owing to governmental censorship.

Yet whatever was done to this particular poem by royal agents, it was nevertheless the case that Jews, praying to the "Ruler of the Universe," knew the difference between earthly rulers and the heavenly one. Ultimate power resided with God, and true love and loyalty were directed there. Religious imagery allowed Jews to mock those who would subject them to the ignominious rule of "earthly" potentates. Importantly, the transcendent deity, the heavenly king, was the moral compass by which the immoral acts of earthly rulers could be judged.

That image of God as the ultimate power, beyond all human manifestations of power, expressed itself in Jewish theology in a variety of ways. This idea of ultimacy could be radicalized. It was possible to take the image of ultimate power and see in it a "beyondness"—God cannot be compared to anything we humans encounter on earth. The nature of God's power, of God's being, is different from anything human sensibility comprehends; God cannot be encompassed through any human characterization. This impulse can equally be traced to Deuteronomy's insistence that God ought not to be worshiped through any physical representations—the book's extreme aniconism—as well as to its message that God is above any earthly power. Add to this Deuteronomy's emphasis that God cannot be seen and that only God's voice, God's teaching, can be comprehended, and one can easily appreciate its leading to the medieval philosophical idea that God's essence is so different from human understandings that it is unknowable.

The medieval Jewish theologian who took this latter idea to its limits was Moses Maimonides (1135–1204). Maimonides insists that all biblical and rabbinic assertions about God, any positive statements we might make, are rhetorical devices—instructional in their purpose but certainly not to be taken literally. Thus, when the Bible speaks of God's mighty arm in Egypt and at the Sea of Reeds, we ought to immediately understand that it is speaking metaphorically. There is no intention to ascribe a physical body to God—God, of course, does not have an arm. It may be that we easily recognize that metaphor as a figure of speech, but this should equally apply to other descriptions of God, like God's anger, or God's might. Indeed, Maimonides is absolutely insistent that anyone who would ascribe any physical aspect to God, or any anthropomorphic description like action or emotions, can no longer be considered a monotheist. God is above any description and cannot be grasped in any image. All human understanding is filtered through the material universe, which inevitably colors and informs human thinking. These human realities prevent us from ever capturing the reality of the Divine. This is equally true of ascribing to God human feelings such as love and regret, anger and sadness, as it is of physical descriptions of the body of God. Our web of language is inevitably caught up in human conceptualizations, feelings, and emotions, yet God is beyond these all too human understandings.

Including this theological idea in his summation of Jewish law, the *Mishneh Torah*, Maimonides carries Deuteronomy's rhetorical puritanism to its logical conclusion:

> Since it has been determined that God has no physical being, nothing that characterizes physical being can occur in God: neither attachment nor separation, neither space nor dimension, neither ascent nor descent, neither right nor left, or forward or back, not sitting nor standing. Nor is God found in time, that it might be said that God has a beginning or an end or a span of years. God does not change at all, nor is there anything that could effect a change in God. God does not die, nor can it be said that God lives as any living being. God is neither foolish, nor wise like a wise man. God neither sleeps nor wakes. God is neither angry nor laughs, is neither happy nor sad, and is not silent nor speaks like a human being.[2]

How, then, to talk about God? Maimonides sees his negative theology as the only means we have to describe the ultimate power of God. All we can say about God is a series of negative statements—what God is not: God is not a material object; God does not die.

But in the building up of these negative statements, we begin to capture some sense of God. Maimonides would argue that out of all the negatives, some measure of God's glory and majesty may be experienced.

Maimonides insists that he is taking Deuteronomy with absolute seriousness. Over and over again Deuteronomy is adamant that to identify God with any physical representation is to demean the concept of God. What God is cannot be captured by any icon, just as the Josianic revolution proceeded by tearing down even traditional monuments that might lead people to identify any aspect of Divinity with a physical image. It is Deuteronomy that asserts that even at Sinai, even at the supreme moment of revelation, Moses and the people saw nothing of God. Maimonides extends this Deuteronomic program of purification even to verbal imagery, and thus moves what is implied in Deuteronomy to a new level. Even the assertion that God is omnipotent or omniscient—that is, the ascription of ultimate power to God—places God within human categories of understanding and is therefore incorrect.

Thus, Maimonides takes the teaching of Deuteronomy as his template. All words descriptive of God are iconic images, useful in poetry but not to be taken literally; when speaking philosophically they are to be discarded. In both his insistence on the absolute purity of our theological assertions about God and his concern for not falling into idolatry, Maimonides, who lived more than fifteen hundred years after the Deuteronomist, has fully imbibed the latter's message—though, of course, the Deuteronomist was not imbued with medieval philosophy and might quickly retort that he never meant to go that far. We should not be surprised that of all the books in the Bible, Maimonides' philosophical summa, *The Guide of the Perplexed*, cites Deuteronomy most often.

Yet if we do not have words to describe God, how do we arrive at an understanding of God at all? The best Maimonides can offer is that we begin our religious lives by meditating on the single Deuteronomic verse, "Hear O Israel, *Adonai* is our God, *Adonai* alone." The contemplation of God's uniqueness, of God's oneness, the breaking through from verbal language to reflection on God in silent meditation becomes the starting point for the religious journey on which we are to embark. Just as Deuteronomy begins the movement from Temple worship to prayer, so Maimonides would move from prayer to meditative contemplation—and the starting point of this contemplation is this quotation from Deuteronomy.[3]

At the same time, Maimonides is insistent that the attempt to achieve "true human perfection" cannot be accomplished solely through solitary meditation. One must cultivate a life in society in order to practice an ethical way of life. "Most of the commandments serve no other end than the attainment of this species of perfection."[4] Even Maimonides, who would strip other understandings from our knowledge of the Divine, retains the ethical as a crucial moment in the development of the religious life.

Maimonides is the most radical of those thinkers who are in a direct line of descent from the Deuteronomist. But Deuteronomy's aniconic message has shaped so much of later Judaism, even that of medievals who rejected Maimonides' philosophical bent and engaged in more mystical contemplations of the Godhead. Medieval mystics who wanted to visualize God had to define their Judaism in relation to the unseen God of Deuteronomy, the one who is beyond physical representation. And if they wanted to talk more personally about God, they had to straddle both sides of the fence — simultaneously talking of both the perceptible emanations of God and of the Infinite One who is beyond being caught within human imagination. The mystics could tell stories of the inner life of God, but ultimately they would have to admit that these were only pointers to awaken the imagination to a beyondness that could not be grasped.[5]

Paradoxically, then, Deuteronomy has both engendered the concrete imagery of God enthroned in heaven, an imagery that underlies much of Jewish liturgy, and equally has inspired in Jewish philosophy a sensibility evoking the beyondness of God.

COMMANDMENTS

Deuteronomy declares that there is a sum of commands, a totality that describes God's will and that must be obeyed for one to find favor with God. "If you do obey these rules and observe them carefully, *Adonai* your God will faithfully maintain for you the covenant made on oath with your ancestors" (Deut. 7:12).

In the third century, surveying the legislation embodied in the Five Books of Moses, the talmudic sage Rabbi Simlai taught: "Moses was given 613 commandments, 365 negative ones, like the days of the year, and 248 positive commandments, corresponding to the organs of the human body."[6]

Rabbi Simlai's teaching is a play on the accepted wisdom of the ancient world. The 365 days of the solar year corresponded to the common calendar of the Roman Empire, and the number 248 was then a commonly accepted sum of human organs. Rabbi Simlai was making an artful comment about humans as physical beings who exist in time and the need to see both the physical and temporal realms as dedicated to God. In this formulation, the entire human body becomes an instrument of doing God's will, and each day of the year is the field in which one may labor to observe these commandments. At every moment, one's whole body may serve God. It is a theological statement; Rabbi Simlai never meant for the calculation of 613 to be taken as the literal count of divine commands.

But once having been uttered, the statement took on a life of its own. Rabbi Simlai's dictum came to be seen as expressing the exact number of commands to be found in the Bible. And so, commentators proceeded to find the correlation between the specific injunctions of the Torah and the number 613.

In a certain sense, the Deuteronomist would have been pleased with the talmudic and medieval rabbis' efforts to enumerate and articulate exactly what it was that God had commanded. Specification allows adherents to feel that they may meticulously observe God's rules, and thus merit being in accord with the divine will at all times. Certainly in arriving at their count, these later sages included not only the instructions in Deuteronomy but those in all of the Five Books. As they saw it, if God has indeed commanded us to fulfill the divine will, we should surely know all that is commanded. The greater that specification, the better able we will be to comply with God's will.

Indeed, there is something quite satisfying about this attitude. Most of us want to know what is required of us to fulfill our obligation in being on this earth, and it is easier to discharge specified obligations than generalized ones. If demands are stated amorphously, they can have infinite implications, with infinite possibilities of violation, whereas a finite number of rules and responsibilities has the possibility of being accomplished. To put it another way, delimited commandments, commandments with fixed boundaries or limits, are a way of containing guilt: I know what I am responsible for and what I have and have not done. Equally, they are a way of experiencing joy: I am fulfilling the will of my creator.

In some ways Rabbinic Judaism is the inheritor of this attitude.[7] The Mishnah, the authoritative compilation of Jewish law edited at the beginning of the third century, was the first to attempt to present the totality of these commandments topically and systematically. There are six "orders," and the tractates within each order are arranged by subject.[8] Interestingly, on the one hand, the Mishnah explicates rules regarding everyday behavior, practical matters ranging from ritual questions such as what constitutes work that violates the Sabbath to how far from city limits need one place a foul-smelling tanning factory. On the other hand, it includes laws regarding purity and Temple worship, though it was written at a time when the Temple did not exist. In this way it sought to describe the totality of Jewish law, and it became the authoritative statement of Jewish law for subsequent generations.

Yet the codification process left out of the compilation differing traditions, source material, legal reasoning. Subsequently, talmudic commentary—both in the Land of Israel and in Babylonia—sought to restore these elements, but these efforts only served to broaden the tradition yet again. This is especially true of the Babylonian Talmud, so much so that one leaves the complexity of a page of talmudic discussion confused as to what constitutes the law, or how indeed to behave. This was most troubling once centralizing institutions lost their authority and written texts came to have the authority that living teachers once had, for it meant that one needed further direction in religious life.

Then, once again, almost precisely a thousand years after the composition of the Mishnah, Maimonides engaged in an innovative attempt to arrange the totality of these laws.

Combing the Five Books of Moses, Maimonides listed the 365 negative commandments and the 248 positive ones, thus taking Rabbi Simlai's metaphor of 613 commandments quite literally. He then arranged all the commandments in fourteen general topics and specified the incumbent detail in their observance.

Maimonides titled his code of Jewish law the *Mishneh Torah*. Shades of meaning and allusions are at play. Deuteronomy uses the phrase *mishneh torah* to mean "copy" in the verse commanding the king to carry a copy of "the Book" with him. The phrase can also mean "a second Torah," for etymologically the word "to copy" means "to make a *second* edition." The term *mishneh torah* is additionally an alliterative play on the related word *mishnah*, meaning "study," which significantly is the title of the normative collection of Jewish law edited by the second-century rabbis. Maimonides had all these meanings in mind. He writes in the introduction: "I have called this work the second Torah, *Mishneh Torah*, since a person may read the written Torah and afterward read this and then know the entire oral teaching, and need no other book between them." One book could contain all that God wants from us.

And there is a reason for this need of specification. In his other major work, *The Guide of the Perplexed*, Maimonides explains that the reason for many commands is to ensure that the worship of the Divine remains pure—that we do not slide back into idol worship. If you will, the law is a way of disciplining us to ensure the purity of our belief and our worship. This, too, accords with the Deuteronomic imperative of ensuring the purity of divine worship.

Subsequently, many Jewish thinkers have since radicalized this view of the law, seeing the sole purpose of the observance of Jewish law as offering fealty to God, and eschewing any attempt to find practical reasons for observance.[9] To these thinkers, the only purpose of the law is adherence to God's will. It is not for us to attempt to understand why specific laws have been legislated by the Divine; what God desires from us is obedience, for God knows what is good for us and for the world. The true religious path allows God, and God's goodness, to totally rule our lives. We are to subjugate any of our individual desires to divine will and desire. This is what it means to serve God "with all one's heart." Adopting the language of Deuteronomy, these theologians argue that the Torah presents commands that we are to fulfill. It is not for us to question their reasoning. The test of loyalty is our willingness to obey commands even though we do not understand their justification.

For instance, this is the view of Yeshayahu Leibowitz, a well-respected twentieth-century Israeli scientist and philosopher. "The reason for the commandments is service to God and not the satisfaction of a need or human interest."[10] Indeed, he argues that if we believe the law fulfills human needs or human goals, then it is not done for God's sake but for our own. It is the selfless service of God, performed day in and day out, that constitutes the religious approach to the Divine. Leibowitz argues that this was the position of Maimonides, of rabbinic tradition, and of the Bible itself. Note how the Deuteronomic notion of obeying God's command is brought to its extreme conclusion.

One should not think that Leibowitz is alone in pursuing this philosophical line of reasoning to its limit. Many texts come close to presenting this point of view. One such example can be found in the writings of the early twentieth-century Hasidic master Abraham Weinberg. In his opening comments on Genesis, interpreting the command to Adam not to eat from the Tree of Knowledge of Good and Evil, Weinberg asserts that the reason for the command was to teach Adam not to

depend on his own understanding and reasoning but that he wholeheartedly observe what God had commanded him even though he was not given any reason or explanation. This is the path which a Jew must steadfastly hold to in the service of God, for without this, one would step backwards in the face of particular circumstances because one would imagine that in this time one could not behave as previous generations did, etc., just as Adam did when he forsook responsibility regarding his sin, excusing himself saying, "the woman that you gave to stand beside me...."[11]

In this view, Adam in the Garden represents a paradigm of what God desires from us: obedience. Our own reasoning only leads to our offering excuses for our behavior or apologies for doing less than God desires. We were exiled from the Garden for the very reason that we were seduced by human reason, which finds explanations for letting ourselves off the hook. The way back to the Garden is simply to obey the voice of God.

Deuteronomy casts a long shadow. In so many ways, these later thinkers are Deuteronomy's children.

THE BOOK

It is not accidental that later Judaism, following the Deuteronomist's lead, found that the need for specification of the commands made the production of books a necessity. A book, a code, can specify what is required—all I need do is look in the proper section and I can know how to direct my life. The Deuteronomic impulse is to denote commands and to write them down as if to say: roll through this scroll and all you need know to live a proper life will be revealed. We should recall that Deuteronomy teaches that the king must have the scroll of the law with him, so that he might constantly be reminded of what constitutes rightful behavior. By extension, books allow each of us to know what is rightful behavior.

The report of Josiah's revolution in the book of Kings centers on the finding of a book, authenticated by the prophetess Huldah. "I have found the Book of Instruction, *Sefer Hatorah*, in the House of *Adonai*," declares Hilkiah, the priest, and with that discovery the Josianic reform begins. This is not simply *a* book of instruction but *the* book, the work that contains the final teachings of Moses, the summation of God's word to Israel. No other book need be consulted; rather, here one can find not only the fundamental plan for Josiah's revolution but that which should speak for all time.

Deuteronomy's view that a single document, a book, contains the summation of the word of God, articulates God's will, and encompasses all that God desires of us was later widened to include the entire Pentateuch, and the word Torah became synonymous with all five books. The injunction of Deuteronomy, for instance, not to stray to the right or to the left—"Be careful to do as *Adonai* your God has commanded you, do not turn aside to the right or to the left"—was understood to apply to the entire Torah, understood now as "the Five Books of Moses."

As noted earlier, many scholars believe the opening and closing chapters of the book of Deuteronomy were later additions to the book. These chapters represent the first understandings of the implication of Deuteronomy—that it contains God's message for all generations. These additions prepared Jewry for what in later times became the injunction to study and immerse oneself in the words of the Teaching:

> Every seventh year ... Gather the people—men, women, children, and the strangers in your communities—that they may hear and so learn to revere *Adonai* your God and to observe faithfully every word of this Teaching. Their children too, who have not had the experience, shall hear and learn to revere *Adonai* your God as long as they live in the land that you are about to cross the Jordan to possess. (Deut. 31:9–13)

The word of God is not only the possession of priests or confined to instruction of the king; rather, it is to be read to all the people who will learn thereby what God demands of them. The Babylonian Hammurabi's Code may have been issued for the elucidation of future kings and their law courts, but the *Sefer Hatorah* is meant to be studied, contemplated, and memorized by all. It is the prime instrument for understanding the divine will, containing within it the record of God's revelation, and it is the means for recapturing the original revelatory moments that established this people.

So, while the authors of the words just quoted may have had only the book of Deuteronomy itself in mind, the injunction regarding instruction came to be applied to the entire Pentateuch: knowing and studying this law, memorizing and constantly keeping it in mental view, became a supreme Jewish value. The Deuteronomic injunction to "take to heart these instructions. . . . Impress them upon your children; recite them when you stay at home and when you are away, when you lie down and when you get up" (6:6–7) was later understood to have a wider application than the Decalogue or the book of Deuteronomy itself; instead, it was applied to the entire corpus of Jewish religious study. Every one of the people Israel must study, remember, and hold each word of this teaching as close to their heart as they can. Thus, the later Rabbis of the Talmud interpreted Deuteronomy to mean that each member of the people Israel was commanded to write a personal copy of the Torah that would be in their possession.

Which takes us back to an earlier thought: Deuteronomy is a public book, a clearly delimited set of instructions and law that can be studied and referenced and transmitted again and again, intergenerationally. It is a book, published, memorized, constantly and repeatedly taught and recited, meant to guarantee that the next generations would no longer overthrow the reforms of the previous ones. In the last additional chapters of Deuteronomy, Moses instructs that his teaching should be written down as a book and placed beside the ark—that is, the ark that contained the stone tablets Moses had brought down from the mountain: "When Moses had put down in writing the words of this Teaching to the very end, Moses charged the Levites who carried the Ark of the Covenant of the Lord, saying, 'Take this book of Instruction and place it beside the Ark of the Covenant of the Lord, your God, that it remain as a witness against you'" (Deut. 31:24–26).

In other words, this teaching is given the same status as the original revelation on Sinai. And while the author may have been referring to the book of Deuteronomy, or one of its essential parts,[12] Jews in later generations understood that the entire Pentateuch had the same status as the Decalogue. Jews are known as "the People of the Book," seeing in the book, the Torah, the meaning and particulars of God's revelation.

Words need to be understood; books need to be interpreted. The idea that the word of God was now captured in a book gave rise to a new class of people: the scholarly students of the book. Sages, teachers, rabbis now served as replacements for the priests and prophets who had formerly mediated the people's relationship with God. The Judaism that lived on was that of the People of the Book, and these teachers guard its instruction.

Yet there is a strange quality of the written word: on the one hand it is inscribed, fixed; on the other hand, the words need to be explained, interpreted. This is especially true as time passes and the original context of the writing is lost. Sages are needed to interpret meaning. Thus later sages developed an expanded idea of Torah influencing Judaism to our own day. To be sure, there is a written book, the Torah/ the Instruction, but there is also an interpretative tradition alongside it, the oral teaching. In some understandings, this oral instruction was given by Moses alongside the written material he conveyed. In other interpretations, the oral teaching constitutes all the implications subsequently drawn out of the Written Law. In this latter conception, the Written Law is both a precise instruction and also a template to be used to direct behavior in situations not covered by the original teaching.

In either formulation, there is a knowledge of the insufficiency of the written word in and of itself to anticipate future exigencies — not to say its inability, even in its own time, to cover all areas of life. As such, the very notion that Deuteronomy sets in motion of a book encompassing the totality of God's will is constantly undercut by what a book necessitates: interpretation — readers' understanding of its meaning in their own times.

Myriads of books were then written to close this gap, but these latter would similarly prove insufficient, if only because times and life conditions change, and new technologies spark new understandings, new ways of seeing, and new questions. The Deuteronomic imperative gave birth both to the glorification of the text and to an expansion well beyond the text. That is the fate of a book that sought to encompass a totality.

Books give rise to more books, requiring more study and interpretation. In fact, in rabbinic thought, study of Torah becomes as important as the performance of ritual and ethical acts. One finds debates in the Talmud as to which is more important, study or action, and in one such discussion the matter is decided in favor of study, for it is both of spiritual value in and of itself and also leads to right behavior. As the contemporary commentator Chaim Saiman remarks: "The decision to entwine a demanding system of regulation within a sanctified framework of religious study and creativity has allowed *halakha* to survive and thrive under a vast array of . . . cultural settings."[13] In other words, Judaism as a way of life has survived because of its emphasis on study, both the valorization of canonical books and the necessity of interpretation: the making of new books.

A Book of Instruction, the portable word, the written Torah, would serve Israel well in all its diasporas. The Children of Israel would carry into exile the notion of a book that contained God's teaching (rather than a place of pilgrimage where one went to discover God's will, or an inherited caste that could communicate God's contemporary wish). This notion allowed them to hear the word of God even when the Temple was no longer in existence.

It was Deuteronomy that gave rise to "the People of the Book," and the People of the Book have marched to new places with books in hand.

The reforms instituted by the book of Deuteronomy did not last into the next generation. Josiah, the reforming king, was killed at age thirty-nine, at Megiddo (known as Armageddon in later literature, undoubtedly gaining its apocalyptic overtone from this reference), while trying to stop the Egyptians from advancing northward. He was caught between superpowers as they waged war with each other.

By this time Assyria itself had become a vassal state—Babylonia had first successfully revolted against Assyrian rule, and subsequently, after having gained independence, subjugated its erstwhile conqueror. Historically, Judea looked to Babylonia as an ally.

Almost a hundred years earlier, Josiah's great-grandfather, Hezekiah, had allied himself with Babylonia against Assyria and thereby lost much of Judea's autonomy when Assyria defeated the Babylonians. Some years later, Hezekiah's son Manasseh had joined with the Babylonians and Egyptians in trying to overturn the Assyrians, but the alliance was defeated and Judea was forced to become a meek subject state. However, by the end of Manasseh's reign, the forces arrayed against Assyria were effective—the tables were turned and Assyria itself was conquered, never again able to rule as the world power it once had been. Babylonia, its southern neighbor, overpowered Assyria and was soon to become the dominant power in the Middle East.

In the interim, while Babylonia consolidated its victory over Assyria, no major imperium ruled the western Fertile Crescent. The vacuum allowed Judea to expand: settling some of the territory formerly belonging to the Northern Kingdom and moving back again toward the Mediterranean coast, while building fortifications in the Negev to protect itself against its neighbors. It was this expanding kingdom that Josiah had ruled. Rather than simply an insignificant city-state nestled in the mountains, for the moment Judea was a player in the international politics of the Middle East, although the region would soon, again, be dominated by a single power—Babylonia.

In an attempt to check the expanding power of Babylonia and expand his own empire, Pharaoh Necho led the Egyptian army north. En route, Josiah, probably in coalition with Judea's traditional ally, Babylonia, tried to stop Pharaoh Necho's march north across the coastal plain, which Judea now considered to be under its own hegemony. But Josiah had overreached. The Egyptian army rolled through the Judean countryside and Josiah was killed.[1]

The march against the Egyptian forces may have been motivated not only by traditional political alliances but by fear of Egyptian political and cultural dominance in this part of the world. For Josiah and the Deuteronomic reformers, foreign interference was the greatest threat to both independence and the purity of the faith—at various times Assyrian hegemony and Egyptian influence had dominated Judea, and in the view of the reformers and prophets, these in turn had polluted Temple practice. Earlier Jeremiah had preached against any foreign alliances: "What then is the good in your going to Egypt to drink the waters of the Nile? And what is the good of your going to Assyria to drink the waters of the Euphrates?" (Jer. 2:18). So Josiah's march against the Egyptians, his attempt to stop them from fending off the Babylonians, may have been part of an effort to achieve a balance of power that would ensure the independence of Judea and the continuation of reform.

Indeed, the loss did mean the end of Judean autonomy. The book of Kings records that it was Pharaoh Necho who determined which of Josiah's sons would rule after their father's death, deposing the chosen successor, Jehoiachin, and substituting another son, Eliakim. Thus, Josiah's defeat resulted in Judea's becoming a vassal state subject to Egyptian rule, and a few years later, when the Babylonian army finally arrived in full force in this part of the Middle East, Judea was captured and became subject to its rule. The death of Josiah marked the end of Judea's short-lived independence. Subsequent efforts to assert its freedom from Babylonian dominance would lead to its total ruin.

The figure of Josiah was now idealized in the memory of the reformers. The book of Kings certainly treats him in a very special way, viewing him almost as what would later be considered a messianic figure. Aside from its encomium to Hezekiah, the biblical author considers Josiah to be the most pious king of Israel since Solomon's day: "Before him, there was no king who turned back to *Adonai* with all his heart and soul and might, in full accord with the Teaching of Moses; and afterwards none arose like him" (2 Kings 23:25). Even Solomon and David, the progenitors of the dynasty, are portrayed as sinners, while Josiah's reign and reforms are depicted as the ideal of piety.

A hint of how shocking Josiah's death was to his generation may be gleaned from the book of Kings. When the prophetess Huldah authenticates the book of Deuteronomy as God's word, she announces that though Israel and Judah will be punished for the sins of their forebears, Josiah will die quietly in his bed. She could not imagine that Josiah would not be rewarded for his actions, and her prophecy is preserved, even though the same book of Kings records Josiah's violent death at the hands of Pharaoh. The expectation of the proper reward for the just king was so great that even the historical facts could not excise the prophetess's words.

But Josiah did die ignominiously, and with him went the people's faith in a central tenet of the reform: the proposition that *Adonai* alone could protect Israel. Thus, Josiah's death brought an end to reform as both official creed and the dominant religious frame. We know from the book of Jeremiah that soon after his death, the very practices that had been extirpated were resumed—Jeremiah, for instance, inveighs against the reinstitution of child sacrifice in the valley of Hinnom, just below the Temple precinct.

A few years later, Judea, now a vassal of Egypt, suffered defeat at Babylonian hands as the latter marched against Egypt. Continued revolt against Babylonian hegemony would only bring further suffering: Jehoiachin, king of Judea, was carried off to Babylonia, and his uncle Zedekiah was appointed in his place. But revolt continued to ferment in Jerusalem, and eleven years later the Babylonians burned the Temple: "They slaughtered Zedekiah's sons before his eyes; then Zedekiah's eyes were put out. He was chained in bronze fetters and he was brought to Babylon" (2 Kings 25:7).

Zedekiah was the last king of Judea, but the book of Kings does not allow itself to end that way. Instead, it includes a final scene of Jehoiachin, in exile in Babylonia, being raised up, appointed a member of the Babylonian king's court. So it concludes with the hope of a future royal restoration: a hope that lived on in Jewish history but was never fulfilled.

The Babylonian policy of conquest and imperial control was to move defeated peoples to different geographic locales, thus quieting the urge for independence yet utilizing the labor of the subject populations. The Babylonians expected that the exiled peoples could be more easily controlled if they were not living in their ancestral lands. In accordance with this policy, a sizable population of Judea, especially its leadership, was removed to Babylonia. Communal leaders and craftspeople were especially chosen for exile, since Babylonian policy was to leave a leaderless community of peasants who would not cause political trouble.

This Babylonian policy differed from that of the Assyrians. While the latter dispersed their conquered people throughout their empire, the Babylonians settled the Judean exiles in one locale, an area between the Tigris and Euphrates.[2] Thus, whereas the dispersed exiles from Northern Israel became known as the "ten lost tribes," the exiles in Babylonia were able to form a vibrant community and continue their Jewish life.

It is with these exiles that our story continues.

Part III

Revolution in Babylonia

10 Priests, Prophets, and Scribes in Exile

"By the waters of Babylon, there we sat" (Ps. 137). Much of the population of Judea was in exile, the Babylonian conquerors having removed most Judeans to the area along the Euphrates that is modern-day Iraq.

Since joining the dominant culture has so often been part of Jewish history, we might well imagine that some, perhaps even most, of the Judean exiles fulfilled their captors' expectations: assimilating to the local population, relinquishing hope of return to the Land of Israel, identifying their Divinity with that of the Babylonians, adopting local practices including religious worship. But a significant number of Jewish exiles in Babylonia maintained their loyalty to the God of their ancestors and preserved a distinct and separate identity from the majority population among whom they now lived. They took up permanent residence in distinctly Israelite enclaves. Indeed, they were able to transmit that separatist identity intergenerationally: those who stayed loyal to their people formed the beginnings of the long and continuous community that has lived along the banks of these rivers down to our own time.[1]

Since it was Babylonian policy to single out and exile the elite— government officials, communal leaders, influential persons, those critical to the economy such as craftspeople—the small population left in the Land of Israel was a largely leaderless group of poor farmers. Whereas this community in the Land of Israel was disorganized, the exiled community in Babylonia was held together by much of its traditional leadership. A common area had been designated for their settlement, though many lived in the capital city, perhaps serving governmental functions.

These exiles who retained a sense of Judean identity not only preserved their received tradition but engaged in a profound rethinking and reworking of that tradition. They first of all had to ask themselves what had gone wrong. Why had exile been their fate? How could *Adonai* desert the people of Judea and allow the seat of the Divine, the Temple in Jerusalem, to be destroyed? They needed to know what to do differently upon their hoped-for return to prevent a future exile. In other words, what ought the new Jerusalem, the return to the land, look like?

There were a score of answers, based on a variety of interpretations of the traditions they carried with them. As the biblical scholar Michael Fishbane writes regarding the exiles who later returned to the Land of Israel, it was "a community of communities, a variety of Judaisms, each one laying claim to the received pre-exilic Torah traditions — through their separate and separating interpretations of them."[2] Distinct religious groupings had differing responses to the problems posed by exile and hoped-for restoration. With no recognized head of the community, and no monarchy to decide between factions, the different institutional claims, the varieties of theological responses, could be voiced simultaneously, exist side by side.

ROYAL SCRIBES AND DEUTERONOMY

Certainly, the Deuteronomic reformers who lived with the memory of the vibrancy of Josiah's reign had their answer. The book of Deuteronomy they upheld had incorporated the prophetic admonition that sin would lead to exile. In this spirit, the prophet Jeremiah had argued that the citizens of Judea and the inhabitants of Jerusalem should not depend on the belief that God would not destroy God's own house; rather, sinfulness would inevitably lead to punishment, to exile: clearly, exile was the consequence of the "heterodox" religious practices that had characterized life in the land.

The Deuteronomic reformers felt that the warnings incorporated in that book had been validated. The theology they had insisted on in the reign of Josiah had been justified. The sins of the people, their turning to other divinities and their "heterodox" practices, had indeed led to exile as had been foretold.

These Deuteronomists edited and arranged the history of Israel to reflect this judgment. The worship of many divine forces and worship outside of Jerusalem's Temple practiced from the beginning of Israel's history until its exile had led to punishment; thus, religious life needed to be reformed along the lines promulgated in the reign of Josiah. We can imagine that especially governmental officials and monarchists who at one time had administered this code preserved its traditions, hoping to return as the agents of its implementation. They were joined by priests and prophetic circles who had themselves participated in the reform.

These people who had always considered themselves reformers saw the book of Deuteronomy as a sacred teaching of critical instructions. It may well be that they were the ones who added the command at the end of Deuteronomy that this book should lie alongside the Ten Commandments in the Holy of Holies—that is, when the Temple would be restored. Similarly, it was probably these scribes who placed a new introduction at the beginning of Deuteronomy also echoing this theme of apostasy and punishment—the story of the people's defection in the desert even as they had just been freed from Egypt—thus emphasizing the way apostasy had been part of this people's history from the very beginning, resulting in the wandering in the desert.

With this theology in mind, the history of the people from its entrance in the land to the exile was edited in the series of historical books known as the former prophets: Joshua, Judges, First and Second Samuel, and First and Second Kings.[3] Especially Kings reflects the consistent theme of sin and punishment: each king of Israel and Judea is judged by the Deuteronomic standard of purity of worship.

Deuteronomy thus formed a spine for a historical body of literature that was now edited in exile. Altogether, these books constituted not only an analysis of past misdeeds, an explanation of how we got here, but a program for the future: a map for the return to Jerusalem that, this time around, would be upheld by the proper observance of the covenant.

Most likely the students and children of royal scribes and priests who had originally propagated Deuteronomy were the ones, while in exile, who continued enunciating this message, canonizing it in this new expansive library that preserved the royal tradition of First Temple times. They imagined a return of royal rule dedicated to the God of Israel. It is a good guess that this traditional elite maintained the loyalty of many of those in exile, who looked to them for continued guidance. Their influence is apparent, as witnessed by the preservation of their literary output, which forms a major segment of what later became our biblical canon.

PRIESTS, PROPHETS, AND A RECONSTRUCTED TEMPLE

But other groups as well articulated visions of return. Priestly circles continued to preserve ideas about the centrality of Temple ritual, editing their traditions regarding proper sacrifice, purity and impurity, and priestly roles. Not only for priests but for almost all exilic Jewish groups, the sadness of the loss of home centered on the Temple and a vision of restoration dominated their dreams. Virtually all the literature of the period—prophetic sermons, psalmic hymns, and the manuals of the priestly writers themselves—reflect the centrality of the Temple and the priesthood. Ezekiel, both priest and prophet whose anointing as a prophet begins on the banks of the rivers of Babylon, ends the book that bears his name with a precise description of worship in a reconstructed Temple. The Temple, for him, is an essential focus. The righteousness of its priests and their proper service is the goal of return. This reconstructed Temple will be free of corruption, filled with priests punctilious in their observance. Alongside them, a people acting justly would once again have God dwelling in their midst in a visible way.

Ezekiel's was a new prophetic vision. He joined an imagined reconstructed Temple with a vision of a reformed political life: a just society (albeit one that did not include a return to monarchy).

The idea of priest and prophet represented in one figure was hardly the norm of First Temple Judaism. Many of the remarkable scenes of classical prophecy picture the opposition of priest and prophet. Prophets were critics of Temple practice; they inveighed against corrupt priests and frequently pointed to the ways in which practices in daily life were as important as Temple ritual. Even the first Isaiah, who among the classical prophets may have been a priest himself, and who preached long before the exile, did not picture the Temple as central to a righteous life. During the time of the monarchy, priests were primarily concerned with the sanctity of the Temple environs and the meticulousness of the divine service, while prophets emphasized the ways the people and society's elites had strayed from Israel's God and corrupted society. The joining of these two differing perspectives in one person demonstrates how central the notion of a reconstructed Temple had become in exile — even capturing prophetic circles. Equally, it demonstrates how important prophetic theology, with its concerns for larger societal conditions, had become to priestly circles.

On the one hand, we can see Ezekiel using classic prophetic rhetoric to describe the reasons for the fall, delineating the moral and religious failure of the generations that preceded the destruction of the Temple:

Every one of the princes of Israel in your midst used his strength
For the shedding of blood.
Fathers and mothers have been humiliated within you;
Strangers have been cheated in your midst;
Orphans and widows have been wronged within you.
You have despoiled My holy things
And profaned My Sabbaths.
Base men in your midst were intent on shedding blood;
Upon the mountains they have eaten their sacrifices;

They have practiced depravity in your midst.
Amongst you they have uncovered their father's nakedness;
Amongst you they have ravished women during their impurity.
They have committed abhorrent acts with other men's wives;
In their depravity they have defiled their own daughters-in-law;
In your midst, they have ravished their own sisters, daughters
   of their fathers.
They have taken bribes in your midst
To shed blood,
You have taken advance and accrued interest;
You have defrauded your countrymen to your profit.
You have forgotten Me—declares *Adonai*, God. (Ezek. 22:6–12)

This is an almost complete summary of the ethical sins that classical prophets had excoriated. Yet, as remarked, the book of Ezekiel ends with the listing of the precise measurements of the Temple and its accoutrements and the description of the proper order of service to be performed there. This is a new synthetic vision, previously unarticulated in prophetic circles, one that combines notions of purity and of Israel's specialness, and calls for justice and ethical behavior alongside visions of a perfected Temple and priesthood:

Then he led me, by way of the north gate, to the front of the Temple. I looked and lo! The Presence of the Lord filled the Temple of the Lord; and I fell upon my face. Then the Lord said to me: O mortal, mark well, look closely and listen carefully to everything that I tell you regarding all the laws of the Temple of the Lord and all the instructions regarding it. Note well who may enter the Temple and all who must be excluded from the Sanctuary and say to the rebellious House of Israel: Thus said the Lord God: Too long, O House of Israel, have you committed all your abominations, admitting aliens, uncircumcised of spirit and uncircumcised of flesh to be in My Sanctuary and profane My very Temple when you offer up My food—the fat and the blood. (Ezek. 44:1–7)

Yet other prophets offered different visions of reconstruction, of return, and of Temple life.

In his dream of return, the later Isaiah of Babylon declined Deuteronomist explanations, arguing that suffering is not proportionate to sin but is rather a cleansing, not only of one's own sins but of the sins of the world. According to Isaiah, Israel will always remain beloved by God—the relationship of love is not broken because of sin. His vision of a reconstructed Temple—a center of worship for all people (for all will come to know God) and for a priesthood (those privileged to serve in the Temple precincts) extending beyond current dynastic lines to include the peoples of all nations—fundamentally disagrees with Ezekiel's vision of the people Israel's exclusiveness. What Isaiah has learned in exile is that suffering is a necessary aspect of the process of redemption, and that God is present everywhere and among all peoples. His vision of a common humanity and a God who cares and loves all has stirred peoples around the globe as it stirred the exiles in Babylonia. Yet one should note that even for Isaiah when articulating a universal message, a reconstructed Temple is central to his vision, though not a Temple recognizable to the current priesthood.

This mixture of traditional prophetic motifs united with visions of a reconstructed Temple was not limited to the exiles in Babylonia. A few years later, those prophets whose vocation was in the Land of Israel would articulate the same message. These prophets preached after Persia had conquered Babylonia and allowed the rebuilding of an altar and the restoration of religious worship on the Temple Mount in Jerusalem. Malachi, Zechariah, and Haggai, prophets of the late sixth century before the Common Era, tried to bestir the remaining dispirited population of Judea as they witnessed the beginning of a revival under their new Persian rulers. Though they could not immediately envision a day when foreign rule would end, these prophets combined messages of the centrality of the Temple with appeals for moral regeneration. Zechariah, for instance, expresses the traditional prophetic indictment of First Temple Judaism, enumerating the ethical sins that led to the destruction:

Thus said the Lord of Hosts: Execute true justice; deal loyally and compassionately with one another. Do not defraud the widow, the orphan, the stranger, and the poor; and do not plot evil against one another. But they refused to pay heed. They presented a balky back and turned a deaf ear. They hardened their hearts like adamant against heeding the instruction [Torah] and admonition that *Adonai* of Hosts sent to them by His spirit through the earlier prophets and a terrible wrath issued from *Adonai* of Hosts. (Zech. 7:9–12)

In Zechariah's reading, the lack of morality caused the destruction of the First Temple, and a moral turn was needed to accompany the reconstruction of the new Temple. Zechariah refers to this as "God's instruction" — Torah. Here, Torah is not a book but a moral teaching. Here, God's instruction is not anything like the Deuteronomic listing of commands, a written constitution for the people Israel, but rather a calling, a looking toward transformation of the way of being in the world — a true heart leading to just actions. The content of Torah, God's instruction, is the prophetic call for justice and return to the exclusive devotion to God.

Along with these expressions of moral zeal, Zechariah instructs the people to listen to the authority of the new High Priest and to vigorously support the Temple's reconstruction: "Assuredly, thus said *Adonai*: I graciously return to Jerusalem. My House shall be built in her — declares *Adonai* of hosts" (Zech. 1:16). In this Zechariah is like Ezekiel and the later Isaiah: combining the older prophetic tradition of moral vision with the hopes embodied in a new, second Temple. Alongside the rebuilding, there must be a change of heart on the part of the people. They need to internalize the moral instruction at the very center of God's message to God's people.

Similarly, Malachi, another of the prophets preaching in the Land of Israel, excoriates corrupt priests who led to the destruction, but equally envisions a new beginning in which God will again be enthroned in the Temple, corruption will be uprooted, and children will be reconciled with their parents and parents with their children. The prophet appeals to the covenant made by Moses at Horeb (Sinai), but nowhere mentions or alludes to the Deuteronomic covenant on the Plains of Moab. Indeed, the dual concerns of proper support for the Temple and moral existence seem to preoccupy these prophets remaining in the Land of Israel. None of them even allude to any other legal matters or elements of what would later be seen as critical parts of the Pentateuch or even of Deuteronomy.

What one has to imagine, then, is different communities trying to explain the calamity and trying to provide a roadmap for the return. Many old elites found new justification in contemporary events for their received ideology. Court figures and royal scribes, joined with some priests, continued to look toward the restoration of the monarchy, wrote the history of Judea's and Israel's kings, and emphasized the royally promulgated Deuteronomic reform. Priests saw the rebuilding of the Temple in Jerusalem as critical for renewal, recorded and preserved manuals of proper ritual practice, and wrote prescriptions for a cleansed Temple and a priesthood that would be able to serve with authority because of its purity (many priests may have imagined a life in the land without a monarchy). Prophetic circles continued to emphasize the moral turn the people must make. To be sure, there was much overlap between these groupings. Ezekiel offers both a classic priestly vision of restoration along with his prophetic critique of society; and Isaiah, while offering a new understanding of the meaning of suffering, pictures a future of a Temple open to the world. What we see happening is the beginning of the congealing of the tradition into a set of assumptions that blend into one another—a sense that there is a commonly inherited tradition that is both moral and cultic, and that views proper civil governance as a divine concern. Yet at this early stage, one can still detect different emphases and expressions in each of the classic elites. Priests, prophets, scribes, and royal officials continued to function as respected leaders. In exile they each produced a literature of memory and hope that reflects their divergent and converging interests.

Out of this mix emerged another constellation of exilic leaders: historically anonymous but eminently significant. Like so many others, their inspiration reaches back to preexilic times. Literary evidence indicates that they may have formed as a faction during the reign of Manasseh and that their ideas had some influence on the writing of Deuteronomy.

Now, in exile, the work of this faction of dissident priests congealed into a new teaching.[4] Ideas that had been birthed in the latter years of the monarchy now achieved their full flowering and articulation in exile. The conditions of exile allowed these reforming priests to further their thinking, and the lack of clear authority allowed their ideas to gain ascendancy. Influenced by the prophetic message of personal responsibility and ethical behavior as critical elements in religious life, they combined these ideas of the need to reform the entire society with their understanding of the place of sacrificial offerings and sacred worship in constituting holiness.[5]

We know these anonymous priests only by their handiwork. They authored the part of the Five Books of Moses we call the Holiness Code: most of the latter half of the book of Leviticus and parts of the book of Numbers. These reformist priests saw the classic priestly vision as too limited in its sole concentration on the purity of ritual and Temple space as in the early chapters of Leviticus. They believed that the prophets had conveyed an important message: if society was unjust, there could be no true worship of the Divine. They taught that ethical lapses convey impurity as much as dead bodies, and so they emphasized the need for societal reform and individual transformation as central concerns of holiness. God's presence is to be achieved both by proper ritual observance and through righteous activity in the workaday world. Both priests and people, sacred places and the land itself, ritual moments and the everyday, have to equally accord with God's order. Holiness is to be cultivated not only by a priesthood but by each member of the people Israel, in the daily rhythm of their lives. Proper worship in a reconstructed Temple (and perhaps in multiple local temples dedicated to God) need be accompanied by a people who live a holy life on the land.

These priests enunciated their program in instructional codes. They chose to write in the genre of law and judicial narrative, though as we will shortly see, their conception of law was quite different than what had come before.

Interestingly, their work does not accord a place to monarchy; nor does it have very much to say about any other civil institutions. It is the work of people who have no political power but who are great visionaries, trying to fashion a religious agenda for a not-yet-existent independent Judea. In exile their ideas gained the full power of expression, for the exilic experience showed there was a way of maintaining some measure of a functioning community without central governmental institutions. The civil authorities of the preexilic community had proved to be corrupt, and these new visionaries had no model from which to articulate what a reformed society should look like. Yet they could dream—dream of a pure and holy people.

The Covenant Code, contained in the book of Exodus, had briefly alluded to the idea that Israel was to be a holy people, and defined that holiness simply as cessation from eating the plundered animal flesh in the field—a notion that accords with priestly ideas of purity. Years later Deuteronomy had expanded on this brief note found in the Covenant Code to elaborate a theology of the Jewish people. For the Deuteronomist, Israel's "holiness" meant that it was to be a distinguished people, a people treasured by God, a people serving as God's intimate courtiers. Jeremiah, who preached during the reign of Josiah, used the term *holy* in the same way—that which is special, set aside.

The writers of the Holiness Code took this evolving notion of a holy people and gave it a new meaning by expanding it beyond its purely nationalist frame. In their view, one might imagine concentric circles of holiness emanating outward from God, to the priesthood, to Israel, and to the world.[6] Not only are places or priests holy, not only are the Temple service and ritual acts holy, but holiness can be described as a way of life, a system of behavior. The practice of traits such as justice, mercy, compassion, and love reflects divine qualities. The authors of the Holiness Code begin by saying, "You shall be holy because the Lord, Your God, is holy" (Lev. 19:2). Holiness may be the defining characteristic of the Divine, but it can also be cultivated in each individual person, for we are all created in the image of God. Holiness is an imitation of the Divine, an extrusion of divine qualities into human activity.

Here, in Leviticus, holiness is not bestowed by divine favor as it is in Deuteronomy. Certainly it is not achieved automatically, in dynastic genealogies, as priests might affirm. Rather, it is a trait that needs to be developed. But while it is achievable by all humans, Israel is especially called upon to perfect it—if Israel is to be close to God.

Those elements of holiness that are among the defining traits of God—justice, mercy, purity, and above all, love—are accessible to human activity and the human heart. Thus, the central chapter of the Holiness Code, chapter 19 of Leviticus, begins its ethical precepts with the most simple and public of acts—setting aside the corner of one's field for the poor so that they may partake of the harvest—and reaches its high point by describing that which can be most intimate—loving one's neighbor as one's self. The land, the people, and one's heart are all the loci of holiness.

This view is easily distinguishable from the earlier sections of Leviticus, which express little moral concern, talking only of aspects of cultic practice and laws of purity. There, the sanctuary is the sole locus of holiness. There, holiness indicates a certain numinous power—the mystery at the very heart of the universe that can only be encountered with great care, in purity, with proper ritual practice, in a place solely dedicated to the encounter of God and humanity and mediated by people chosen for the task from birth. In the Holiness Code, something new is enunciated—the pursuit of holiness within the secular realm by everyone. That pursuit has first of all an ethical quality.

Jacob Milgrom's magisterial commentary on the book of Leviticus has this to say about the ethical instruction in the Holiness Code: "YHWH[7] has symbolically taken the poor and alien into His domain.

Hence anyone who disobeys his commandments concerning their care are desecrating, as it were, his holiness. . . . The implication is clear: YHWH is the protector of the defenseless, and only those who follow his lead can achieve holiness."[8]

The quintessential perspective of the language of holiness is priestly. The word *holy* is a concept associated with priesthood: priests are set aside, and holiness is associated with the sanctuary. In priestly thought, it is in the Holy of Holies that one meets the Divine. Something revolutionary has happened here in moving the locus of holiness beyond the most sacred space.

Characteristically, the Holiness Code uses as its main form of address the expression "ish, ish" — each and every person; what is written here is meant for you and you and you. This is not a law for an elite but one directed toward each individual in Israel, equally. All have the status of "persons," and therefore all have religious responsibility. Holiness is no longer only a matter of Temple concern or of priestly function; it extends to the entire people, in their daily lives.

What is more, this code applies not only to the people Israel. Its reach is explicitly extended throughout to include all those who dwell in the land, non-Israelites as well. Chapter 19 warns against oppressing the stranger and then offers near the conclusion of the chapter the extension of the law of love to "the stranger who dwells in your midst" (verse 34). This idea, it goes on to say, should not be foreign to the people Israel: remember that you were once slaves in Egypt and were mistreated as outsiders by the regnant society. Indeed, the reason for God's "mighty hand" in the Exodus of the people Israel from Egypt is the creation of an alternate society, a society ruled by God's justice and love (verses 36–37).[9]

The earlier legal codex in Exodus (except for its appendix) is almost entirely secular in approach. Its subject matter is the civil and criminal code of society, its rhetoric is that of crime and punishment, and its form is similar to legal codes in other ancient Near Eastern societies. (It is distinctive in many other ways, especially in expression of greater social equality.) Building on Exodus, Deuteronomy incorporates prophetic moral and monotheistic themes but is still recognizable as a secular legal document. In contrast, the Holiness Code introduces religious terminology throughout, for all worldly relations — relations to the poor, relations to the land, the administration of justice — are matters of holiness. In Exodus, sexual and other crimes are frequently understood in monetary terms; for instance, a violation of virginity involves the payment of the bridal price to the father. In Deuteronomy the rape of an engaged woman is a criminal offense subject to capital punishment. The Holiness Code decrees that even the rape of a slave woman — something the ancients seemingly considered a nonjudicial matter — has rent the relationship with God asunder. The offense in this case is not a monetary transgression against property, for which the perpetrator would now pay the owner of the slave woman for the damage caused. Rather, it is a sin against God, and so a sacrifice — in essence, a confession of sin — must be offered. As seen in this case, personal injury has moved from the category of civil law to religious law. (Our modern sensibility would demand much more, but one should see how, in its historical context, this is a considerable ethical advance.)

Deuteronomy ends its enumeration of laws with a series of curses of those who commit evil in private, away from the scrutiny of witnesses, and therefore avoid earthly punishment. The enumerated crimes committed out of public view, which will never reach the courts, range from sexual relations with one's daughter-in-law (a domestic violation that may never be reported to the authorities) to purposely giving the wrong directions to a blind person. The Holiness Code, too, decries sins committed away from the public eye, and it too decries putting "a stumbling block before the blind," but adds, "Do not curse the deaf" (verse 14). The person who is deaf does not experience the insult, no one else may have heard it, and so no human legal system can punish such behavior, but a violation has been committed; human dignity has been assaulted. If no one else, God has heard this voice and is offended. Unethical behavior even when seemingly without consequence is a matter of concern.

The medieval commentator Nachmanides (1194–1270) extends this insight, explaining that the injunction with which the Holiness Code begins, "You shall be holy," refers to those matters that are beyond the law—"Make yourself holy in those things which are permissible."[10] He senses that the understanding of holiness has gone beyond what law itself can proscribe, that the Holiness Code is concerned with something quite different from the priestly regulations, the explicit commands of the Deuteronomic Code, or the regulations of the Covenant Code in Exodus. The Holiness Code attempts to define the law in areas that reach beyond that which can be adjudicated. It is the expression of a personal ethic as law.

Sitting in exile, these reforming priests were envisioning an ideal return. What ought our community look like to be beloved of God? When we reestablish our polity, how should we behave in order to avert God's wrath? How can we create a society in which a second exile will never occur? Israel must become "a nation of priests and a holy people"[11]—that is, a people dedicated to God, a true community of care concerned with the imitation of God, with the symbol of the presence of the living God, the sanctuary, at its center.[12]

Certainly, one reading of the cause of the exile was that worship in the Temple had not been performed properly. That was clearly the perspective of many priests, who now envisioned a return that would ensure the purity of Temple activity. They set about collecting traditions and teachings that articulated priestly duties and standards along with formulas for the sacrificial system, and writing prescriptions for appropriate worship. Although the materials themselves most likely reflect preexilic practice, the arrangement and editing of these materials dealing with priest and Temple that became the opening chapters of Leviticus took place at the time of the Babylonian exile. Those priests who edited the cultic materials that constitute the latter part of Exodus, the first half of Leviticus, and many sections of Numbers saw proper cultic practice as central to the building of the new Jerusalem. But the authors of the Holiness Code, though clearly deeply immersed in priestly culture, accepted the prophetic critique that it was not only the impurity of worship—the sins of the priesthood, the desecration of the Temple with foreign images, the adoption of pagan religious practices—that caused the destruction of the Temple. And since the corruption and sinfulness that led to destruction was not only a matter of improper worship, restoration was not simply dependent on the purification of the cult. Needed as well was a thoroughgoing cleansing of all relationships in the society, a new set of attitudes, the creation of "a new heart."

The prophet and priest Ezekiel used the latter metaphor, intermixing the descriptions of priestly purification and of personal repentance on the part of each member of the House of Israel:

> I will sprinkle clean water upon you, and you shall be clean: I will cleanse you from all your uncleanness and from all your filth. And I will give you a new heart and put a new spirit into you: I will remove the heart of stone from your body and give you a heart of flesh; and I will put My spirit into you. Thus, I will cause you to follow my laws and faithfully to observe My rules. Then you shall dwell in the land that I gave to your fathers, and you shall be My people and I will be your God. (Ezek. 36:25–28)

This passage abounds in priestly imagery with its central metaphor of cleanliness and impurity, but its concerns are prophetic: a new heart, a new spirit, a new life in dwelling with God. Though Ezekiel was not a part of the circle of priests who authored the Holiness Code, when one reads his message one sees to what degree the ideas those authors adopted are now part of the spirit of the age. The authors of the Holiness Code ask of all Israel, "Love your neighbor as yourself," to walk on the path of holiness.

The anonymity of these priests leaves the exact chronology up in the air; what remains is their teaching. In the ferment of exile the nature of the religious responsibility of the people Israel and their relation to a priesthood and to religious rituals come to the fore. Reformist priests envisioned a society in which the hearts of all Israel were transformed: a new society of people whose core was loving, and whose inner life was therefore at one with what was essential to Israel's God. Only when the people Israel acted with the same purity as a reformed priesthood properly performing sacrificial ritual would sacred space and holy people be in accord, and only then would the harmony that God had envisioned in creation be realized. It was this line of thinking that produced the Holiness Code. And in the end, this perspective would be placed near the very center of the Torah.

We will now look more closely at that code, the handiwork of these reformist priests.

11 The Holiness Code

The Holiness Code receives its name from its most salient teaching, found in chapter 19 of the book of Leviticus: the command to "be holy, because the Lord Your God is holy" (verse 2). Most of the subsequent chapters in Leviticus, many chapters in Numbers, and individual teachings throughout the Five Books can be identified as part of this code. These texts share an overriding theological conception: an emphasis on the practice of holiness even outside of the Temple confines, amid all of the people. Certain phrases (which we will shortly examine) are also characteristic of this code.[1] Finally, the Holiness Code conveys its set of regulations in a very different style from any other law code in the Torah, as we will soon demonstrate as well.

At first glance the book of Leviticus may appear seamless, but in fact, the more one studies the book the more pointed the linguistic differences and the differences in concern in its various parts become clear. Until we come to the Holiness Code, Leviticus centers on sacrifices, the priesthood, laws of ritual purity and ritual practice. But in the middle of Leviticus, the subject matter changes: the average citizen of Israel is now center stage. Instead of the land or the sanctuary or laws of ritual purity, the topics at hand are personal behavior, everyday life, and civil society.

Not incidentally, the earlier chapters of Leviticus are said to have been revealed by God to Moses in the sanctuary in the desert—the priestly locus of revelation—but elements of the Holiness Code are said to have been given by God on Mount Sinai, that is, in the presence of all the people.

Most of the code can be found within Leviticus in chapters 17–25 (chapter 21 is a priestly document inserted within the Holiness Code and chapter 23 seems like a priestly document edited by these Holiness Code authors). In light of the uniqueness of the language used in these portions, other portions of the Five Books of Moses, especially many parts of the book of Numbers, can be identified as having been written by the same group of authors.[2]

The first half of Leviticus is solely concerned with sacrifice, the priesthood, and issues of purity and impurity. Through most of it, Moses informs his brother Aaron, the High Priest, of the directions—the regulations—to follow. The revelation of these laws takes place in the Tent of Meeting, which is identified with the portable sanctuary elsewhere in the Torah. In this priestly theology, after God reveals the Decalogue at Sinai, all subsequent divine revelations take place only in the sanctuary. The very opening words of Leviticus are, "*Adonai* called to Moses and spoke to him from the Tent of Meeting, saying. . . ."; from there the book proceeds in the next several chapters to spell out the various kinds of sacrifices and the procedural directions for their offering in the sanctuary. Although at the beginning of Leviticus, Moses is told to speak to the entire people Israel regarding the laws of sacrifice, in the subsequent chapters Moses is addressing Aaron and his priestly family.

And then we meet the Holiness Code. In its central moment, chapter 19, it begins with Moses being told to address the entire people, and the subject quickly moves from sacrificial concerns to personal behavior, societal relations, and, in subsequent chapters, the land. In chapter 25, we are told that the site of revelation is not the Tent of Meeting; rather, like the Decalogue, it is Mount Sinai.[3]

THE EXTENT OF HOLINESS

The authors of the Holiness Code are priests who try to combine their calling with prophetic perspectives and critiques, synthesizing and translating the two into a vision for a future society. While their rhetoric is formed from the priestly language of holiness and purity, it incorporates the prophetic demand of the centrality of personal behavior on the part of each person in serving God. As we will see, these priests are influenced by the Covenant Code, but while they sometimes expound the same subject matter, they represent an entirely different school and outlook. The Holiness Code frequently ignores the innovations of Deuteronomy, such as legislation regarding the king or an exclusive central place of worship. Instead, it delineates a unique outlook that nonetheless retains the attitudes of Deuteronomy and later prophets such as Ezekiel in emphasizing individual responsibility. In essence, the faction that authors the code rethinks the tradition, borrowing concepts from previous biblical law codes and prophetic conceptualizations yet giving them a new theological frame.

Chapter 19 of the book of Leviticus is the centerpiece of these laws of holiness. It opens with the pure expression of the code's theology: "You shall be holy because the Lord your God is holy." It is addressed to all of Israel, not only the priesthood. Moses is told to "speak to the whole Israelite community" (verse 2). It includes several of the most ethically sublime assertions of the Bible, culminating in verse 19, which many have seen as the high point of biblical law: "You shall love your neighbor as yourself."

To justify and help secure the extension of the purview of holiness beyond the sanctuary's precincts, and to anchor this code within an older tradition, many of the initial prescriptions are reminiscent of the Decalogue both in content and vocabulary. For instance, we cannot hear verse 3 of chapter 19, "Each person should be loyal to their father and mother, and observe my Sabbaths," without remembering the way these two commands sit side by side — in reverse order — in the Decalogue. Similarly, the next verse, "Do not turn to idols or make molten gods for yourselves: I, *Adonai*, am your God," is a recapitulation of the opening lines of the Decalogue.[4] It is as if these priests are laying out their initial argument: God's central revelation was at Mount Sinai. It was delivered to the entire people. It included both the admonition regarding the proper worship of God and instruction on Israel's proper behavior. God gave this primal revelation to the entire people. The people Israel are the ones who are to carry out God's message. They are the ones who can come close to God—"become holy"—through their actions. Both the observance of ritual moments and ethical behavior constitute obedience to the divine order. Therefore, we priests need be concerned with the people and their behavior along with our punctilious observance of sacrificial ritual.

Next, the argument that the people are a critical subject of holiness is supported from a different tack. The following three verses turn to the law of sacrifices, particularly the free-will offering, as the authors argue with their fellow priests on their very premise: the holiness of the sacrificial system.[5] The delineation here is an almost exact recapitulation of the law as enunciated in the earlier priestly portion of Leviticus (chapter 7). The repetition is totally unnecessary—nothing has been added to laws that have already been enunciated—and for that reason we can assume it is an intentional quotation. Unlike other sacrifices, such as the sin offering, the free-will offering is partially consumed not only by the priests but also by those who donated the sacrifice. And it is the only sacrifice that may be eaten outside of the sanctuary, at home, away from priestly supervision. It is as if the holiness writers have an underlying agenda and are saying to their fellow priests: You know, after all, that holiness can exist outside of the sanctuary, for you allow laypeople to participate in this holy act—which can only be celebrated in purity and within ritual constraints—outside of the sanctuary. Even in your thinking, holiness can be maintained outside the sanctuary, and laypeople can be trusted to be the conveyors of holiness—you, yourselves, have said that—so now listen to the other ways holiness exists among the people outside of the sacred realm of the sanctuary.

Having proven their case from the revelation at Sinai and sacrificial offerings—the two core sacred realms that can be appealed to in which Israel and the Divine come into direct contact—the authors then give concrete expression to the way in which ethical relations, along with the sacrificial system, constitute the ground of holiness. Provisions are to be made for the poor and the stranger in the harvest, laborers are to be treated fairly, and justice is to be properly rendered. Ultimately though, the ethical turn revolves around a demand for personal transformation. The exhortations of this chapter reach their height in the very center of the chapter, where we read, "You shall not hate your kinsfolk in your heart" (verse 17) culminating in the command, "Love your neighbor as yourself" (verse 19). At work in the hands of these authors is a powerful reinterpretation of what it means to approach the Divine. This instruction offers an entirely new understanding of the Decalogue's prescription not to be jealous of one's neighbor, for in the positive formulation found here, so much more is being asked. It is nothing less than a call for personal transformation, a profound change in the way one relates to the world.

Notably, some of the chapters surrounding chapter 19 also contain the characteristic expressions and concerns of this chapter. They too are addressed to the entire people, and their concern, as well, is personal morality: the proper care of the body as well as the land so that God remains in relation to the people—all frequently couched in the language of holiness. Modern exegetes have therefore come to think of this entire section, from chapter 17 on, as a separate law code.

(That said, as pointed out earlier, a few intermediate chapters, like chapter 21, seem to have the same priestly concerns as the earlier sections of Leviticus and may not be original parts of the Holiness Code. They may have been woven into this section to help create an air of unity for the entire book of Leviticus.)

GOVERNANCE

Interestingly, the Holiness Code does not recognize any current institution of government or any political elites. Unlike Deuteronomy, there is no mention of a king or of kingship. Nor is there any mention of other authorities, national or local leaders such as city elders, or the heads of clans, as in the Covenant Code. Neither priests, nor tribal figures, nor royally appointed officials or men of renown are designated as judges. In the minority of cases where punishment is specified, the naming of an exact judicial body is vague. Thus, for instance, in chapter 20, when punishment is specified, "the people of the land" are to administer it. By contrast, both Exodus and Deuteronomy offer very specific instructions for the establishment of a judiciary, as well as specifications of the qualities expected of judges. Priestly passages in earlier chapters of Leviticus refer to the judicial functions of the priesthood—not so the Holiness Code.

Rather than identifying human authorities, the Holiness Code frequently and explicitly mentions God as the one who will carry out punishment for violation of a law. Sometimes the Holiness Code simply adopts the priestly formula for punishment of sins that only perpetrators would know they committed and where there is no possibility of judicial ruling. As an example, if one eats of the sacrifice when one has not undergone proper purification, the priestly text asserts that God will "cut off the sinner from the nation"—*v'nikhr'tah ha-nefesh hahi mi-yisrael* (e.g., Lev. 7:20). The later Rabbis understood the term to mean that God would end the sinner's life early, and many contemporary scholars agree with the rabbinic understanding of the intent of this term. Rather than a court providing the death penalty or other punishment, the violator of the law faces God who exacts punishment for the burden of sin. Along these same lines, many times we hear God saying, "I will turn my face toward that person," meaning God will favor this individual, or "I will turn my face away from that person," meaning disaster will follow. In these passages, reward and punishment are meted out in the direct relationship of God and the human; no other entity intervenes. In this fashion the Holiness Code announces the punishment for necromancy: "I will set My face against that person, whom I will cut off from among the people" (Lev. 20:6). For the most part, then, this is a religious code, establishing a direct relationship between the individual and God: "You should be holy for I, *Adonai*, Your God, am holy."

Similarly, in the Holiness Code sometimes the land itself, rather than human judicial authority, becomes the instrument of punishment. Thus, summarizing the admonitions against adultery, the punishment enunciated is "lest the land vomit you out" (Lev. 20:22). Here, as in some parts of Deuteronomy, the land is the instrumentality of God's reward and punishment for ethical or criminal acts, not any human agency.

In chapter 19 of Leviticus, the centerpiece of the Holiness Code, almost all the laws are stated as a direct speech from God to the people: "Be holy for I am holy . . . ," "You shall . . . ," "You shall not. . . ." Only a single law in each of the two halves of the code is the kind of legislation we have come to call casuistic—if you do "x," then the consequence is "y." As previously noted, throughout the ancient Near East, such formulations of casuistic law are the characteristic expressions used in handbooks for judges. Here, though, the directness of language is more reminiscent of the Decalogue than of legal systems.[6] Accordingly, analyzing these passages, the contemporary Israeli scholar Baruch Schwartz has argued that the sentence structure is frequently akin to the poetic passages of the Bible.[7] These, then, are not judicial formulations: the author is not thinking in practical terms of the direct application of law. Rather, these are exhortative claims, being made of each individual. In essence, chapter 19 establishes a code describing the relationship of God and Israel, but it has none of the formal characteristics of the enactment of a constitutional arrangement or the establishment of a legal corpus. We are in the world of poetry, of vision, of law enunciated as a religious ideal. Legal formula here surpasses itself and becomes something more, something prophetic.

In the same vein, the exhortations prescribed by this chapter concern matters that ultimately cannot be controlled or imposed by legal institutions. "Love thy neighbor as thyself" is not enforceable by a court of law. Even the more detailed and objective legislation is hardly enforceable. For instance, the later Rabbis were probably right in saying that the injunction in chapter 19:9 to set aside a corner of one's field for the poor was a case of a law being stated without delineated amounts;[8] how much is a corner? That these later sages were at a loss to define it reflects the fact that the law was not written as a legislative formula but as a personal imperative. Compare this to other parts of the Bible, such as the law of tithing, which is quite specific as to the amount one is required to contribute.

In sum, these passages in chapter 19 live in the realm of individual personal aspiration, of religious ideal, not judicial praxis—and it is precisely these private, personal, extrajudicial areas that the Holiness Code seeks to include within the realm of religious legislation. The medieval commentator Nachmanides may have had deep insight into the psychology of the authors of the Holiness Code when he interpreted the exhortation "Be holy" as aimed at including within the law that which is beyond the law. He remarks that one can fulfill all the commandments and still not be a pious or good person. To be a religious person is to be able to understand how one ought to behave in those areas of life that are not subject to codification, to exact juridical definition.

In the Decalogue, God announces, "I *Adonai* your God, who brought you out of the land of Egypt," and this becomes the summary verse for the Holiness Code, "I am *Adonai*, your God who freed you from the land of Egypt. You shall faithfully observe all my laws and my rules: I am *Adonai*" (Lev. 19:36b–37).Ultimately, what is being imagined is the negation of the mentality of Egypt, of the imperium. The Holiness Code is a reinterpretation of the Exodus and Sinai. Its aim is not only a just society but one in which each individual becomes holy, comes close to the Divine. We are no longer slaves—inconsequential in the eyes of the taskmaster—but have the possibility of incorporating within us that which is of most consequence: qualities of the Divinity.

Like Ezekiel telling the exiles that they will be given a new heart, the authors foresee a time when human hearts will be transformed, but their program is even more radical than the vision of the restored Temple, an uncorrupted priesthood, and an ethical life of the people imagined by that prophet. One must see it not as legislation meant to be implemented in the here and now, not as a set of laws negotiated between contending political factions, but as a wondrous vision of what might be and what ought to be: an imagined reality by religious reformers wishing that, upon return, God's kingdom might be established.

This is the work of people out of power who have no investment in traditional elites. Thus, the style of the Decalogue, a direct form of speech between God and the human, becomes the basis for all its law. The recurring chorus in the Holiness Code is "I am God." That is the reason for the law. It is insistent on the direct relation of God and the people Israel. The ultimate trust is in this relationship, not in the mediation of recognized communal authorities.

THE SABBATH

It was in exile that the Sabbath achieved a new prominence. Sitting in Babylon, without a Temple, there were limited ways in which people could feel close to the Divine. The Sabbath provided the means by which the exiled community of Israel could share in a regular, weekly sense of sanctity.

Earlier biblical codes give the Sabbath much less prominence and a much different meaning than does Leviticus's Holiness Code. The word Sabbath means to stop, specifically stopping certain kinds of work. In Exodus (chapter 23) when the laws of festivals are enunciated, the seventh day is given a purely economic and social function—it is a day of rest for servants and animals; presumably householders may do what they will. Some biblical scholars argue that until the Babylonian exile, rest on the seventh day did not necessarily mean the weekly Sabbath; rather, one of seven days of work was mandated as a day off for workers. Each employer could decide which day that would be.[9]

In Deuteronomy's version of the Decalogue—there is only one other reference to a Sabbath in this fifth biblical book—the seventh day is proclaimed a memorial for the Exodus: that is, an end to slavery. Unlike the parallel codes in Exodus and Leviticus, Deuteronomy's chapters 15 and 16, which enumerate the festivals, do not even include the seventh day in their list.

But something changes when we turn to the Leviticus listing of the holidays in chapter 23. There, the weekly Sabbath is introduced in order to establish it as the model for all the other festivals, which are also to be characterized by the cessation of work. Every holiday is now to be a "Sabbath." The way one is to understand the cycle of time is through the lens of the Sabbath. The spring harvest holidays (from Passover, with its offering from the barley harvest, to the celebration of the first fruits of the wheat harvest) are to be separated by a count of seven weeks—that is, seven times seven days.

Most especially, it is only in the Holiness Code that the Sabbath is given a divine function: "It is a Sabbath dedicated to God, throughout your entire settlement" (23:3). So in the Holiness Code the Sabbath achieves a new prominence and different orientation.

This change regarding the way the Sabbath is viewed accords with the distribution of the mention of the Sabbath among the succession of prophets. The earlier (eighth-century BCE) prophets Amos, Hosea, and Isaiah of Jerusalem each voice only a single parenthetical mention of a Sabbath, and scholars have even debated whether these refer to the seventh day or a midmonth festival of the full moon (Micah has no reference at all to the Sabbath).[10] But in the exilic teachings of Isaiah of Babylon and Ezekiel, the Sabbath has a prominent place.[11] Ezekiel, for instance, equates the violation of the Sabbath with ethical corruption—"Fathers and mothers have been humiliated within you; strangers have been cheated in your midst; orphans and widows have been wronged within you. You have despised My holy things and profaned My sabbaths" (Ezek. 22:7–8)—and calls the Sabbath "holy" (20:20).[12] Both he and the later Isaiah use the same vocabulary for the violation of the Sabbath as was classically used for the violation of the sanctity of the sanctuary. One can guess that the force of exile created the conditions elevating the institution of the Sabbath to a new prominence: equating it with the sanctuary.

In exile it was no longer possible to experience holiness directly in the Temple. While some returned to the Land of Israel, most exiles remained behind in Babylonia and could not participate in the sacrificial and priestly system of holiness directly even when, under the reign of Darius, a modest altar and Temple was reestablished in Jerusalem (520 BCE). It was the Sabbath that provided the arena in which holiness could be apprehended. Thus, the Sabbath became not only a day of rest for one's workers—that is, a day whose importance is primarily economic and social. The Sabbath became a day that is "holy unto God"—a phrase that can be translated as "dedicated to God," and that can also carry the connotation "a day in which one can come closest to the Divine."

It may well be that the Sabbath became the day in which the exiles gathered and listened to what was believed to be divine instruction—whether prophetic sermons or instructional material, texts that were later gathered into what we know as the Torah. Certainly, the later Rabbis credited to this period the institution of the synagogue and the establishment of days of gathering to hear the Torah read and taught. It may well be that their mythic historical memory accurately portrays a historical development, though we have no concrete evidence to support this view.

Whatever its communal function—how the community functioned is shrouded by a historical veil—the place of the Sabbath accorded by the Holiness Code represents the fulfillment of the theological impulses inherent in that code. It is noteworthy that in the delineation of the festival law, the celebration of the Sabbath is specifically directed to take place "in your dwellings" (Lev. 23:3), in contrast to the commemoration of other festivals so connected to land and Temple, agricultural celebration and pilgrimage. The Sabbath is observed by all of Israel: it is not the special domain of the priesthood. It allows for an extra-Temple means to experience the Divine. Moreover, it provides a recurring ritual moment when holiness is achievable for all of Israel, thereby acquiring a status perhaps equal to the Temple itself. That is why it is precisely this holy day that could survive and gain importance in exile.

Most scholars assign the first chapter of Genesis describing the Creation of the world to priestly authors. One has only to compare it to the second and third chapters with their story of the expulsion from the Garden to realize the stylized and formal nature of the language: a characteristic of priestly materials. We are presented with a mathematical and almost "scientific" description of Creation. Each day concludes with "It was evening and it was morning. . . ." The first three days and the next three days stand in exact parallel. To begin, days one and four deal with the same matter: light. Light and darkness are created on the first day; sun, moon, and stars containing light are formed on the fourth. Days two and five address the same matter: water. The upper waters and lower waters are separated on the second day; fish and fowl that swim in the sea and fly in the air in the space between heaven and earth (which contain the two bodies of water) are created on the fifth. Days three and six concentrate on what emerges and what lives in water and on land. Dry land appears on the third day; and animal life and humans striding the land are created on the sixth. The six days are an ordered mathematical system, and at the end of the sixth day we are told that God found everything to be "very good."

But the language of the seventh day is entirely different.[13] The stylized linguistic elements characterizing the first six days are gone. Instead, we find that the day is "blessed," that God makes it "holy," and that God is refreshed on the seventh day. Most biblical scholars agree that this description of the seventh day is a later addition to the unfolding story of Creation. Its incorporation of the language of holiness points to the authors of the Holiness Code as the later editors who added this material. The Holiness Code demands that our lives be imitative of God's qualities, and now our rest on the seventh day becomes imitative of God's own inner life. God rested on the seventh day, and so should humans.

In a similar vein, the final editors of the Pentateuch surround the laws for building the sanctuary in the desert in Exodus with laws regarding the observance of the Sabbath. The contiguity inevitably establishes a relationship between Sabbath and Temple.[14] Here, too, the Sabbath is called a day that is "holy to *Adonai*" (Exod. 31:15, 35:2). Making this connection, the Sabbath becomes a portable sanctuary.

The effect of this new understanding of the Sabbath is to move the religious realm to the inner life. Rest, cessation from work, and contemplation can create the possibility of reaching toward the Divine. It is the breathing space that Divinity, God's self, took after completing the work of Creation, and it is our spiritual breath of life.[15]

This new understanding of religiosity is the gift of exile.

THE SABBATH OF THE LAND

Living in exile, what preoccupied these authors was the dream of return, of once again living autonomously in the Land of Israel. Sitting in Babylonia but longing for their homeland, the writers of the Holiness Code formulated a theology of the land. In their vision, the land, too, is an actor in the drama of holiness—the land must observe the Sabbath.

As such, the Sabbath is not only to be understood as having been given to the human in imitation of divine activity; the Sabbath is an inherent idea governing nature. "When you arrive in the land ... the land itself shall cease work and celebrate a Sabbath dedicated to God" (Lev. 25:2). Of course it is the people who must observe this Sabbath, it is they who must stop work, but the instruction is phrased as if the land itself is animate—its needs must be fulfilled, its laws observed. It, too, celebrates a Sabbath.

The earlier injunctions regarding the seventh year are economic and social. The Covenant Code declares that in one year out of seven the produce of the land is to be left for the poor and the animals in the wild (Exod. 23:11); and in Deuteronomy, the sabbatical year is not agricultural but financial, a time when outstanding debts are canceled. But in the Holiness Code, the rest given the land is for divine purpose. Borrowing some of the language from Exodus, it adds this conception and enjoins:

> When you enter the land that I assign to you, the land shall observe a sabbath for *Adonai*. Six years you may sow your field and six years you may prune your vineyard and gather in the yield; but in the seventh year the land shall have a sabbath of complete rest, *a sabbath for Adonai*: you shall not sow your field

or prune your vineyard. You shall not reap the aftergrowth of your harvest or gather the grapes of your untrimmed vines; it shall be a year of complete rest for the land. But you may eat whatever the land during its sabbath will produce—you, your male and female slaves, the hired and bound laborers who live with you, and your cattle and the beasts in your land may eat all its yield. (25:2b–8)

Note that though the specifics of not sowing or pruning, not gathering or harvesting, are taken from Exodus—the passage even ends with the quotation from the Covenant Code that the wild beasts may eat off the land—the provision of the seventh year is no longer for the sake of the poor; rather, it is for the land itself. In Exodus this is simply called the "seventh year"; in Deuteronomy this seventh year is called the *shemitah*—that is, the "cutting off, stopping" referring to the cancellation of debts; but in the Holiness Code the seventh year is called the Sabbath. For the animate—owners, laborers, farm animals—the Sabbath occurs every week; for the inanimate—the Land of Israel—it occurs every seventh year. It is a "sabbath for *Adonai*"—that is, the cessation of work on the land returns creation to God. Thus all, both animate and inanimate, both people and land, must be governed by a Sabbath. The human Sabbath is celebrated in its microcosm of the week; agricultural days of work are measured in the macrocosm of years. Both can partake of holiness.

At the very end of Leviticus, curses for nonobservance of the law are enumerated, with chapter 26 emphasizing that exile will be the ultimate punishment. This passage describing the exile seems to give voice to the land: "Then shall the land make up for its Sabbath years throughout the time that it is desolate, and you are in the land of your enemies; then shall the land rest and make up for its Sabbath years" (Lev. 26:34). This is a new explanation of the exile: you became refugees because you did not know how to religiously care for the land. The land needed its Sabbath, and since you did not provide it, it spewed you out. God says: I forced the expulsion of the inhabitants, the desolation of the land, so that the land might have its rest and peace. In exilic imagination, the land itself becomes an actor in the drama of exile and redemption. The land has been violated; desolation allows for the Sabbath of the land you should have observed.

JUBILEE

The portrayal of the original division of the land in the book of Joshua—part of the Deuteronomic historical cycle—was seen as the initiation of a just society. Each family unit was apportioned its share, distributed by lot at the time of the conquest. This is the historical vision now included in the book of Numbers. As Moses is about to hand over leadership to Joshua, who will lead the people into the land, a census is conducted, and then we read: "Among these shall the land be apportioned as shares, according to the listed names: with larger groups increase the share, with smaller groups reduce the share. Each is to be assigned its share according to its enrollment. The land, moreover, is to be apportioned by lot; and the allotment shall be made according to the listings of their ancestral tribes" (Num. 26:52–56).[16] There is an imagined equality in the original distribution of the land.

The authors of the Holiness Code envision that share as an eternal portion. Should any family have to sell land because of poverty, that property will return to that family in the jubilee year. And so there will be both a Sabbath of the land every seventh year and a Sabbath of Sabbaths, a jubilee year, after seven times seven. This will complete a full cycle of time, after which shares in the land will return to their original equal distribution.

In this imaginative leap, the return from exile includes an idealized picture of time and space. The land will rest every seven years, as stipulated in the Covenant Code in Exodus; but equally, in the fiftieth year, the land will return to its original condition, to the moment when the people Israel first entered it. In the fulfillment of a complete temporal circle—seven times seven—all of society can start over again, as equals. In the beginning, we were all equal, and so it will be, again and again — every fifty years.

At its core, the mythic origin story of the equal division of the land is based on the exilic community's understanding of Israel's history. It has come down to us as the story of the occupation of the land, recorded by an author who viewed history through a late imperial lens. This story of the conquest of the land as told in the book of Joshua recounts that in seven years the land is denuded of its native Canaanite population and distributed to its new Israelite occupants by lots. The land becomes a tabula rasa on which the story of a new society can be written.

But as noted earlier, another very different historical record survives — the chronicle of the conquest as presented in the book of Judges, where a Canaanite population lives side by side with an Israelite one, where Israelite tribal society appears to consist of a relatively weak hill people entering into local alliances, and where members of the native population marry into the society or join with Israelite leaders. That depiction is closer to the prophetic assertion in Exodus that the conquest could not possibly take place all at once, but "little by little" (Exod. 23:30).

The book of Joshua may have been written shortly before the exile, perhaps during the reign of Josiah — notice the play of names — but in exile it came to have special resonance. Its retelling of Israel's history shaped a romanticized view of the people Israel and the land. In this understanding, when we first entered the land, it was almost immediately made ours. It is as if the land were a blank slate on which the people's history was written. Since daily life in Israel, full of constant contact and mingling with the surrounding population, was no longer a lived reality, Israel's history could be mythically retold and believed. And this story of origins became the story of return. These exiles could feel that the land had now been emptied and was just waiting for their return: when we go back, each of us will have our rightfully inherited share restored to us. The way it was when we originally entered the land will be the way once again when we return.

The mythic past becomes a map for the future.

The law of the jubilee year—the claim of the eternal property rights of the original Israelite owners and the return of the land every fifty years to its original owners—is then a vision of an imagined society ruled by justice and equity, but not a description of any actual historical moment. It represents a new understanding. The functioning of a jubilee year is not recounted in any other biblical text. The jubilee year is not applied to any biblical calendrical dating system—that is, no prophet says that he spoke in the first or the fifth or the tenth year of the jubilee; nor does any king date his reign by a reckoning of the jubilee year. There is never any mention of some family having returned to their ancestral lands in the jubilee year; on the contrary, the constant prophetic jeremiad against the impoverishment of the rural population points to the opposite conclusion—people pushed off their land, without recourse, permanently impoverished. In reacting to these economic hardships, no prophet mentions the jubilee as a legal requirement for returning the land to the poor or castigates Israel for nonobservance of the jubilee. In fact, other than its original formulation in the book of Leviticus, the word *jubilee* in the context of referring to a fiftieth year is mentioned only one other time in the Bible: in the last chapter of Numbers (36:4), in a passage that picks up on matters discussed earlier in the book and serves as an appendix that may well have been written by the final editor, one of the authors of the Holiness Code. All other uses of the Hebrew word for jubilee, *yovel*, refer not to a period of time but to the sounding of the horn blast. For instance, in Exodus, in the revelation at Sinai, we read, "When the horn [*yovel*/jubilee] is sounded, they shall go up to the mountain" (19:13).

Perhaps there is an internal biblical midrash here. The jubilee is a celebration of liberation, signaling not only the freeing of the land from its acquisition by the wealthy and its return to the displaced poor, but also the liberation of all Israel from oppression and the creation of an egalitarian society. The jubilee year is a kind of sounding of the horn voicing an ultimate message of equality, marking the difference between the oppressive slavery of Egypt and the newfound freedom

God promises. It represents a rereading of the story of liberation and the entrance into the land in its assertion that a holy people is one in which every family of the people Israel can share equally in the land. The book of Deuteronomy had stated in connection with the law of the sabbatical year that debts should be canceled, "for the poor will never cease from the land" (Deut. 15:11), and thus instituted a system of caring for the poor. The Holiness Code, instead, dreams of a system whereby poverty indeed ends, and the chance to begin again with capital, with the land that one's ancestors originally owned, is afforded to all.

Interestingly, once the notion of jubilee was propagated, it became a focus of redemptive dreams. In the Second Temple period, the idea of the jubilee became so deeply ingrained that a writer did try to reimagine Jewish history in cycles of jubilee years. His work, the Book of Jubilees, sees time through the lens of the system of sabbatical and jubilee years, restating all of early biblical history in cycles of fifty years. The Qumran community that sequestered the Dead Sea Scrolls appears to have considered it a sacred book.[17]

The preexilic silence regarding the jubilee year and the postexilic exuberant expansion of the concept are witnesses to the lack of evidence regarding the jubilee in earlier times, in contrast to the moment of its invention in exile. Once it enters the imagination, it becomes a critical idea and a means of calendrical accounting.

Nevertheless, even though it fired the imagination of the returnees, the Rabbis of the Talmud report that the jubilee year was never observed in the Second Temple period. They explained that no one could any longer determine when the jubilee year actually occurred. Nevertheless, there may have been a more fundamental reason for its lack of implementation—the sheer inability of a society to carry it out.

Thus, the law of the jubilee was never observed in all of Jewish history but remained as an idealized economic program for a perfected society. It was a dream conjured in exile by authors imagining the return to the land in accordance with prophetic demands for equality and protection of the poor.

But though it was never implemented, memory of the jubilee year survives actively in Jewish observance and imagination. The Day of Atonement ends with the blowing of the shofar—understood to be the biblical horn, *yovel*—in fulfillment of the biblical command to announce the jubilee year by blowing the horn at the beginning of that year. Each year, as the service of atonement is completed, the ancient dream is made living once again. May this be a year of the jubilee. May this be the year in which justice reigns. May this be the year of true freedom and equality.[18]

THE STRANGER

By living in the land, "the stranger" enters into the circle of holiness.

Deuteronomy, too, had extended its protections to the stranger and awarded the stranger the same rights as the "poor in Israel." Nevertheless, Deuteronomy differentiates between Israel and the nations roundabout, warning against intermarriage and emphasizing a differential treatment regarding loans—in the seventh year, loans to Israelites, but not to "foreigners," are to be remitted.[19] Similarly, while the foreigner passing through your land may be charged usurious interest, your "brother" is not (Deut. 23:21); Deuteronomy shows remarkable compassion for the "stranger," a non-Israelite living among this people.[20] In the speech that constitutes the prelude to the Deuteronomic Code, Moses bids us to "love the stranger" (Deut. 10:19).

The Holiness Code continues on this path but goes beyond Deuteronomy in the care of the stranger, saying that the stranger should be treated as a citizen: "When a stranger resides with you in your land you shall not wrong him. The stranger who resides with you shall be to you as one of your citizens; you shall love him as yourself, for you were strangers in the land of Egypt: I, *Adonai*, am your God" (Lev. 19:33–34).

The Holiness Code is constantly insistent that the law in the Land of Israel is to apply equally to the citizen and the "stranger who dwells in your midst."[21] That equality is now extended from the secular realm to ritual law—that is, the stranger may enter into the realm of holiness.

The sacrificial law is applicable to the *ger*/the stranger, so that when talking of the desert sanctuary—held up as an ideal moment—the *ger*, too, may bring a sacrifice there.[22] Negative prohibitions regarding holiness apply to the stranger as well. Like an Israelite, a stranger may not eat the blood of an animal (Lev. 17:8–10).[23] The *ger* may also participate in that most intimate of rituals, the Pesaḥ remembrance of the going out of Egypt, the memorializing of Israel's primal history. Over and over again we hear that the law applies equally to full citizens and "the stranger" (e.g., 19:34, 24:16, 24:22).

In regard to the Passover offering, though, we may be witness to contending forces within the circles that authored the Holiness Code. In the passage in Exodus attributed to them, we find the explicit instruction that the non-Israelite must be circumcised to participate in the rite, while in the passage in Numbers attributed to these authors, where we are told that the stranger may be included in the Passover celebration, for "one law shall apply to you and the stranger dwelling in your midst" (Num. 15:14), the need to be circumcised is not mentioned.

And in addition to the stranger's inclusion in certain rituals, the stranger is equally included in what is forbidden: forms of worship that the stranger may have previously practiced before coming to the land but are anathema to the worshipers of *Adonai*. The punishment is the same for the Israelite and the non-Israelite who engage in child sacrifice, or in magical practices. In other words, the stranger's welcome is an invitation to join the circle of worshipers of *Adonai*, with the understanding that other worship is excluded for all those living in the land.

The book of Numbers includes two stories in which Moses does not know the law and must inquire of God as to what is to be done, both of which many scholars attribute to the Holiness Code authors. One involves an adult son of an Egyptian father and an Israelite mother, who in biblical law is not considered a member of the people Israel. In the midst of a fight with an Israelite, he curses *Adonai*. Moses does not know whether the law stipulating punishment for cursing God applies only to Israelites. God responds that the same punishment should fall on an Israelite or a non-Israelite in the camp, for the same law applies to a "citizen and a stranger/*ger*" (Num. 24:16). This incident is part of the wandering in the desert, outside of the land. Here the question is not the holiness of the land, but the holiness of the camp: the holiness of the people as they travel together. The community itself ought not to be defiled; and within the physical bounds of the community, the honor, the worship, and the praise of *Adonai* must be preserved even by one who is not a member of the people Israel.

The second incident is that of an Israelite who collects wood on the Sabbath in violation of the law against making a fire on that day. When Moses, again unsure of the law, inquires of God, he is again told that the punishment should be the death penalty (Num. 15:32).

The two stories, told in the same way, represent two themes of the Holiness Code authors. The first regards the holiness of the camp and the inclusion of the stranger in the circle of holiness; the second concerns the observance of the Sabbath, the critical foundation in the code's building of a system of holiness.

Imagined here are overlapping areas of holiness. The sanctuary is holy, the priesthood is holy, the Land of Israel is holy, the people Israel are holy, the seventh day and the seventh year are holy as well. All are intertwined. All those who dwell in the Land of Israel must maintain the holiness of the place. Only *Adonai* must be worshiped. If the land is to remain holy, no foreign worship ought to be practiced within the realms of holiness, even by a stranger.

But along with this restrictive rule is a broadening of the concept of the worship of *Adonai*. The celebration of *Adonai* is no longer exclusive to the people Israel—all may now participate.[24] The faith of the people Israel is open to the stranger: those who live among you may participate in the worship of *Adonai* but they may not worship other gods. Though it is the entire universe that reflects God's presence, it is in the Land of Israel that the holiness of God's creation is to be made manifest. All people who live in God's land must accord with God's law.

That law has a moral content, demanding the equitable distribution of the land and the just use of its produce. The land need reflect

God's harmony, God's grace, God's peace and rest, for holiness can be found in all aspects of existence — among all people, in all that is animate, even in soil and sand. Time, too, can be made holy. The realm of holiness extends from microcosm to macrocosm, from the priesthood to each person, from the Land of Israel to all of creation, from the Sabbath to all the days of the year, from the seventh year to the jubilee and from there to all time.

The authors of the Holiness Code dreamed a great dream. It is a dreaming induced by exile, repeated again, throughout time, by so many refugees. It is the dream of return, of no longer being estranged. It is the dream of peace and perfection after loss and wandering. Holding out the promise that the loss can now lead to a new beginning, the authors write with the intention that this time, we will not be expelled from the Garden.

12 The Heritage of the Holiness Code

Beginning with the Covenant Code, Israelite religion embodied its ideals in law. As fundamental organizing principles, both the Covenant Code and Deuteronomy combined civil jurisprudence with ethical and prophetic imperatives. The Holiness Code added to this understanding its own insistence on the need for personal transformation and its dream of a utopian society. As we will see in the last part of this book, authors influenced by the Holiness Code were the final editors of the Torah, so that the sensibility of the Holiness Code permeates the entire Pentateuch and, in turn, later Judaism's self-understanding.

Most law is written to regulate behavior; its concern is with what people do. Not so the Holiness Code. On many occasions, it enunciates an ideal, a view of what ought to be. Implicit is an acknowledgment that its vision may not be currently implemented. It is a dream of future possibility: its gaze is fixed on a distant future with little hope of current fulfillment, but enunciating its ideal transforms the way one sees and acts in the present. Such is the Holiness Code's law of jubilees and equally, its command that we love our neighbor as ourselves.

This mixture of responding to what is current reality while holding on to a dream of an ideal world had a decisive influence on the development of Jewish law, the halakhah.

We can see it in the very opening phrases of the first teaching of the Mishnah, the postbiblical compendium of Jewish law (edited around 225 CE) that serves as the foundation text of all subsequent rabbinic rulings. In this text we find a concern with the religious life of each person, as well as the articulation of a dream of an ideal world—a world centered on a restored Temple, just rule, and service of the Divine.

The first tractate of the Mishnah, called *Berachot,* deals with issues of prayer: it organizes the liturgy and declares the proper setting and time for prayer. The very first teaching begins with the question of determining the proper moment for the recitation of the evening *Shema.* By the time of the Mishnah's compilation, the rhetorical phrase in Deuteronomy 6:7 that "you should speak of them[1] . . . when you lie down and when you rise up," embedded in the paragraph known by the first word of the opening sentence, "Shema/Hear," had become the source of a tradition of reciting these words (in fact, the entire paragraph Deuteronomy 6:4–9) twice daily: early in the morning and at the onset of evening.[2] Since in ancient rabbinic teaching the calendrical day is calculated from one evening to the next, the first Mishnah inquires as to when evening begins: When is the beginning of the new day, and so when exactly should the recitation of the *Shema* take place? Its opening words are:

> When can one recite the evening *shema*? At the moment when the priests enter [their home] to eat their portion of the tithe. (*Mishnah Berachot* 1:1)

We might reasonably be struck by the esoteric oddity of this response. Asking for a set time, we would expect an easily identifiable boundary time in response, such as "when the sun sets" or "when the stars appear"; and in fact, other texts from this period that speak to this question do offer more readily defined times of this kind.[3] Some further background is called for.

Priests could only partake of the tithe when they had been cleansed from impurity. A priest who had touched someone who was impure became impure himself and needed to bathe, washing away the impurity that would last for a day, until nightfall; then, at nightfall, he could go home to eat food prepared from the tithe, which needed to be eaten in purity. Yet one might live in a town where there were no priests, or perhaps the priests in one's town had not become impure, in which case one would not see a priest coming home after purifying himself to eat the evening meal. Moreover, at the time of the Mishnah, there had not been a Temple in existence for 150 years and priestly functions were largely suspended. Thus the standard being enunciated for determining the proper liturgical time is not a reality one could necessarily encounter, but a vision one could hold in mind. In that way, the dream of the proper service of God, of Temple life, is ever present.

Though the Temple was no longer in existence, having been destroyed by the Romans in 70 CE, the dream of restoration persisted. More than half the text of the Mishnah concerns Temple activity: the daily and festival sacrifices, the rules of purity and impurity. Even when discussing festival observance—ritual moments that by now had completely devolved on family and communal celebration and worship—the Mishnah devotes inordinate space to the appropriate procedures regarding Temple rituals appropriate for that day, though they could not be performed in their time. For instance, the tractate of the Mishnah concerned with the Day of Atonement devotes its first seven chapters to the Temple service and role of the High Priest in honor of the day; only in its eighth and last chapter do we encounter the regulations regarding fasting and the ascetic practices incumbent on each individual. And, finally, only at the conclusion of that chapter, which is the conclusion of the tractate, do we find instructions regarding personal repentance, which in these sages' minds is the post-Temple means of atonement.

So something else is happening here other than the practical explication of the law. An ideal vision of society is delineated side by side with the rules for living in the concrete reality of our religious lives here and now. The text holds onto an idealized vision of the Temple even as it recognizes the need for ordering a religious life—a holy life—without a Temple. One may not see a priest living in one's town—certainly, one may not necessarily observe him as he returns home to eat the tithe after having bathed to wash away impurity—yet in one's mind's eye one holds on to this vision of priests living a life of purity. We live our lives in this world, pursuing holiness in the reality of everyday life, while we yet dream of a purity beyond, a purity that could never be achieved in our current condition. At times, the Talmud—the ancient Babylonian commentary on the Mishnah—can decide a question on the basis of seeing what people do, in other words, based on current reality: "Go out and see what people are saying."[4] Religious regulation ought never to go far beyond what its adherents can accomplish; extreme piety cannot be the rule for everyone. Yet alongside that reality we can dream of a different world—one that has a greater closeness to the Divine, one that comes nearer to God's desires.

There's more at work in this first Mishnah when it declares that the individual reciting the evening *Shema*, fulfilling what is seen as a biblical obligation of profession of faith, is analogized to a priest consuming holy food. Here we find the long shadow of the Holiness Code, which understands holiness as applicable equally to acts committed by priests and nonpriests. Holy moments may be experienced beyond the confines of the sanctity of the Temple, or by others than the priests designated to serve there. Through a literary device, the Mishnah has created an equivalence between priests and every lay person faithfully fulfilling their religious obligations.

Both impulses—the wish to see holiness in the everyday, and equally the dream of a perfected world when the Divine truly dwells among us—are found in the Holiness Code. The purpose of the former is to achieve the latter. In this world, certain moments can touch on holiness. In the world that is coming, holiness will mark our way of life. The Mishnah, and by extension all subsequent formulations of Jewish law, echoes these themes.

PERSONAL TRANSFORMATION

One characteristic expression of the Holiness Code is *ish ish*, "each person"—the extension of the notion of holiness beyond the Temple and its priesthood to everyone. While priestly documents in the Torah denoted priests as the guardians of holiness and declared them to be the mediators of divine instruction, the priestly authors of the Holiness Code expanded this circle.[5] This democratization of holiness, the assumption that holiness, a characteristic of God, was not only bestowed on consecrated individuals but was open to all of Israel, became a critical element in later Jewish thinking.

Articulating this different understanding of holiness, the Mishnah boldly declares that a learned teacher who may be the scion of an adulterous union—technically a "bastard/*mamzer*"—takes precedence over an ignorant High Priest: for instance, if both are captured by brigands and need to be ransomed, we redeem the teacher before the High Priest. The High Priest is no longer seen as the most prestigious of Jewish leaders. Although lineage defines who may be a priest, inner qualities—learning, piety, personal ethics—determine who takes precedence. Everyone, even the most lowly or the most scorned, can become the one most deserving of respect, a noted scholar. This is certainly a radical reorientation of values.

In fact, the learned teacher becomes a symbol of that which is perceived as most holy. Referencing the verse in Exodus (25:11) that describes the wooden ark as covered with gold on both its outside and inside, the Babylonian Talmud remarks, "Any Torah scholar whose inside is not like his outside, is not to be considered a Torah scholar."[6] That is, his inner life must be the same as the teaching he is representing. Like the ark that holds the tablets, the teacher holds the Torah. As the ark is pure, so, too, the teacher. Once the ark was the center of holiness, now the Torah scholar is, but only when his person is indeed representative of holiness.

Ultimately, the Holiness Code calls for a transformation in the way *each person*—not only a scholarly elite—conducts their lives. Its concern about, its care for, the human heart—"Do not hate your brother in your heart. . . . Love your neighbor as yourself"—accorded the inner life equal status with the performance of religious acts. This understanding placed characterological issues front and center in religious life. Kindness, awareness of the other, the sacredness of each individual became religious values that each person needed to cultivate.

Accomplishing this required a new understanding of the importance and value of the inner life—one that extended beyond the Decalogue's negative injunctions not to steal or not to murder. Not only should one not act out of envy or jealousy; one should act out of love. The desired achievement was a profound inner realignment: from not living with resentment and hate to, most importantly, manifesting care and empathy in relationship to others. An equal and perhaps simultaneous objective was to develop an inner life conscious of God's presence.

It was this emphasis on the inner life that induced later commentators to reinterpret other verses in the Torah. In the ancient Near East, love of a ruler was not about an inner state of being but rather a call for loyalty: you are not to join with other powers. Thus Deuteronomy's injunction, "You shall love *Adonai*, your God" (6:5) was originally a demand not to worship foreign gods or other deities but to be loyal servants of God, obeying God's commands.[7] But later Judaism understood these words differently. For instance, in one line of thought, these verses regarding love of God were understood to call for the cultivation of an attitude that appreciated God's goodness in all one encountered.[8]

The priestly documents of the Torah imagine the High Priest encountering God in the Holy of Holies. In this view, only the High Priest could have a direct experience of the Divine; it was dangerous for anyone else even to try. The democratizing perspective of the Holiness Code led directly to the medieval conception that the experience of the Divine was open to everyone, and indeed it would well be pursued by everyone. Both medieval philosophers and mystics came to understand the contemplation of the Divine by everyone who is able as the ultimate fulfillment of the religious life. Maimonides suggests a system of meditational techniques so that one can achieve the pure contemplation of the Divine. Jewish mystics developed other techniques to achieve a mystical experience of the Divine. In essence, the revolution of the Holiness Code in extending the possibility of holiness beyond the priesthood and the Temple was the universal inheritance of both philosophers and mystics, though they contended with each other regarding how to implement this goal.

Bahya ibn Pakuda, an eleventh-century Andalusian Jewish theologian and one of the most influential Jewish thinkers, named his work

Guide to the Duties of the Heart. (The Hebrew translation simplified it to *Duties of the Heart.*) The title captures the thesis: what is needed first of all in the religious life is the dedication of the heart. This is the foundation of the religious life, the fundamental attitude with which we need go through our day.

Here, then, we find the radicalization of the ideas that the Holiness Code set in motion. In Ibn Pakuda's view, this inner transformation is the very foundation of the law: if one does not pursue it, one lacks a fundamental understanding of the purpose and meaning of the religious life. His guide, originally written in Arabic but soon translated into Hebrew, proved to be one of the most popular medieval works and is reprinted and studied to this day. His emphasis on characterological issues formed the basis of an entire genre of Jewish literature known as *musar*—the Hebrew word means "education"—an instruction centrally concerned with individual virtues. Over and over again, teachers of *musar* have argued that observance of the law has little meaning when it is not accompanied by characterological development.

The call to transform one's heart is a call to embark on a continuous journey, for the human personality is always developing, always unfolding, always encountering new situations. The call to holiness is then understood as a constant progress, a relentless struggle, a lifelong undertaking. In *Duties of the Heart,* Ibn Pakuda argues that the rightful compass is buried deep within each person; uncovering it is like digging for a well, for which one may have to dig for a long time. He tells of a wise person who said, "I have been digging for it [a pure heart] for twenty-five years."

ENCOUNTERING THE DIVINE IN
CONTEMPORARY JEWISH THOUGHT

In our own time, the great twentieth-century Jewish philosopher Martin Buber (1878–1965) has offered a corrective to this view, while writing in the spirit of the Holiness Code. Buber does not focus on the turning inward, the self-examination and personal development that must take place in order to reach toward a holy life. Instead, he emphasizes the need to appreciate the other, elevating the crucial encounter with "other." In essence, Buber's thought is an extended unfolding of the meaning of "Love your neighbor as yourself." In his philosophy of meeting, Buber argues that when the "I" and the "You" come to understand each other as different, yet constituting a common humanity, then the Divine becomes present for them. This interhuman love is what manifests the Divine presence in the world. As such, the aim of the religious life is not the cultivation of personal religious experience but rather the stance one takes in encountering the world, which leads to the consciousness of the presence of God. In fact, it is not only our interhuman relationships that uncover the Divine presence but the way we encounter everything we meet, animate and inanimate, which can reveal the Divine presence in the world.

The teachings of the Holiness Code are manifest in Buber's thinking, even as certain aspects of medieval understanding are discarded. The fusion of the religious realm with the lived life and the possibility of the world's perfection is Buber's constant theme. "The living spirit wishes . . . spirit and life to find the way to one another; it wishes spirit to take shape as life, and life to be clarified through spirit."[9] The legacy of the Holiness Code is manifest: one can experience the Divine in the everyday world; everyone can participate in this experience; and empathy itself, the reaching out to the other, is the throne room of the Divine presence.

Even more so than Buber, the theologian Abraham Joshua Heschel (1907–1972) captures the spirit of the Holiness Code. He talks about religious acts as leading a person into the consciousness of God's presence; equally, of worldly acts as furthering justice, which similarly manifests the Divine presence. Famously joining with Martin Luther King Jr. in the march for racial equality in Selma, Alabama, he said about the experience, "I felt my legs were praying."[10]

Like the Holiness Code itself, Heschel proceeds out of a critique of priestly religion that would limit religiosity only to the cultic activity.

"Religion has always suffered from the tendency to become an end in itself," he writes, "to seclude the holy, to become parochial, self-indulgent, self-seeking; as if the task were not to ennoble human nature but to enhance the power and beauty of its institutions or to enlarge the body of doctrine."[11] For Heschel, holiness is not a priestly concern—that is, primarily interested in building and preserving religious institutions. Holiness is, rather, a matter of transforming the heart, so that one empathizes with the vulnerable in our society and sees God everywhere in each person.

But Heschel also recognizes how religious ritual is equally part of the road to holiness. Central to the message of the Holiness Code is the Sabbath as an instrument of the Divine. It is not incidental that in the Roman world Jews were called the Sabbath observers, sometimes mockingly, sometimes as a purely anthropological observation. It was *the* characteristic by which Jews were known: being keepers of a strange institution unknown to Romans. The Sabbath ensured both a secular literal rest and a dedicated day for reaching toward the Divine, thereby affirming the human dignity of all: householder and servant, patrician and field-worker alike. Observance of the Sabbath and experience of its spiritual richness did not demand great philosophical capabilities or extraordinary human sensitivities. The Sabbath worked its magic on all.

Heschel finds in the Sabbath the quintessential expression of Jewish religiosity. "Perhaps Sabbath is the idea that expresses what is most characteristic of Judaism," he writes, and then proceeds to combine both the secular and religious in explaining its meaning:

What is the Sabbath? A reminder of every person's royalty; an abolition of the distinction of master and slave, rich and poor, success and failure. . . . The Sabbath is an embodiment of the belief that all people are equal and that equality among people means the nobility of everyone. The greatest sin of a person is to forget that they are a prince. . . .

What is the Sabbath? The presence of eternity, a moment of majesty, the radiance of joy. The soul is enhanced, time is a delight, and inwardness a supreme reward.[12]

And, much as implied in the Holiness Code, Heschel captures both the sense of journey and the ineffable when he writes:

This is what we mean by the term *spiritual*: It is the reference to the transcendent in our own existence, the direction of the Here toward the Beyond. It is the ecstatic force . . . turning arrivals into new pilgrimages. . . . It is impossible to grasp spirit in itself. Spirit is a *direction*, the turning of all beings to God: *theotropism*. It is always more than—and superior to—what we are and what we know.[13]

Ultimately, the authors of the Holiness Code dreamed a dream of such power that one can feel its pull millennia later. These twentieth-century Jewish sages write their theology in its shadow.

Part IV

The Last Revolution

13 The Torah

Jerusalem was astir. The governor, appointed by the Persian court, was promulgating new regulations.

He had come with royal authority to rebuild the walls of Jerusalem, almost 150 years after they had been torn down. That, in itself, had proved controversial.

After its destruction by the Babylonians in 587–86 BCE, Jerusalem was in ruins. The Persians had, in turn, conquered Babylonia in 539 BCE and had allowed exiled Jews to return to the Land of Israel and rebuild an altar on the Temple grounds, but only a few returned. And because the Babylonians had exiled the political and religious elite, the craftspeople, anyone of influence, the Jews who had remained were mostly small farmers. Thus, the Jewish population of the Land of Israel was largely impoverished, and internecine politics had interrupted previous attempts to rebuild the city walls. These farmers and the Jewish returnees from exile faced new opposition from a local population who had moved into the decimated land during the Babylonian exile. The foreign settlers, known as Samaritans because they mostly settled into the northern province of Samaria, had falsely reported plots of Jewish sedition to the Persian authorities, which had led to the suspension of the program to rebuild Jerusalem.

According to the biblical account, the new governor, Nehemiah, a courtier of the Persian king Artaxerxes, was a Jew who had achieved success in the royal court and gained the ear of his monarch. Deciding to use his position as a trusted court official to revive Jewish life in the Land of Israel, Nehemiah fixed on a project of rebuilding the walls of Jerusalem, and the king, whose empire extended over almost the entire Middle East, granted him the authority to do so. And so, the new governor arrived in the city probably in 445 BCE with the charge to rebuild the walls.

Jewish residents may have cheered, but Samaritans opposed the building project. Again and again they tried to undermine it, sometimes threatening to attack the work, sometimes reporting to Persian authorities that the walls were being rebuilt as part of a Jewish plan to revolt. Nehemiah, though, proved to be an assiduous leader, organizing Jewish inhabitants for both defensive purposes and as work gangs engaged in the rebuilding, as well as using his influence at court to insulate the project from Samaritan canards. Not incidentally, the draft of workers and soldiers led to economic privation and opposition from the impoverished Jewish residents as well. Nehemiah's full powers of persuasion were needed to calm protests among his Jewish constituents even as he fended off the machinations of the non-Jewish inhabitants.

Nehemiah's persistence ensured that the wall was indeed built. But that led to yet another conflict with the Jewish residents, as Nehemiah, a Babylonian Jew, used the rebuilt walls for a new purpose: to thwart what he decried as Sabbath violations practiced by the residents of Jerusalem. Nehemiah reports:

> At that time, I saw men in Judah treading winepresses on the Sabbath, and others bringing heaps of grain and loading them onto asses, also wine, grapes, figs, and all sorts of goods, and bringing them into Jerusalem on the Sabbath. I admonished them there and then for selling provisions. . . . When shadows filled the gateways of Jerusalem at the approach of the Sabbath, I gave orders that the doors be closed, and ordered them not to be opened until after the Sabbath. I stationed some of my servants at the gates so that no goods should enter on the Sabbath. (Neh. 13:15–16,19)

It is evident, then, that the people resident in the Land of Israel did not observe the Sabbath as the newly arrived Persian Jews did.

They saw nothing wrong with work going on outside the city limits, nor with traders entering the city on the Sabbath day. They appeared to know nothing of the kind of Sabbath observance that Nehemiah assumed was required.

THE SABBATH AND RELIGIOUS REFORM

As remarked on earlier, the Sabbath as we know it became an important institution for Jews exiled in Babylonia. Bereft of the Temple, the Sabbath became a means of experiencing a closeness to that which was holy. The authors of the Holiness Code, writing in exile, had stressed the Sabbath as a day dedicated to God, and now Babylonian exiles returning to the land, imbued with the new Sabbath sensibility, were insisting on a new strictness in the people's observance of the seventh day.[1]

The people of Jerusalem recognized none of this, experiencing it as a new and foreign ritual demand, while Nehemiah used his policing power over the gates of Jerusalem to forcibly impose his sense of the requisite observance on the people.

This was part and parcel of a general religious reform that now became the order of the day. Nehemiah was not alone in bringing a new Jewish teaching to Jerusalem. Ezra, a priest, had organized a group of Levites to return to the Land of Israel.[2] He and his cohorts joined with Nehemiah to promulgate "the Torah of Moses" to the people of Jerusalem. Nehemiah called for an assembly of "all the people" (Neh. 8:1) and designated Ezra to read this new teaching aloud. As the book of Nehemiah recounts:

> On the first day of the seventh month, Ezra the priest brought the Teaching [*Torah*] before the congregation, men and women and all who could listen with understanding. . . . Ezra the scribe stood upon a wooden tower made for the purpose. . . . Ezra opened the scroll in the sight of all the people for he was above all people; as he opened it, all the people stood up. . . . The Levites explained

the Teaching to the people, while the people stood in their places. They read from the scroll of the Teaching of God, translating it and giving the sense; so they understood the reading. (Neh. 8:2,4,5,7–8)

This reading and teaching from the scroll went on for seven days. For the people of Jerusalem this was indeed a new teaching—which we can glean from Nehemiah's report regarding another ritual, the observance of the Feast of Booths:

On the second day, the heads of the clans of all the people and priests and Levites gathered to Ezra the scribe to study the words of the Teaching [*Torah*]. They found written in the Teaching that *Adonai* had commanded Moses that the Israelites must dwell in booths during the festival of the seventh month, and that they must announce and proclaim throughout all their towns and Jerusalem as follows, "Go out to the mountains and bring leafy branches of olive trees, pine trees, myrtles, palms, and other leafy trees to make booths, as it is written." So the people went out and brought them and made themselves booths on their roofs, in their courtyards, in the courtyards of the House of God.... The Israelites had not done so from the days of Joshua son of Nun to that day. (Neh. 8:13–17)

The passages in the Five Books of Moses that speak of building booths to celebrate the fall festival occur in both Deuteronomy and Leviticus. The former gives little detail other than calling it the Festival of Sukkot, that is, booths. Only in the latter description in Leviticus, in a passage identified as part of the Holiness Code, do we read of the gathering of agricultural materials and the dwelling in booths for seven days in celebration of the festival.

These laws of festival observance were unknown to the people of Jerusalem. Indeed, the text in Nehemiah emphasizes how new this observance is by stating that it had not been done since the days of

Joshua—that is, for the past half a millennium. The Torah as a complete set of instructions, the Pentateuch as we know it, was foreign to these people of Jerusalem. Both Nehemiah, coming from exile, and Ezra, a priest who led a group of exiles back from Persia, proclaim to the people of Jerusalem the rituals in the Pentateuch—rites that we in our modern days may know, but of which generations of Jews who had remained in the Land of Israel knew nothing.

Not only was the institution of this new religious regime met with opposition by his fellow Jews, but Nehemiah also reports of non-Jews who fought his political program. In particular, he mentions three opponents—Sanballat the Horonite, Tobiah the Ammonite, and Geshem the Arab—all non-Jewish residents of the Land of Israel and nearby lands who saw this new Jewish resurgence as a threat. Interestingly, Jews also joined with them; as Nehemiah reports:

> I saw that Jews had married Ashdodite, Ammonite and Moabite women; a good number of their children spoke the language of Ashdod and the language of those various people and did not know how to speak Judean [i.e., Hebrew].[3] I censured them, cursed them, flogged them, tore out their hair, and adjured them by God, saying, "You shall not give your daughter in marriage to their sons, or take any of their daughters for your sons or yourselves."... One of the sons of Joiada, the son of the High Priest Eliashib, was a son-in-law of Sanballat the Horonite; I drove him away from me. (Neh. 13:23,24,28)

First there is the question of the preservation of Jewish culture, of the Hebrew language: citizens of Judea were using the language of their more dominant neighbors, probably Aramaic (possibly Phoenician), as their common tongue, forgetting Hebrew.[4] But equally there is the mention that the grandson of the High Priest had married into a prominent Samaritan family that had actively opposed Nehemiah's project. Nehemiah now insists on separating the Jewish community from these peoples: "They [the Levites] read to the people from the

Book of Moses, and it was found written that no Ammonite or Moabite might ever enter the congregation of God [Deut. 23:4]. . . . When they heard the Teaching [the *Torah*] they separated all the alien admixture from Israel" (Neh. 13:1,3).

In a similar vein, Ezra in his book stresses that intermarriage, especially among the priesthood, is of critical concern. He prays that the people may change their ways:

> Now then, do not give your daughters in marriage to their sons or let their daughters marry your sons. . . .
>
> While Ezra was praying and making confession . . . then Shechana son of Jehiel of the family of Elam spoke and said to Ezra, "We have trespassed against our God by bringing into our homes foreign women from the peoples of the land. . . . Now then, let us make a covenant with God to expel all these women and those who have been born to them." (Ezra 9:12, 10:1a,2a,3)

The returning Babylonian exiles bring a new teaching and a new nationalism to the Jews of the Land of Israel, affecting their religious lives, their domestic lives, indeed their very identity and sense of self.

THE TORAH

The later prophets of the Land of Israel who lived a generation or two before Nehemiah — Haggai, Malachi, and Zechariah — do not mention any of the teachings just discussed. They do not refer to the Torah in the way Nehemiah does. They do not quote from the Pentateuch or refer to it. Their proclamations are not that different from First Temple prophets. At times they echo the message of earlier prophets preaching moral reform. They call for ethical uprightness and the restoration of proper worship in the Temple, sometimes arguing that it was moral and religious corruption that led to the destruction of the First Temple. These prophets talk about loyalty to Zerubbabel, a scion of the House of David, and to Joshua, the High Priest, but their message does not ring with calls of Sabbath observance or obedience to the Torah. The Pentateuch as a fully edited text is the work of Babylonian Jewry. In the Land of Israel, it is only when we meet the figures of Ezra and Nehemiah, exiles who come to Jerusalem from Babylonia, that we have a call to return to the norms of the Torah as we know them.[5]

The Pentateuch begins with the story of exile, the primal exile, of Adam and Eve wandering east of the Garden because of their sin, and the Pentateuch ends with the Children of Israel waiting to enter the land but not yet there. It captures a moment of expectancy, of being outside and trying to gaze in. Structurally, it is a story that resonated with the exilic community of Babylonian Jewry, sitting outside the Land of Israel.

And it was priests in Babylon who did the work of editing it. In exile they took on new roles, beyond those of ritual functionaries and judges of purity and impurity. Ezekiel is both prophet and priest, authoring some of the most fantastic and imaginative visions in all of prophetic literature along with concrete, detailed plans for the reconstruction of Temple worship. As priest-prophet he seems to have exercised an important communal-leadership function. For instance, he describes one of his visions as taking place in his home with "the elders of Judah" meeting there (8:1). In a similar vein, upon Ezra's return to Judea, we never see this exilic priest functioning in a priestly ritual role; rather, Nehemiah describes him as reading and explaining the Torah to the people, that is, performing an instructional role. He is a priest who is also called a scribe.[6] Priests have taken on new leadership positions.

We are not told exactly what is meant by "scribe," the appellation Nehemiah gives to Ezra and his peers. We can imagine the scribal function of some of these exilic priests as collating the religious documents of the community, working to preserve its religious heritage. They were, simultaneously, archivists and artists who shaped the vision of return, taking the memory of the past and giving it coherence as a contemporary ideal. They also functioned somewhat like lawyers in our own society—judges, legislators, counselors—propounding the law, interpreting it, and executing it as well. It is hard to say what religious functions they fulfilled given that they were not serving in the Temple but acting as leaders of their community under foreign (Persian) domination. In so doing these scribal priests were both preserving religious traditions and corporate Jewish memory and creating a new religious synthesis celebrated with appropriate rituals. Rabbinic sources have always assigned a special role to Ezra and his associates in the work of formalizing the tradition and instituting related practices, and these later sources may well have preserved a historical truth.[7] This much can surely be said: the very name "scribe" now given to Ezra and his priestly associates implies a relationship to a written tradition — a written text.

This model of priestly leadership taking on larger political and religious roles was to survive and develop further throughout the Second Temple period. A little more than 250 years after Ezra, Simon the Maccabee, a member of the family that sparked the revolution against the Syrian Greek overlords, would not only take on the role of High Priest but also political leadership, and his descendants would serve as kings of Israel. Almost 250 years later, after the destruction of the Second Temple in 70 CE, it would be Johanan ben Zakkai, an important priest himself, and his court, all of whom were priests, who would organize the emergent Rabbinic Judaism that sustained Jews through their Diaspora sans Temple. Eventually, the new role of interpreters of the law would come to overwhelm the tribal prerequisites of priesthood, and the learned sage would replace the hereditary priesthood, but that process would take hundreds of years. Meanwhile, priests were often the recognized communal leaders.

In the center of the Torah is the sanctuary in the desert. The instructions for the building of the sanctuary, the rules for sacrifice and for the priesthood, and finally, the dedication of the sanctuary occupy almost half the text of the Pentateuch. Pride of place is given to this portable sanctuary; it is the apex of the Five Books.[8] The Pentateuch takes great pains in describing the sanctuary as being at the very center of the Israelite camp in the desert; the tribes are arranged in four directions surrounding it. This, then, is a document that reflects priestly theology, one that sees Temple worship at the center of Israelite life.

In this these priests were not alone. Virtually all the literature of the exilic period—prophetic sermons, psalmic hymns, and the manuals of the priestly writers themselves—reflect the centrality of Temple worship in the ideology of almost all Jewish groups. There is a sense of sadness over the loss of home centered on the Temple.

Ezekiel and Isaiah, living in Babylonia, envisioned a reconstructed Temple. The prophets in the Land of Israel, like Malachi, live at a time when they can see the rebuilt altar on the Temple Mount but know that it is hardly the stuff of dreams; rather, it is a somewhat humble construction. So they envision a moment when a full and complete reconstruction will take place. The future need contain a purer faith.

The religious life that the priestly editors of the Pentateuch espouse, the faith represented in Temple worship, is unequivocally monotheistic. Unlike Deuteronomy, the Pentateuch does not begin with Moses and the Exodus from Egypt; nor does it begin with a folk history, the patriarchal narrative, the ancestral origins of the people Israel. Rather, it begins with the Creation of the world. Babylonian Jewry had experienced God as being everywhere—with them even in exile—for the whole world was God's. In other words, if God was with this people exiled from their land, it was because there was one God who created the earth and ruled it, a being who was not a local god. It was not Jerusalem, or the Land of Israel, or even the Temple that bore witness to God's presence; it was all of creation, the stars, the sun, and the moon. To the exiles in Babylonia, Isaiah preached:

Ascend a lofty mountain,
O herald of joy to Zion;
Raise your voice with power,
O herald of joy to Jerusalem—
Raise it, have no fear;
Announce to the cities of Judah;

Behold your God!
... Do you not know?
Have you not heard?
Have you not been told
From the very first?
Have you not discerned
How the earth was founded?
It is the One who is enthroned above the vault of the earth. . . .
The One who brings potentates to naught,
Makes rulers of the earth as nothing. . . .
(Isa. 40:9,21–22a,23)

The prophet emphasizes this theme by having God's self voice these thoughts:

Will you instruct Me about the work of My hands?
It was I who made the earth
And created human beings upon it;
My own hands stretched out the heavens,
And I marshaled all their host. (Isa. 45:11–12)

In accordance with this theology, any allusion to other divine beings that may have been characteristic of Israelites who had lived before the destruction of the Temple is totally absent from the Pentateuch, save for the occasional mention of angels, direct messengers of God. In Psalms, and other books of the Bible such as Job, we find remnants of stories reminiscent of pagan mythologies, primal wars between God and other divine and semidivine figures—Tiamot and Leviathan, for instance—but such mythological understandings are totally absent from the Pentateuch.[9] Similarly, while archaeological evidence has uncovered widespread worship of the dead in ancient Israel, such practices are totally absent in the Torah. Indeed, there is no discussion of an afterlife or a netherworld in the Torah. We may surmise that the biblical authors and editors wished to indicate that there were no other spiritual forces in the universe that deserved to be worshiped.[10]

It was a universal monotheism that preserved the distinctive identity of the exiles in Babylonia, and that now triumphed as the center of Israel's religious identity. And it was the one God, the God of Israel, who ensured the Israelites' return. This was the common faith of the exiles in Babylon, enunciated by priests and prophets alike. The sanctuary that is at the center of the Torah, the sanctuary that traveled with the Israelites in the desert, is dedicated to this one God.

Following the lead of the pioneering biblical scholar Yehezkel Kaufmann, the contemporary Israeli scholar Israel Knohl emphasizes that the sacrificial system described in Leviticus is minimalist regarding pomp and ceremony. No musical or liturgical accompaniments are ordained as part of the sacrificial system. No incantations are mentioned, though these are present in other ancient Near Eastern texts delineating prescribed worship.[11] Along the same lines, in other cultures we encounter the flesh of sacrifices or other offerings being left as consumption for the gods even as the supplicants may have believed that this was only a symbolic gift; here, the animal flesh is burnt on the altar with the remainder eaten by the priest or the supplicant. None of the flesh is left for God—the Divinity clearly does not eat flesh. At most, regarding the offering, we find the ambiguous phrase "a sweet savor, burnt for *Adonai*." There is a purity and simplicity to this description of the offerings in accordance with the new purified notion of divinity that emerged from prophetic circles and triumphed in the exile.[12] The faith espoused by the Torah has monotheistic purity. A significant segment of the Jerusalem priesthood may have persistently articulated this kind of pure faith even before the exile.

The vision of the sanctuary that stands at the center of the Torah is not that of a baroque building but of a portable tent, which the Israelites carry with them in their march through the desert and which, at each resting place, is set up once again in their center. In the book of Kings, Solomon's Temple is described as an elaborate structure, built with the forced labor of Israelites and the help of foreign craftspeople. The portable desert sanctuary is made possible by free-will donations and crafted by Israelites using available materials. This contrast accords with a general attitude displayed in the text: royal elements have little place in the Pentateuch. While the role of the priesthood is elaborated, that of a king is not. Except for the passages in Deuteronomy that place limits on the power of kings and see the reign of royalty as a foreign innovation, there is no mention of kingship in the Torah. Only in one or two poetic passages—ancient songs whose words could not be changed—is God referred to as king, though that appellation would have been most natural for a divinity; psalms, for instance, frequently refer to God as king. We can only conclude that this commonly used appellation was deliberately left off by the final editors of the Torah. The emphasis on the purity of worship places a religious outlook at the center of a program of return but does not put its hope in a Davidic dynasty. We should remember that Moses is a prophet, sometimes functioning as a priest, but not a king. The Torah is a priestly, not a royalist document.

These priests who edited the Pentateuch were either themselves members of the group that authored the Holiness Code or else heavily influenced by them. They conclude the six days of creation with the seventh, the Sabbath, the crown of creation. They surround the instructions and construction of the sanctuary in the desert with the laws of the Sabbath. They place the Holiness Code next to the regulations for the portable sanctuary, the sacrificial system, and the laws of purity. Immediately following the description of the High Priest entering the Holy of Holies—the closest one can come to the Divinity—we find the commandments addressed to all of Israel: what can be eaten, whom one can marry, the injunction to be holy.

But along with giving prominence to their own perspective, these priests saw themselves as preservers of a tradition greater than their own. They were leaders who needed to speak to all the people, and permeating their vision was a notion of reconciliation: of all Israel being a united people. Mythically, this vision was symbolized by the falling out and eventual mutual reconciliation of Joseph and his brothers. In exile, the wars between Judea and Northern Israel could be seen as one of the critical causes of the downfall of these two kingdoms. The words of Isaiah of Jerusalem regarding the destructiveness of tribal warfare, preached more than a hundred years before Judea's exile, rang true for them:

> Next, the people became like devouring fire:
> No man spared his countryman.
> They snatched on the right, but remained hungry,
> And consumed on the left without being sated.
> Each devoured the flesh of his own kindred
> Manasseh Ephraim's and Ephraim Manasseh's
> And both of them against Judah! (9:18–20)

And so, in Genesis's telling, it is the rivalry between Joseph and his brothers that brings the children of Jacob down to Egypt—just as in the eyes of the exiles, it was rivalry between Northern Israel and Judea that contributed to the destruction they had suffered.

The book of Kings tells the story of the breakup of the united kingdom after the death of Solomon. Jeroboam leads a revolt against the harsh administration of Solomon's son Rehoboam. According to Kings, the prophet Ahijah of Shiloh, encouraging Jeroboam's breakaway rebellion, tears Jeroboam's new robe into twelve pieces and says, "Take ten pieces . . . for thus said the Lord, the God of Israel: I am about to tear the kingdom out of Solomon's hands, and I will give you ten tribes" (1 Kings 11:29). Northern Israel was composed of ten of the twelve tribes of Israel and sometimes referred to itself as the descendants of Joseph, while Judea was eventually joined by the single tribe of Benjamin but retained the name of its chief tribe. It may hardly be coincidental that a torn robe plays a crucial role in the Joseph story. The brothers who have sold Joseph into slavery show his torn and bloody robe to their father and ask, "Do you recognize this?" The coat of many colors that their father had gifted Joseph becomes a symbol of the brothers' jealousy; the torn robe of Ahijah reminds us that the split in the kingdom is a war of brothers.

Indeed, the later Rabbis were to remark that what had happened in the patriarchal age was entirely symbolic of what would happen to their descendants. These Rabbis attributed the destruction of the Second Temple to the hatred of one brother for another. They may well have seen the Torah as offering a subtle reading that the war between brothers had adumbrated the downfall of the First Temple. Along these lines, we may view the final reconciliation of Judah and Joseph in the Genesis story, their mutual recognition, as a metaphor for the hoped-for unified return, a dream animating the people Israel in exile.

The tale of Joseph and his brothers is remarkably carefully balanced. Readers continue to argue about how to read the story—whether the central hero is Judah or Joseph. Is Joseph cold and cruel, hiding his tears until his brother Judah's speech breaks through his protective shield—the power of his office—and transforms him? Or is Joseph an educator, a righteous figure, teaching his brothers to recognize how they had wronged him? Amazingly, the storyteller seems not to take sides with either Joseph—representing Northern Israel—or Judah—the surviving southern kingdom whose progeny were in exile in Babylonia. The war of brother against brother has brought this family to Egypt where, in the end, they will all be enslaved together. Ultimately, both Northern Israel and Judea suffered the common fate of exile: one by the Assyrians, the other by the Babylonians.

But the Torah offers a measure of hope, for ultimately there is forgiveness. Even though after their father's death the brothers still do not trust each other, nevertheless they are on the way to reconciliation, for their descendants will be the Children of Israel who experience a common slavery that knits them into a common people. These tribes are to carry the bones of Joseph out with them as they leave Egypt. It is they, the collectivity, who stand at Sinai—who are commanded, finally, in the last of the commandments, not to be jealous of one another. (They are instructed by Moses of the tribe of Levi, whose members are not to own land in Israel, for the priesthood ought never to be part of internecine warfare.) The Judean exiles, captive in Babylonia, will return to the land; carry with them the memories of the North, of Joseph; and create a united kingdom. Not incidentally, at the center of the Holiness Code, near the apex of the Pentateuch itself, we find the injunction, "Do not hate your brother in your heart." Unlike the following verse, which talks of loving your "neighbor," here the object is "brother." Brotherly hatred was a cause of the destruction, and the overcoming of that brotherly hatred will constitute the redemption.

Underlying these narratives, then, is the knowledge that exile was the fate of both the Northern Kingdom and of Judea, as well as the prophetic hope that all the tribes of Israel will finally be reconciled.

In an earlier time, after the exile of Northern Israel, Isaiah of Jerusalem preached this very message of reconciliation:

> Then Ephraim's envy shall cease
> And the besiegers of Judah shall be cut off
> Ephraim shall not envy Judah
> And Judah shall not besiege Ephraim. (11:13)

We see here the preexilic consciousness that was to triumph in exile. Exile became the common fate of Northern Israel and Judea, and their common tragedy allowed them to finally see that they had a common destiny. The story of Joseph and his brothers foreshadows the dream of the exiles: a return to the land with brothers reconciled. In a passage written after the Babylonian destruction, Jeremiah explicitly promises that a new story can be told:

> See, a time is coming—declares *Adonai*—when I will make a covenant with the House of Israel and the House of Judah. It will not be like the covenant I made with their fathers, when I took them by the hand to lead them out of the land of Egypt, a covenant which they broke. . . .
>
> For I will forgive their iniquities and remember their sins no more. (Jer. 31:31–32, 34)

This spirit of reconciliation animated the priests who compiled the Pentateuch.

The work they edited was an archive of traditional teachings, not a new code that would favor one traditional perspective or another. Inclusiveness marks the entire Torah. Notably, it embraces all three legal codes—the Covenant Code (Exodus), the Deuteronomic Code, and the Holiness Code (Leviticus)—despite the inherent contradictions in doing so. Disagreements between sources remain undecided. Deuteronomy may recommend one way of observing the Passover while Exodus defines a different mode of observance, and their inclusion in the same book would create conundrums for successive generations, but the editors determined not to decide between them. If the sanctuary is at the center of the Teaching, and with it the Holiness Code, then to the right we find the book of the Covenant, and to the left Deuteronomy—it is as if one entered the sanctuary through a gateway defined by two pillars.

Thus, Deuteronomy came to seamlessly occupy its place as the last book of the Teaching, balancing the book of the Covenant on the other side, though Deuteronomy had been promulgated as an exclusive teaching. That sense of exclusivity was now applied to Torah as a whole. Torah would not simply refer to the single book of Deuteronomy, as had the original reference to the Torah that Moses ordered written down (Deut. 31:7–13): the scroll of instruction. Now the Torah would encompass the entire collection of assembled materials: the Five Books.

To accommodate the variety of sources included, these editors were influenced by a literary device that characterizes ancient poetic forms. In biblical poetry, every line is further developed with a second telling that gives a slightly different emphasis than the first; and sometimes the poetic verse has three lines, with the third line developing yet a further thought. In poetry the lines follow on one another. In the Torah the same themes are separated by whole books. Yet as in poetry, in the Five Books of Moses the same story could be told over again—for example, two versions of Creation, two versions of Sarah's being passed off as Abraham's sister, two versions of Moses hitting the rock—but with somewhat different emphases and different outcomes. Similarly, law codes could be recorded with differing directives regarding the same issues. The decision to be inclusive was a way of accommodating the variety of traditions that represented different elites and different geographical origins. Differences achieved a poetic, not a legal solution. The Torah, while a book of instruction, is a literary masterpiece as much as it is a constitution. It places narrative side by side with law codes, and includes many different versions of the same instruction. We might say that the Torah treats law both as prose instruction and poetic creation. As poetry, the law retains ambiguity and mystery, calling forth the need for interpretation on the part of generations of readers.

Critical questions were left undecided. As a compilation edited in exile, it did not have to confront the single-minded decisions necessitated by self-governance. These priests kept both the instruction in Exodus, "In every place where I cause My name to be mentioned I will come to you and bless you" (20:21)—a validation of multiple sanctuaries—as well as the Deuteronomic instruction that sacrifices might be offered in a single place only—understood as a reference to the Jerusalem Temple (Deut. 12:5). In the same vein, they preserved both the first teaching of the Holiness Code that all cattle must be brought as a sacrifice before any part is eaten (Lev. 17:19)—an injunction that could only be observed if there were multiple sites for sacrifice—and the passage in Deuteronomy permitting secular slaughter (in light of the distance the population would need to travel to offer every animal to be eaten as a sacrifice in a centralized sanctuary [Deut. 12:21]).

The decision to be inclusive, to not allow any single faction to define the meaning of the biblical heritage, represented a brilliant compromise, for the politics of religious rectitude was tricky. The scribal descendants of First Temple governmental officials formed a constituency that must have argued that Deuteronomy had a unique imprimatur—it had been promulgated by a king, Josiah, and had served as the last constitution of the people. It is the only one of the Five Books to mention kingship, the reinstitution of which was critical to many exiles' dreams. Furthermore, these descendants of former officials may have hoped to return to their ancestral roles once Judea regained its independence, and so had a personal stake in its preservation.

Another constituency, the remnant of the folk who had remained loyal to their ancestral traditions, had kept their heritage alive in exile by taking on personal acts of piety and retelling their tribal stories. Although Deuteronomy had begun with the Exodus from Egypt and had not included any patriarchal stories, the Torah now included those materials in the first volume—one that counterbalances Deuteronomy.

Jeremiah could see the time in the desert as a honeymoon between God and Israel, but these editors did not romanticize that time. They recorded that history as one of contention, just as they knew that the history of the people Israel had been full of moments of disloyalty—to God, to one another. Still, they could hope that in bringing the totality of traditions together, they could begin the process of reconciliation. They saw themselves as preservers of the multiplicity of traditions. They seemed to recognize that each source reflected moments of spiritual understanding; each could give insight into what God wanted. For the exiles, preservation of traditions was more significant than determining the validity of any single code or narrative. Every received tradition from the past needed to be preserved; it was the totality that would be sustaining.

AFTERMATH

The people standing in the public courtyards of Jerusalem heard Ezra and the priests reading these scrolls. They had not heard these words before. And as the reading came to an end, they heard Moses' warning to the generation who were about to enter the land after forty years of wandering: you will undoubtedly stray, as your parents did. The people in the courtyard knew that their ancestors had witnessed the destruction of Jerusalem, and they could hear that even the time of wandering in the desert was filled with contention. I wonder what the populace felt as they heard the words read aloud by Ezra. Did they experience Moses' warning as directed at them? Did they hope that this time they might get it right—now, they would follow the Teaching and be rewarded with the restoration of independence? Nehemiah reports that immediately upon hearing the words of the Teaching, the people went up into the hills, gathered the willows, and built the huts celebrating the festival. Might they not have felt, "This time we will do God's bidding, follow the teachings of those who represent the Divine"? Or was Nehemiah's report entirely self-serving, and did most people go about their business ignoring him?

For his part, Ezra reports that the people were transformed. He confesses in prayer: "'*Adonai*, God of Israel, You are righteous, for we have survived as a remnant, as is now the case. We stand before You in all our guilt, for we cannot face You on this account.' While Ezra was praying and making confession, weeping and prostrating himself before the House of God, a very great crowd of Israelites gathered about him, men, women and children; the people were weeping bitterly" (Ezra 9:15–10:1).

Nehemiah ends his book with a prayer that his work might be considered valuable and true to God: "O my God, remember me to my credit" (Neh. 13:31). He seemingly saw his commission at an end, and we hear no more of him. We may presume that after he rebuilt the walls of Jerusalem—thereby fulfilling the Persian king's commission—and allied himself with Ezra in a program of religious reform, he returned to Persia, where he continued to serve as an official in the Persian court.

He left behind a community charged to uphold the Torah.

FINAL THOUGHTS

Through the generations, reading the Torah from beginning to end, almost all readers and commentators related to the Pentateuch as a single-minded text telling a unitary story. Primal history and patriarchal narratives in Genesis lead up to the moment at the end of Deuteronomy when the Children of Israel stand ready to cross the River Jordan and fulfill the promises made to their ancestors. The logic of the story is inexorable. Exile from the Garden can be redeemed by a people living in its land with God in its midst.

To be sure, the various apostasies in the desert echo the disaster in the Garden. Moses ends his speech in the closing chapters of the Torah exhibiting a certain pessimism about the future, warning that the people will sin and fall away. Indeed, continuous exile was the fate of the Jewish people—yet succeeding generations held on to the possibility that the people Israel would indeed abide by the covenant, and so the Garden could be recovered. As such, the architecture of the Five Books provided a self-understanding for Jewish communities for thousands of years.

At times the biblical stories are so compelling that we do not notice moments of contradiction, but contradictions and opposition of ideas abound in the Torah. Take a closer look at the unfolding biblical narrative and it begins to show some of its seams. Torah proves to be a patchwork quilt of multiple sources, various threads knit together to form a woven coat of many colors.

In the journey we have taken in the pages of this book, we have followed the path by which different historical eras, different cultural moments, shaped constituent parts of the Torah. Discrepancies range from minor ones, like the slight word changes in the two versions of the Decalogue in Exodus and Deuteronomy, to more consequential ones, such as the differences in the laws regulating Passover observance in Exodus and Deuteronomy, or the differences between texts ruling whether Hebrew slaves may be owned at all—Leviticus says no, in contrast to both Exodus and Deuteronomy. These divergences, although sometimes tucked away in different volumes of the Five Books and therefore not necessarily immediately noticed, are, on reflection, so blatant that one must assume a certain deliberateness on the part of the editors in not taking a stand between vying ideologies. In other words, the final editors, while quite consciously creating a literary unity, understood that they were heirs to a multiplicity of traditions and did not seek to choose between them to create a common orthodoxy.

Only in certain arenas does the text create a single-minded vision. This is especially true of its consistent monotheistic outlook. Critically, there is no consort to God, no sexuality alluded to in relation to the Divine, and no other heavenly force with which the Deity has to contend. The contrary position was true in the world out of which the Torah emerged, but none of these beings are even hinted at in the text.

In almost all other areas, however, the weave of the final editors does not obliterate the variety of threads constituting contrasting theologies, visions, and legal outcomes.

The significance of this point is most easily grasped by considering a specific example, aspects of which we have encountered earlier in this book. According to the Five Books of Moses, the revelation at Sinai is critical for an understanding of the most basic assertions of Jewish belief. It is a foundational moment in the life of the people. The validity of the Torah itself—God's instructions—depends on this moment, for in its view, this is the primal moment of God's revelation. Yet the Five Books of Moses offers us several different accounts of what occurred at Sinai.

While these disparate texts are sometimes placed side by side, more often they occur at different points in the narrative. The several accounts of what occurred at Sinai are so artfully placed in different parts of the Five Books—in separate chapters of the book of Exodus at some distance from each other, as well as in Deuteronomy, where Moses retells the story of Sinai—that their inner contradiction is hardly noticeable while we experience the drama of the overall narrative. Perhaps in this way the editors hoped to lessen the future readers' sense of self-contradiction in the text. But as soon as a reader pays attention to these details, their incompatibility becomes impossible to miss.

At one point in Exodus we read that Moses, Aaron, and the elders sat down at Sinai and ate a festive meal as they viewed God, while later in Exodus we read that no one can possibly see God and live. In one scene Moses alone receives the commandments—going up the mountain and bringing down the tablets written by the hand of God—but in another scene God comes down and voices these words to the entire people. Who then heard God speak these words? All the people? The elders as their representatives? Just Moses? The Torah has moments when each of these possibilities is validated. Similarly, one might ask, did Moses and the elders, or just Moses, have a visionary experience of God, as later prophets claimed they themselves had, or can humans only be addressed by the voice of God but never be vouchsafed a vision of God? Contradictions such as these have impelled the multilayered theory of biblical criticism from its inception in the seventeenth century to today, forming the basis of biblical scholarship for more than three hundred years.

In the rabbinic tradition, these contradictions underlay the interpretations propounded by midrashic masters and Bible commentators, who were compelled to resolve these difficulties because of their a priori understanding of the unity of the Torah. Thus, ancient readers as well as modern ones have had to confront these variations, the only difference being what was considered an adequate solution to the problem. Ancient expositors could explain the contradictions as intentional means of God expressing what is beyond human understanding. For instance, according to one midrash, God spoke the words of the Decalogue in Exodus and their slightly different articulation in Deuteronomy simultaneously—something no human is capable of.[1]

Contemporary Bible scholars do not accept theological turns such as this. Rather, they maintain that different versions either represent different authors writing in different moments in time or differences in the sources available to the final editors.

Some biblical scholars have contended that the final editors were pious, slavish scribes who did not alter their sources and included all that had come before, eliding the differences as much as they could. On the contrary, I have argued here that the inclusion of these differences is quite intentional, and that the success of the final editors depended precisely on their *not* deciding between these disparate theological and legal interpretations. These editors, sitting in exile in Babylon, were seemingly happy to have the main contentions of their ideology universally adopted. They envisioned the Judaism of the return as a pure monotheism with a purified sacrificial ritual life, and laws that fostered ideals of justice and holiness. To arrive at a national consensus, the editors were quite willing to be as inclusive as possible of the variety of movements represented by the religious and political elites that had developed among the refugees. Prophets, priests, royalists and their scribes, refugees from Northern Israel, and Judean elders could all find a home in this text, for all their traditions were incorporated into the Five Books. Altogether, the editors' experience in exile shaped their perspective in ways that may not have been fully conscious. They saw themselves as preservers of a preexilic tradition, not as arbiters of a new Judaism, though through the very act of inclusion they produced something new.

David Weiss Halivni, one of the greatest and most original contemporary scholars of the Talmud and someone I am proud to name as my teacher, takes Ezra as the organizer of this editorial task, as many Bible scholars do, arguing that Ezra was attempting to get as close to the original Torah, the original revelation, as he could.[2] In other words, there was an original revelation that became corrupted in the First Temple period and underwent several different recensions. Ezra tried his best to recreate the original revelation resulting in our variegated Torah.

I believe this view is mistaken, as there was no original moment of revelation of the entire Torah. Rather, Ezra—to use Halivni's historical myth—saw that all these disparate texts propagated in First Temple times and in exile contained a spiritual reality that could form the basis of Jewish life. He incorporated all of them because he did not want to lose their distinct spiritual understandings. Each contained a truth that needed to be preserved. God's manifestation in this world is not singular but multifarious.[3] (I've used Halivni's—and the ancient Rabbis'—portrayal of a near-prophetic role on the part of Ezra to illustrate the point, but more probably it was a collection of priests, not a single person, who edited the final text.)

As the Five Books began to circulate as a completed document, the Torah, some writers did not see this work of editing as finalized. They continued the process of trying to unify these disparate texts by putting together more coherent accounts of the vying traditions. Thus, the author of the apocryphal Book of Jubilees, writing perhaps in the second or third century BCE, reconstructed a history of Israel and the world in which Genesis and Exodus, as depicted in the Pentateuch's account, also fit into a schema of jubilees, forty-nine-year cycles.[4] Contradictions are resolved in this reediting; for instance, the story of Adam and Eve in the Garden, which in the Torah is a distinctly separate account of Creation, is included in Jubilees within the story of the sixth day of Creation.[5] Several copies of the Book of Jubilees have been found among the documents of the Dead Sea Scroll community, demonstrating that it was cherished by these Jews and thought of as a sacred text. In a different vein, that same Dead Sea Scroll community preserved a Temple Scroll—perhaps composed in the first century BCE—that gives a unified account of sacrificial practice, eliding any differences in the Pentateuch and adding details as to procedure.[6] These documents indicate that the Five Books of Moses was not necessarily recognized as having ultimate authority, a monopoly in the canonization of the traditions of the exiles and the returnees. Rather, these other editors attempted to unify the received and disparate tradition in other ways.

Interestingly, though, these more unified and more ideological presentations of Jewish history and law achieved credibility only within sectarian circles. The Five Books of Moses seems to have triumphed in the Jewish community that survived precisely because it did not resolve contradictions but instead incorporated the theologies of numerous traditions and parties. In holding on to its internal contradictions, it preserved a certain mystery, and a profound understanding that contradictory viewpoints and a variety of beliefs provide insight into truths beyond single-minded formulations.

In this vein, a seminary classmate of mine, the distinguished contemporary Bible scholar Stephen A. Geller, argues that the plurality of opinions encompassed in the Torah is an invitation to everyone to read it with a degree of openness: "The Bible must be read with the same freedom one has in all literary, especially poetic, interpretation . . . with delight in the kind of ambiguities that give texts deeper meaning. The later Rabbis recognized this freedom in midrash, and even in matters of halakhic [legal] disagreement sometimes allowed that both opinions were the 'words of the Living God,' a God made living precisely by the play of debate."[7]

Thus the decision to be inclusive, to incorporate vying ideologies and legal sources in a single work, had lasting effect. The editing of the Five Books ensured that though there was a broad direction pointing to a common Jewish life, there was not a single, right pathway to that life, even though many would try to formulate a single-minded summary of Torah.

A major legacy of the process of editing the Torah was a certain tension. On the one hand, the editors presented the Torah as a single continuous text, but, on the other hand, they retained its contending elements. The two differing tendencies continued as oppositional forces within Judaism's self-understanding. The Mishnah, the foundational text of later Judaism, gave direction for Jewish life in a Greco-Roman world. Though it incorporated some differences of opinion, it tried to minimize disagreements. We know this because both the Talmud of the Land of Israel and the Babylonian Talmud comment on the Mishnah by quoting texts recorded at the time of the Mishnah that were not included in it.[8] In other words, the Mishnah tried to present as much of a unified perspective as it could, while the Talmud restored many of the disagreements the Mishnah put aside. Indeed, one often leaves the pages of the Babylonian Talmud—which over time became the more studied and normative text of the two Talmuds—with critical questions undecided. The Mishnah's thrust toward unity is undercut by the plurality of opinions the Talmud reintroduces, refusing to decide between them.

Is difference a blessing or a sign of degeneration? This issue was debated over and over again in Jewish tradition. Some thought that God's word was singular, and therefore differences of opinion as to what constituted proper behavior arose from faulty transmission; others thought that God's infinite knowledge was paralleled in the infinity of interpretation. The very design of the printed page of traditional Jewish texts bears witness to this debate. Most often one sees a bold text running down the center of the page and on the side, in smaller type, are commentaries that expand on the text, argue with other commentaries as to its meaning, and sometimes subvert the text altogether. In his *Mishneh Torah*, Maimonides sought to present a definitive Jewish legal tradition—look at my text and you will know what to do, he said, you need no other—but in almost all printed editions of his work, his text, in bold, is accompanied by elucidations of commentators placed alongside it in smaller type. They explain what Maimonides meant, sometimes question his reasoning, and not infrequently disagree with him while also arguing with other commentators' interpretations and conclusions. Essentially the reader is drawn into a community of argument, even when reading a text that purports to be a final judgment regarding correct behavior.

The Judaism that triumphed and that lasted through millennia has never been able to put forward a single-minded creed, though numerous thinkers have tried. In the Middle Ages, one philosopher after another endeavored to list Judaism's creedal affirmations, but none was able to achieve canonical status. Maimonides issued the most famous attempt, thirteen articles of faith, but later medieval philosophers reduced them to three and then to one—belief in the one God—thus affirming monotheistic faith as the underlying message of the Bible but going no further.

Even that most basic affirmation, the belief in one God, has been subject to contention, for there are many varieties of monotheistic belief, as is reflected in the Five Books themselves. The Torah includes both purified priestly notions of the Divine, which limited God's appearance to one sacred site—the Holy of Holies—as well as folkish views in which humans could experience the Divine or messengers of the Divine suddenly appearing and disappearing.

In later times, any single-minded formulation about the nature of the one God has encountered equal difficulty in gaining ascendancy. The purity of Maimonides' vision, which argued that ultimately God could only be understood in negative theology—we can only say what God is not, not what God is; as Exodus says, "No one can see My face" (33:20)—was undercut by medieval kabbalists who developed elaborate mythic images of the Godhead. Similarly, those who insisted that God is transcendent, wholly other, could be debated by those who maintained that God is fully present, walking in the Garden beside us, as in the Bible when God smells the sweet savor of the sacrifice. Maimonides insists that God is not characterized by emotions; others argue that God's concern, God's suffering, and God's love form the very essence of the Divine. In every age, each of the opposing schools of Jewish thought could point to verses in the Five Books of Moses validating its position. Each side in a debate could justify itself by appealing to different parts of the Torah.

AN INTERPRETATIVE COMMUNITY

The plurality of viewpoints found in the Torah sets in motion a directionality and some specific institutional structures, but ensures that the community of its followers will have varied outlooks, varied perspectives on critical theological issues, and varied practices. One cannot point to any period of postbiblical Jewish history in which there were no contending theological camps, rites, and practices.

And so, the inner contradictions and discrepancies, the differing ideologies represented in the Torah, ensured that Torah alone would never be sufficient for directing Jewish life. Judaism did not develop as a Bible-centered religion in the sense that defines some contemporary Protestant sects. One could not simply look in the Bible and find "the answer." Some measure of interpretation has always been necessary, at the very least to explain away or decide between the internal contradictions. Judaism developed as an interpretative community. An almost infinite number of rereadings of the tradition could be adduced, and all could point to some elements in the primal text that supported their position. The internal history of the Torah we have traced reflects this process: one code built on another, interpreting for its time the meaning of the prophetic, priestly, and cultural viewpoints it encountered. In later generations, each historical single-minded formulation, each uniform classical text, proved insufficient in itself. Something more had to be brought to the text to give it life in a different era.

The failure of consensus also means that in our day, Jews observing the same rituals may have very distinct consciousness regarding their acts, and even the same individual might engage in that observance out of different motives at different times. There are moments when I understand the performance of a religious act as following a command—I do the religious act because we, Jews, are enjoined to. There is a sense of awe in the performance. God's voice, perhaps experienced as some inner voice, is commanding me—this is what God wants of me, and I serve the Divine by doing this act. At other times I sense that the obligation occurs because of my initial agreement to enter into this Jewish religious life, and because the benefits I now experience from being a part of this culture, this people, this faith necessitate that I undertake participation in all its facets, even those whose meaning is not immediately obvious to me. That is my understanding of being a member of a covenanted people. At other moments, I perform the same act thinking that it brings me closer to the Divine, that the behavior transforms my life so that I experience myself as entering a holy realm. I do what I do to enhance my soulfulness. In that regard, I engage in Jewish practice because I believe these religious acts increase my capacity for love—love of others, love of the world, love of God, perhaps even appreciation of my own selfhood as in the image of God. (At such moments, the love themes of the Song of Songs may be seen as reflecting my own inner reality.) The Torah in its inclusiveness allows for the legitimacy of all of our varied feelings and motives throughout a lifetime and lifetimes.

The Torah not only validates this internal pluralism, but as argued earlier, it also ensures that no single overall interpretation of Judaism will triumph—Jewish sectarianism is necessarily part of a living Judaism. Because of the difficulty Judaism encountered in formulating a common creed, many thinkers argue that Judaism is not a philosophical religion. What is universal for Jews is not a belief system but a way of life, a common practice. But this formulation fails to recognize that theology is not the sole field of contention; the meaning and the specifics of the law are as well. A common text, the Five Books of Moses, set the ground for continuing debate regarding both theology and practice.

This understanding of Torah should ultimately impel an underlying acceptance of difference. Through the expression of different, varying formulations, Torah is made whole. As such, those of us nurtured by this inherited text called Torah are not meant to simply leave each other alone—you do it your way, I'll do it mine. Rather, we are to engage each other, argue with each other, wrestle with each other over the "rightness" of our way, and finally, at our best, learn from one another. Each individual interpreter of Torah reflects an aspect of God's truth, and through the collectivity, God's truth is made known.

THE IDEAL AND THE REAL

One of the characteristics of the Pentateuch's anthologizing of the range of visions and imperatives necessary for the implementation of God's teaching is the inclusion of laws that can be immediately and practically implemented alongside those beyond the range of current implementation. While Deuteronomy, instituted in the reign of Josiah, was promulgated as a constitution, and while the Covenant Code in Exodus may have been promulgated and enforced as law, other biblical passages, especially those of the Holiness Code, are almost impossible to ever implement. One can accept and strive toward realizing the imperative to love one's neighbor in one's heart, but it would take a community of saints to actually achieve such a vision. Yet one would not want to expunge this passage because of our failure to implement it. Holding up the ideal energizes the striving that moves us beyond the ordinary.

These two polarities, the attempt to create a living law for a contemporary community and the vision of the law as creating an ideal society, have always continually contended with each other in Jewish life. The contemporary Orthodox theologian Joseph Ber Soloveitchik has argued that the great continuous attraction of Talmud study is the attempt to achieve an ideal formulation of the divine will. He sees Torah study of this kind, a constant working through of the intricacies of Jewish law with a vision of an ideal future as much as the practical present in mind, as a means to achieve an ideal society here on earth.[9] But the achievement of that final goal always remains in the distance. The law always stumbles over contemporary realities—misreadings, human failings, limits to understanding. Every effort to fully perfect the vision, explicate its intricacies, live out the ideal formulation of God's will within any historical time has inevitably been limited by the circumstances and perspectives of its age.

The Torah incorporates the secular laws of Exodus, the practical constitution of Deuteronomy, and the ideal formulation of the Holiness Code. How, then, should the law be decided? Should it make ideal demands or make its peace with contemporary practice? Perhaps this was at the root of the fundamental divide between two factions of early Rabbinic Judaism, the House of Hillel and the House of Shammai—the former recognizing the limits of most people's capabilities, the latter wanting to create a pious elite—but this debate can be heard throughout Jewish history, not least of all in our own contemporary world.

The conflict between these two ways of seeing the purpose of the law—as realist and as idealist—has always conveyed a sense of incompletion about Judaism. The Torah ends with the vision of the land that the Israelites are about to enter, but they are not there yet. Most Jews who see the Torah as foundational to their lives still recognize, as I do, that we do not have it quite right yet—we have not grasped Torah's truths in their entirety because the parts do not ultimately quite fit together. This is the very opposite of a creedal religion that maintains that adherence to certain fundamental concepts gives one certainty regarding issues of faith and salvation. Even as we attempt to comprehend every jot and tittle of the Torah, there is always a beyond to which it points.

This indeterminacy emanates from the vicissitudes of Jewish history as well. The Second Temple was destroyed like the First, but unlike the First, was never replaced. After the destruction of the Second Temple, the Five Books, which place the sanctuary and the sacrificial system at the center, could never be fully implemented. Its architectonic structure pointed away from any reality that Jews encountered in daily life. The Temple's destruction ensured a deep and permanent sense of incompletion. Jews even today pray facing toward the Temple that has not yet been rebuilt. Every moment of prayer is thus a reminder of incompletion. Talmudic Rabbis argue and then resolve their disputes by saying that in the messianic age it will become clear who is in the right; meanwhile we must live in a world where two opposite opinions are held and their contradictions unresolved. We labor in an imperfect world even as we reach for something more.

The ending of the Five Books, anticipating entering the land but not actually doing so, proved to be a prototype of the experience of future Jewish generations, who anticipated fully observing the Torah but never really could. Judaism became a religion that was always "on the way."

As the Five Books of Moses leaves off, Moses dies; Joshua is to succeed him. A new generation born in the desert, none of whom experienced slavery, is to attempt to fulfill the promise of the Exodus. There is an air of expectancy. The moment of entrance to the land is a hinge. Where will this path lead—to redemption, or to another sinful fall?

Indeed, what has led up to this point is the alternating saga of new beginnings and dashed hopes. Sin and the exile from Eden soon follow the story of Creation. In ten generations the earth has become so degenerate that God brings the Flood, wiping out all but a saving remnant of earth's inhabitants. A new covenant is made with Noah and his descendants, but shortly after, this family, too, proves disappointing. There is a need to disperse humanity, to multiply their languages, for when human beings at this early stage form a common community, they see God as their adversary.

Then there is yet another new beginning, with Abraham and his seed. But each generation of this family has to be further refined. Ishmael is sent out to the wilderness, Esau disinherited. And when we finally encounter the twelve brothers who are to be the eponymous progenitors of the tribes of Israel, they battle one another. The Exodus and Sinai are to constitute a new start, this time for an entire people, but here too the generation of the Exodus is caught up in the nexus of a slave mentality, and so this new effort fails as well. The march through the desert is fraught with revolts, internecine argument, and apostasy.

There is a constant falling away, but also a constant hope for a new beginning. In his last speeches in Deuteronomy Moses is pessimistic—the Children of Israel have not proved themselves up to the task, they hardly deserve to be called God's people, having contested Moses' leadership conveying God's demands throughout the desert march. Yet this deeply flawed people is to enter the land and Moses is not. For all that Moses has experienced, he will not participate in the future. He can never know what will happen, for the nature of the future is that it is always an opening to a new story, a different telling than what has gone before.

While the Five Books of Moses leaves us on the verge of the entrance to the land, some scholars have argued that we should really speak of a Hexateuch: the conquest under Joshua was meant to be the completion of the tale and the book of Joshua forms the logical conclusion to the Five Books. In that story, the land is finally conquered, distributed to, and settled by the twelve tribes. But the Torah does not end that way. It is not a tale with a definitive novelistic ending. In the way the Five Books have come down to us, the story of Joshua is left to the later histories. As the Torah ends, we are anticipating the future, open to the possibility of a new future, even as that hopefulness is shrouded by a sense of foreboding. The Torah is a text that always stands poised at a moment before completion.

The very form of Torah gave birth to yearnings that go beyond the text. There is a constant longing to resolve the inner contradictions, to reach beyond the mysterious clouds, to engage in a reading that will explain it all. If you will, it is a desire to enter the land, to settle there once and for all. It is a longing endlessly defeated by the text itself, which constantly inspires new interpretations, new beginnings.

The full embodiment of the Torah is always just out of reach. Always there is a new midrash, a new line of interpretation we need to write for our own time so that the paradoxes of Torah may be synthesized for us, here, now. The spiritual life that its authors uncovered continues to speak to us, and so as we implement its institutions and practices in our own time, we offer our own understandings of their meaning. And surely, our efforts, too, will be found lacking and in turn lead to a new rebirth.

The life of Torah is an ongoing series of revolutions, an ongoing series of revelations.

Notes

1. For instance, this describes the stated approach of Lester Grabbe in 1&2 *Kings*.

2. Many scholars argue that a number of different hands were at work editing the priestly materials; some scholars have talked of four different layers of priestly material. The older source-critical model took the position that the priestly layer reflects the work of exiles; more recently, the idea that these materials are preexilic has been dominant in scholarly approaches. The fact that Ezekiel, writing in exile, several times offers a different version of Temple ritual than we find in the Pentateuch means, at the very least, that many Temple matters remained fluid into the exile.

3. *JPS Hebrew-English Tanakh*. JPS has provided me with a manuscript of a gender-neutral version of its translation of the Torah and I have used that version, changing only the name of God to conform with the style in this book.

PRELUDE

1. Genesis 16:19 mentions the Kenizites as one of the ten nations settled in Canaan. Joshua 14:14 credits Caleb, the Kenizite, with conquering and occupying Hebron.

2. The reference in verse 23:28 is to "the Hivites, the Canaanites, and the Hittites."

3. The discrepancy between the depiction of Hazor's destruction in the time of Joshua and its prominence in the time of Deborah has fostered an ongoing debate among archaeologists and biblical historians who have tried to square the circle.

4. Finkelstein and Silberman, *Bible Unearthed*, 97–123.

5. See, for instance, Sperling, *Original Torah*, esp. 52; he attempts to read this reconstructed history as a major theme of the biblical narrative.

6. There is a reference to Baal Hashamayim (the Lord of Heaven), who was probably considered the head of a pantheon in the Phoenician city of Byblos. Rollston, "Transjordan," 290.

7. Knohl, *Bible's Genetic Code*.

8. Freud, in his *Moses and Monotheism*, was dependent on this theory. There is some debate as to whether this revolution was indeed monotheistic or a centering of Egyptian religion *primarily* on the sun god.

9. See Knohl, *Bible's Genetic Code*, 75.

10. Habakkuk 3. These sources are quoted by Knohl, *Bible's Genetic Code*, 74.

11. Many scholars would say that the biblical author(s?) we call "J" lived at the time of David or Solomon, although others, such as Knohl, believe that "J" came later (oral communication).

12. Finkelstein and Silberman, *Bible Unearthed*, 208, maintain that during this early period Judea did not develop cities and the entire population of the highlands numbered no more than forty-five thousand, while Northern Israel may have grown to 350,000.

13. Grabbe, *Ancient Israel*, 76, summarizes some of the archaeological evidence.

14. These city-states constantly warred with the Israelites. The two groups, Sea Peoples and Israelites, arrived at the same time and were natural rivals. In the time of the Judges, Samson fought the Philistines, who imprisoned him in Gaza. Later, the Bible reports that after Jonathan's death at Philistine hands, David lamented: "Do not tell of it in Ashkelon, do not report it to Gath" (2 Sam. 1:20), thus naming Ashkelon and Gath as the quintessential enemies of the kingdom.

15. Finkelstein and Silberman, *Bible Unearthed*, 149–68. "Currently there is a dearth of monumental and other inscriptions that are associated with a functioning state until the ninth century" (Grabbe, *Ancient Israel*, 115).

1. ELIJAH'S VICTORY

1. Baal is a generic name, meaning "Master" (or "Lord"), which the Bible gives to many foreign gods. It was a common name for Canaanite gods, usually associated with a head of a pantheon. The term Baal is usually followed by a descriptor as in Baal Hashamayim, the Lord of Heaven.

2. From the Semitic meaning "new city"—*ir hadash*.

3. At a later time, Moab also threatened Israel. Mesha King of Moab boasts that he defeated Israel in several battles, as recorded in the Mesha Stone, ANET, 320.

4. Herodotus 2:44 and see, most recently, Quinn, *In Search*, on the spread of the worship of Melqart.

5. The Bible itself (1 Kings 16:33) refers to Israel's having adopted the worship of Astarte alongside the worship of Baal under Jezebel's influence.

6. Similarly, the Bible reports that David founded a new capital city, Jerusalem, to unite his kingdom.

7. The preface to the book of Amos dates his prophecies to the reign of Jeroboam II.

8. Jehu was forced to pay a tribute to Assyria, ANET, 280.

9. ANET, 320.

10. ANET, 279, 281.

11. That's the position of Lester Grabbe in his commentary 1&2 *Kings*.

12. Exodus 23:17 dates the start of the new year at the final fall harvest, "when you collect your grain at the end of the year."

13. Some of these stories can be dated as having been authored much later than the patriarchal period when they are said to have taken place. Certain allusions are a giveaway; for example, though the patriarchs are described as having flocks of camels, camels were not domesticated in the Near East until the turn of the millennium, long after what is thought to be the patriarchal period.

14. The biblical scholar Shalom M. Paul, for instance, dates the legal portions of the code to the premonarchal time of Israelite history; see his "Book of the Covenant."

15. See, for instance, Propp, *Exodus 19–40*, 306–8. Deuteronomy 27:2–3 exemplifies this process: "As soon as you have crossed the Jordan . . . you shall set up large stones. Coat them with plaster and inscribe upon them all the words of this Teaching."

2. THE COVENANT CODE

1. The other two major civil codes incorporated in the Torah are dependent on the Covenant Code. The two, Deuteronomy and the Holiness Code in Leviticus, rework some of Exodus's ideas and its wording and so are dependent on the Covenant Code, while also putting forth their own legislation. The Holiness Code, mainly located in Leviticus, also includes some laws found in the book of Numbers.

2. Although chapter 24 combines different accounts, verses 3–8 are most explicitly connected to the preceding law code and constitute the covenant

between God and the people. Verses 1–2 and 12–18 speak of Moses alone going up to God and receiving the two tablets—seemingly the Decalogue. Verses 1–2 and 9–11, which talk of Moses and the elders going up the mountain and feasting as they see a vision of God, constitute a distinctly separate account.

3. In a second telling of the story of the covenant that then follows upon this, Moses is told to go up and receive "the tablets of stone, the *Torah/* Instruction and the commandments which I have written to guide them" (Exod. 24:13–18). The tablets of stone seemingly refer to the Decalogue, but the *Torah* and the commandments refer to something more than that: assuredly the Covenant Code whose words have just been spoken.

4. The biblical scholar Shalom M. Paul has devoted a considerable part of his career to uncovering these parallels. A summary of his work can be found in Paul, "Book of the Covenant."

5. Paul in "Book of the Covenant" asserts that no other ancient law code has this kind of list of ethical and religious teachings stated in apodictic language attached to it.

6. An allusion to this practice is preserved in Leviticus 17:1–9.

7. It is hard to say what is meant by the dedication of the firstborn of humans. Later biblical tradition specifies a monetary redemption of the firstborn (Ex. 34:20), but the passage here may reflect an earlier tradition where the firstborn became the clan's religious leaders, or priests. Note that Samuel is dedicated by his mother to serve in a priestly role. Though he is not the firstborn of his father, his mother vows to consider him a firstborn. Alternatively, some have argued that the dedication of the firstborn is a sacrificial allusion.

8. The scholarly literature frequently labels such belief as "henotheism," the worship of a supreme God along with subservient divinities.

9. It is unclear whether this provision applies only to the spring festival, since the beginning of the verse talks about the offering of the first fruits. Cooper and Goldstein in "Daily Sacrifice" understand the verse this way.

10. Cooper and Goldstein, "Daily Sacrifice."

11. Moses reports what God has taught, but is not the author of these words.

12. "Currently there is a dearth of monumental or other inscriptions that one associates with a functioning state until the ninth century" (Grabbe, *Ancient Israel*, 115). It is difficult to assume that a code would have been promulgated before this time—the dynasties of Omri and Jehu—when there is no evidence of a state bureaucracy.

13. The code ends with a promise of a "divine messenger" who will lead the people into the land—might this be a reference to a political leader such as a monarch who is appointed by God? Is there a hint here of the divine appointment of leadership? Ought we to have in mind the book of Kings' description of Elisha's anointing of Jehu to overthrow Omri's dynasty? (2 Kings 9:1–13).

3. HERITAGE OF THE COVENANT CODE

1. Babylonian Talmud, *Rosh Hashanah* 17b.
2. Babylonian Talmud, *Rosh Hashanah* 17b.
3. Found in almost every prayerbook; see, for instance, *Mahzor Lev Shalem*, 232.
4. "Ki Hinei Kaḥomer" / "As Clay in the Hands of the Potter," an anonymous twelfth-century poem included in almost every Askenazic High Holiday mahzor. The medieval poet quotes the phrase "Remember the covenant" from Psalm 74:20 as the chorus.
5. Hartman, *Living Covenant*, 5.
6. Hartman, *Living Covenant*, 6. Hartman's use of the metaphor of "husband" can be extended to any loving relationship, as he himself does at the end of the paragraph referring to "partners."
7. Cohen, *Jewish History*, 145–56.
8. Adler, *Engendering Judaism*, 169–217.

FIRST INTERLUDE

1. "And Jehoiada solemnized the covenant between *Adonai*, on the one hand, and the king and the people on the other—as well as between the king and the people—that they should be the people of *Adonai*" (2 Kings 11:17). In Judea the idea of covenant is intimately connected with the idea of kingship: God has covenanted with the Davidic dynasty to rule this people. Indeed, in one conception, the Davidic dynasty stands as the intermediary between God and the people.
2. When the Northern Israel prophet Hosea declaimed, "The many teachings I wrote for him [Ephraim, i.e., Northern Israel] have been treated as something alien" (8:12), perhaps he meant an assemblage of individual scrolls.
3. Cogan and Tadmor, *II Kings*, 161.
4. E.g., the redemption of a slave (Lev. 25:47–55).

1. Ahaziah is the full name, the letters of God's name forming the ending. A seal from this time mentioning the king also uses the shortened form of the name.

2. 2 Kings 16:6. The Masoretic reading of *Aram* is a corruption as can be seen from 2 Chronicles 28:17; Cogan and Tadmor, *II Kings*, 186–87.

3. At this distance it is hard to say what this actually involved — simply a ritualized symbolic offering or an actual human sacrifice. Certainly, nations around Israel and Judea practiced actual human sacrifice at various times.

4. This author used the word *syncretism* in the previous chapters to point to the identification of biblical Israel's religious world with those of its neighbors: for instance, as seeing *Adonai* and Baal as identical or part of the same pantheon. The term *polylatry* (suggested by the scholar Benjamin Somers) here refers to Israelite practice, which accorded power to many divine forces — though none necessarily challenging the ultimate power of the God of Israel. These forces included, at various times, God's consort Astarte, heavenly powers like the sun and the moon, and intermediate divinities like those symbolized by the snake Nehushtan. The term *polytheurgy* (coined here) describes the practices that attempt to influence the many aforementioned forces having divine power. Included in this latter term are child sacrifice or, as it may have developed in Israel and Judea, the symbolic practice of "passing one's son through the fire," as well as rituals meant to placate or ward off the demonic, and practices specifically associated with propitiating the dead. Sometimes in this chapter these practices are referred to as "heterodox," in contrast to the "orthodoxy" of the reformers. While their practitioners hardly thought of them as heterodox but rather as traditional Israelite religion, most of these "heterodox" practices were eschewed by biblical prophets and authors. Some ceremonies described in the Five Books of Moses, like the removal of the sourdough for Passover (devilish forces could reside in it), or the sending of the goat out to Azazel (possibly a demonic power residing in the desert) as a rite of Temple purification on the Day of Atonement, give hints of belief in spirits and divinities, other than the supreme Deity, to be feared or propitiated.

5. The reinstitution of the practice of child sacrifice either in actuality or symbolically is attested to by Jeremiah: "They have built shrines to Baal, to put their children to the fire as burnt offering to Baal" (Jer. 19:5). Jeremiah himself dates this verse as being in the reign of Zedekiah, the last king of Judea.

6. There is archaeological evidence of worship of Yah and his Asherah, where the latter term refers to a distinct being, God's female consort. In 2 Kings 23:7 we read that women wove "houses" to enshrine Asherah, thus associating Asherah as a feminine object of worship. For a different picture of the meaning of *asherah*, referring only to posts, see Sommer, *The Bodies of God*, 44–49.

7. Famously, the Israeli scholar Yehezkel Kaufmann argued that such denunciations were prophetic exaggerations. Recent scholarship has disproven Kaufmann's claim. See, for instance, Israel Knohl's *Biblical Beliefs*, a major theme of which is a refutation of Kaufmann's theses.

8. "The extraordinary tenacity of these proscribed practices in Israel seems to have been an integral part of persistent paganizing trends, with the making of idols (v. 12) as its most overt expression." Andersen and Freedman, *Micah*, 491.

9. The Asaph psalms also abound in references to God as *El* and *Elohim* but are sparing in the use of the personal name of God, *Adonai*. Scholars attribute this rhetorical feature to Northern Israel.

10. 2 Kings 18:18; Isaiah 36:22. The author heard this lineage propounded in the late Prof. Nahum Sarna's class on Psalms when he was a rabbinical student.

11. Both Ezra and Nehemiah mention the Asaph clan. Ezra reports that 128 members of the clan returned with him from Babylonia (2:41), a number confirmed by Nehemiah (7:44), and both ascribe musical roles to this clan.

12. "A severe destruction followed Sennacherib's 701 BCE campaign at almost all sites, excluding Jerusalem" (Stern, *Archaeology*, 165). But Stern then adds, "Between that date and the arrival of the Babylonians, the country enjoyed a period of rebuilding and relative prosperity"—a discovery that accords with the expansion that occurred in the reign of Hezekiah's son Manasseh.

13. ANET, 288.

14. ANET, 288.

15. A tablet describing Esarhaddon's conquests states that he summoned Manasseh to appear before him (ANET, 291).

16. "Assyrian 'palace style' pottery reached even the table of the kings of Judah, as indicated by finds at the palace of Ramat Rahel. . . . Other Assyrian quality goods, such as elaborate metal bowls and glass objects, were also imported into the country" (Mazar, *Archaeology*, 547).

17. The exact date of the beginning of his reign has been contested. Some scholars ascribe his accession as dating from 698 BCE.

1. Many scholars attribute the editing of Chronicles to the time of Ezra and Nehemiah or slightly thereafter; see, for instance, Myers, *I Chronicles*, lxxxvi–lxxxix.

2. It is hard to determine what is meant here by the image of Baal. Baal was the ancient Canaanite chief god, and so this might be a reference to the continuation of Canaanite cult practices throughout the First Temple period. Jeremiah, living at the time, speaks of prophets of Baal (Jer. 2:8).

3. The practice of child sacrifice may have continued into the latter half of the first century BCE. Frank Moore Cross argues that a Phoenician inscription on a shard found in an excavation of Idalion on Cyprus is a report of a child sacrifice in the fourth century; Cross, "Phoenician Inscription."

4. Dever, "Archaeological Commentary," 143.

5. Leviticus is quite distinct as a book containing the sacrificial law and the Holiness Code. It fits in its place in the Pentateuchal order since Exodus tells the story of the building of the sanctuary and Numbers begins with its dedication.

6. The prohibition against *asherot* is woven throughout Deuteronomy; see, e.g., 12:3, 16:21.

7. On straying from the "true" faith, see, for instance, Deut. 13:13–19.

8. According to the introductory chapters of Deuteronomy, which may be a later addendum but are certainly written in its spirit, these other divine beings are given to other nations to worship. See, e.g., Deut. 4:19.

9. "Meat" here refers to farm animals. According to the Covenant Code, wild animal flesh when eaten or touched imparts impurity, but in Deuteronomy (and the Holiness Code) its consumption is declared impermissible. According to the Priestly Code, the thanksgiving offering was the only sacrifice in which laypeople could partake.

6. LAW IN DEUTERONOMY

1. Levinson, *Deuteronomy*.

2. The person who most saliently attached the notion of boundaries to the maintenance of the purity of the camp and the distinctiveness of Israel and its mission was Mary Douglas in her classic work *Purity and Danger*. The argument here follows her lead.

3. The description here accords with the narrative in Chronicles (2 Chron. 35:20–24). Some scholars pick up on the more laconic description of events

in Kings (2 Kings 23:29) to argue that Necho summoned Josiah to a meeting in Megiddo and the latter was assassinated at the meeting.

4. One might wonder if Jehoahaz's name—which includes *Adonai's* personal name, as opposed to *Eliakim*, which includes the old Canaanite reference to God as *El*—tells us anything regarding the change of religious orientation implied in deposing the former king.

7. DEUTERONOMY'S REVELATION

1. The vassal treaties of Esarhaddon, ANET, 534–41. The analysis here is based on Weinfeld, *Deuteronomy and the Deuteronomic School*, 116–29.

2. Weinfeld, *Deuteronomy and the Deuteronomic School*.

3. The only biblical use of this term is found in Ezekiel, who preached in Babylonia and refers to the king of Babylonia, Nebuchadnezzar, as the "king of kings" (Ezek. 26:7).

4. The book of Kings reports that a prophet, Micah, in the time of Ahab tells of his vision of God seated upon a throne surrounded by courtiers (1 Kings 22:19). The book of Kings was undoubtedly written after the prophet Isaiah recorded his vision, and the image may be borrowed from there. In any case, Isaiah's vision is certainly much more elaborate, and more akin to Assyrian reliefs, than that ascribed to Micah in Kings.

5. As noted in the previous chapter, some of the scholarly literature refers to this phenomenon as "henotheism," the worship of one God while not denying the existence of other gods.

6. Of course, we cannot date these psalms with any certainty, save to say they are clearly from the age of kingship. Second Temple Israel had no kings until the rise of the Hasmoneans at the end of the second century BCE.

7. For instance, in the book of Kings, when Solomon dedicates the Temple, it is he who is depicted as the chief functionary.

8. Knohl, oral teaching.

9. Among the prophets, it is Jeremiah, who lived at this time, who most frequently uses cognates of this verb.

10. Moshe Weinfeld offers a complete list of expressions typical of Deuteronomy in his *Deuteronomy and the Deuteronomic School*, appendix A, 320ff. See 336–38 for those referring to command and commandments.

11. In Leviticus 16:2, all that the High Priest can see of God in the Holy of Holies is the cloud—that is, the throne of God, but not the divine self.

12. In both Deuteronomy 25:3–10 and 25:13–15, the entire people are prescribed a liturgy to recite. In addition, Deuteronomy 21:7–8 prescribes a liturgy that the elders are to recite to clear them of responsibility for the death of someone who has been killed in proximity to their town.

8. THE PEOPLE AND THE LAND

1. Later rabbinic culture, trying to square the circle, argues that Deuteronomy only prohibits male and not female Moabites from intermarrying.

2. The expansion of Judea is noted in Stern, *Archaeology*. A school of contemporary scholarship most notably including the Israeli archaeologist Israel Finkelstein would argue that there may never have been a time when the various tribes of the north and south were united in a common kingdom and that the supposed reigns of David and Solomon are a romantic revisioning of the past. While in this author's view they go too far in this claim, it is certainly the case that the archaeological evidence has not supported the Bible's vast geographical claims regarding the extent of the Solomonic Empire.

3. The Holiness Code also speaks of the land spewing out the people because of their sin (Lev. 18). It is hard to say who influenced whom, that is, did the Holiness Code influence Deuteronomy or the other way round?

4. This is an older prophetic trope harking back at least to the age of Hezekiah. Isaiah had come to see Assyria as the punishing instrument of God's design: "Assyria, rod of My anger, / —In whose hand, as a staff, is My fury!— / I send him against an ungodly nation, / I charge him against a people that provokes Me . . . / After all, I have kings as my captains! . . . / Shall I not do to Jerusalem and her images / What I did to Samaria and her idols?" (Isa. 10:5,6,8,11).

9. THE HERITAGE OF DEUTERONOMY

1. Goldschmidt, *Mahzor*, 105–9. The poem is ascribed to one of the most famous of Ashkenazic *paytanim* (lyricists), Shimon ben Isaac of Mainz (eleventh century), and is a reworking of the original by Eleazar Kallir. The English translation of the poem is by the present author.

2. Maimonides, *Mishneh Torah*, 1:11.

3. This is asserted explicitly by Maimonides in the *Guide of the Perplexed*, 3:52.

4. Maimonides, *Guide of the Perplexed*, part 3, ch. 54, 635.

5. E.g., Rabbi Moses Cordovero in his magisterial summation of mystical thought, *Pardes Rimmonim*.

6. Babylonian Talmud, *Tractate Makoth*, 23b. Rabbi Simlai was a Palestinian sage who later in life taught in Babylonia.

7. The sectarians at Qumran also wrote manuals delineating prescribed practice, though none aims at the completeness that characterizes the Mishnah.

8. The Rabbis of this period distinguished between the Oral Law and the Written Law—the latter being the Bible, the former being the interpretations of the Bible that led to their own practice. But Rabbinic Judaism survived because it was written down, and to this day students study these written texts.

9. One can already find allusions to this position in rabbinic texts, e.g., "The only reason for the commandments is to purify people," *Bereshit Rabbah* 44:1.

10. In Eisenberg, *Leibowitz's Philosophy of Jewish Law*, 77.

11. Weinberg, *Blessing of Abraham*, "Bereshit," 2, 16.

12. Some traditional commentators read this verse as referring to Moses' last song in Deuteronomy 32.

13. Saiman, *Halakha*, 248.

SECOND INTERLUDE

1. The dominant view has been that Josiah died in battle, but others, reading between the lines of the accounts in the books of Kings and Chronicles, argue that he may have been assassinated, lured by a ruse to the Egyptian camp.

2. Some documents of Jewish residents of Babylonia have been uncovered; some mention "the city of the Jews." See Horowitz et al., *By the Rivers of Babylon*.

10. PRIESTS, PROPHETS, AND SCRIBES

1. Iraqi Jews were forced to flee in the early 1950s after the establishment of the state of Israel. Neighboring Iran was also the site of ancient Jewish exilic settlement. It is estimated that less than ten thousand Jews still live in modern-day Iran, even after Khomeini's revolution caused the overwhelming majority of Jews to flee.

2. Fishbane, *Biblical Interpretation*, 123.

3. One should be wary of thinking of a single editorial stance for these books; there may have been many authors each with their own perspective. The book of Judges has as its agenda the dangers of tribal anarchy and the necessity of kingship, while Samuel and Kings highlight the danger of kingship. These historical books certainly incorporate earlier sources; they were not so much written in exile but heavily edited in exile. The book of Joshua is an exception and may have been written around the time of Josiah.

4. Milgrom, *Leviticus* lists eleven instances in which the Holiness Code adumbrates ideas in Deuteronomy, but this author finds his arguments unconvincing in all but one or two of these. In the same vein, Fishbane, *Biblical Interpretation* finds one or two instances of literary precedence. Undoubtedly the ideas of the Holiness Code began taking shape in the late Temple period and their influence on some aspects of Deuteronomy is undeniable, but these ideas achieved their complete and fullest expression in exile.

5. Israel Knohl's *Sanctuary of Silence* has been pathbreaking in arguing for these dual influences on the construction of the Holiness Code. Much of what has been said here is based on Knohl's work, although this author disagrees with Knohl in dating the main body of this faction's corpus. He sees their ideas as having been formulated mainly before the promulgation of Deuteronomy, whereas this author finds that many of their central ideas accord with the conditions of exile. Knohl does admit that their work of editing and refining continued through the exile, since he too finds some of their work, especially that of editing, to be clearly postexilic.

6. This idea of concentric circles is specifically elaborated by Milgrom, *Leviticus*.

7. Milgrom uses this standard transliteration for the Hebrew personal name of God, *yod, heh, vav, heh.*

8. Milgrom, *Leviticus*, 1624.

9. Deuteronomy, too, announces "You should love the stranger" (Deut. 10:18) but defines that obligation in terms of ensuring that the stranger is fed and clothed. In the Holiness Code, the love of the stranger is emphasized further: the stranger is to be "as one of your citizens, you shall love the stranger as yourself" (Lev. 19:34).

10. Comment on Leviticus 19:1.

11. Exodus 19:6. This injunction precedes the revelation of the Decalogue in Exodus. Scholars have debated the authorship of this editorial comment; most think it is a Deuteronomic insertion. Whatever the case, the present

argument is not that the authors of the Holiness Code necessarily authored this concept but that they now expanded its meaning.

12. The description of the sanctuary in the desert at the end of the book of Exodus may itself constitute a critique of Solomon's Temple (see chapter 13), and so the visions of religious worship imagined for the return from exile do not accord with the building of a Solomonic-like Temple.

11. THE HOLINESS CODE

1. Israel Knohl, whose work on the code has had enormous impact, tellingly refers to the "Holiness School" rather than the "Holiness Code."

2. In his *Sanctuary of Silence*, Knohl discusses the linguistic elements differentiating the Holiness Code and enumerates the passages to be included. Pages 98–101 list all of the passages throughout the Five Books ascribed to the Holiness Code. On pages 70–95 Knohl gives a detailed analysis of the portions of Numbers ascribed to the code. Both there and in the appendix to chapter 2, 103–6, he shows the extent to which the authors of the Holiness Code reworked the original texts in the Priestly Code.

3. The subject matter there is the sabbatical year and the jubilee law. The switch to a different site for this revelation was so startling to later commentators that Rashi (1040–1105), the most famous among them, immediately asks, "What is the relation of the sabbatical year to Sinai?" The comment itself has become a Hebrew expression used whenever one notices odd juxtapositions.

4. The medieval commentator Abraham ibn Ezra traces the entire Ten Commandments threaded through all of chapter 19. Modern scholars are in disagreement as to whether chapter 19 can be read in this way.

5. The free-will offering (Lev. 16–17) is a sacrifice freely offered by the supplicant. It is not brought to atone for any sin; rather, it marks the completion of a vow.

6. This is a broad generalization. Both Deuteronomy and Exodus include some apodictic statements — especially at the end of the book of the Covenant, which is closer in style to the Holiness Code.

7. Schwartz, *Doctrine of Holiness*.

8. *Mishnah Peah* 1:1.

9. Cooper and Goldstein, "Daily Sacrifice," 1–20; Cooper and Goldstein, "Festivals of Israel and Judah," 19–31.

10. Amos 8:5, Hosea 2:13, Isaiah 1:13. Both Amos and Isaiah mention Shabbat in conjunction with observance of the new moon, supporting the scholarly theory that at this juncture, the Sabbath as a festival day was observed monthly at the full moon.

11. In Ezekiel, chapter 20, the Sabbath is singled out and is equated with the totality of law.

12. In terms of chronology, Jeremiah is a swing prophet. He began preaching before the reign of Josiah and lived long enough to witness the exile. On literary grounds, scholars argue that the extensive prose passage in Jeremiah referring to the Sabbath, chapter 17, is most probably a later addition, a position with which this author tends to agree. Even if it is an authentic teaching, it points to the fact that the Sabbath became a central element of prophetic teaching only in this late period.

13. The division and numbering of biblical chapters did not take place until the sixteenth century. Interestingly, those editors recognized the different linguistic form of the seventh day and the unity of language of the first six days and so assigned the passage regarding the Sabbath, the seventh day, to chapter 2.

14. Indeed, the talmudic Rabbis understood the laws of the Sabbath as deriving from the construction of the Temple.

15. Exodus 31:17. This passage regarding the Sabbath (Exod. 31:12–17) follows the instructions for building the sanctuary.

16. Almost the same language is used in what seems like an appendix to Numbers, chapter 36.

17. Fragments of multiple copies were found amid the Dead Sea Scrolls.

18. Not incidentally, the biblical laws surrounding the jubilee year that talk of the right to buy back the land even before the jubilee year constantly repeat the word *redemption*, even summing up by using the phrase "and you shall redeem the land." While here the word *redemption* is used in a monetary sense, a buyback, *redemption* is also used for divine action related to the return from exile—that is, the return to God's care. The medieval Jewish Bible commentators pick up on this dual meaning. Thus, in one sense, redemption is a process of returning the land to its original owner(s), the families who first were given these plots, but in another sense these property laws return the land to God, fulfill God's intent for the land. This is the spin the medieval commentator Hizekuni (mid-thirteenth-century France) gives to the verse "and you shall give

redemption to the land"—land can never be sold; it can only be handed over to another for guardianship. God is the true owner of the land. We are all resident aliens in relation to God; our ownership is limited and must be practiced within the bounds of God's law, made manifest through a system of justice and Sabbaths. Redemption is the restoration of the land to God's order, and the jubilee is a return to that order. In this view, this is the message of the "Sabbath of Sabbaths": the ultimate return to God's order.

19. Regarding the remission of loans in the seventh year, Deuteronomy declares: "You may dun the foreigner; but you must remit whatever is due you from your kinsmen" (Deut. 15:3).

20. When the word *foreigner* is used, Deuteronomy may be referring to an itinerant trader who is not a permanent resident. It is fair to assume, though, that "the stranger" is not included in the category of a "brother" Israelite.

21. Israel Knohl, for instance, argues that the phrase is one of the telltale signs that the passage was written by the Holiness School.

22. Repeated in Numbers 15:15. Israel Knohl, *Sanctuary of Silence*, 55–56, argues that this chapter is quintessentially the work of the Holiness Code authors.

23. Compare the Deuteronomic instruction specifying that the flesh that Israelites may not eat is to be given to the stranger (14:21).

24. One might reflect on the relation of this to the later Isaiah, who includes the non-Israelite in Temple worship.

12. HERITAGE OF THE HOLINESS CODE

1. In context in Deuteronomy, "them" refers to the Decalogue. However, by the time of the Mishnah it referred to all of Torah, much as the very word Torah had achieved its fuller expansive meaning.

2. In rabbinic teaching, Deuteronomy 11:13–21 and Numbers 15:36–41 were recited alongside this paragraph, although there was controversy over reciting this last paragraph in the evening.

3. The Babylonian Talmud, the ancient rabbinic commentary on the Mishnah, does in fact explain that the time stated in this Mishnah is to be understood as when the stars appear. As an example of more readily defined times in other texts from this period, see Babylonian Talmud, *Berachot* 2b.

4. BT *Berachot* 45a.

5. In Exodus and in Numbers the priestly breastplate is defined as the instrument of judgment. In Numbers 27:21, Moses instructs Joshua that by

the signals of the breastplate worn by the High Priest, the march should proceed or come to a halt.

6. BT *Yoma* 72b.

7. Moran, "Ancient Near Eastern Background," 78–87. Even Deuteronomy in chapters 10 and 11, which speak of love of God and the circumcision of the heart, defines that love as being solely loyal to God (10:20) and as observance of God's laws and commandments (11:1).

8. One can find this understanding enunciated in numerous commentaries. See, for instance, Moshe Cordovero, *The Palm Tree of Deborah*, chapter 5; Menahem Nahum of Chernobol, *Meor Eynayim, parashat* Shimini.

9. Buber, *Israel and the World*, 92.

10. Quoted by Heschel's daughter Dr. Susanna Heschel: "When he came home from Selma in 1965, my father wrote, 'For many of us the march from Selma to Montgomery was about protest and prayer. Legs are not lips and walking is not kneeling. And yet our legs uttered songs. Even without words, our march was worship. I felt my legs were praying'" (https://forward.com /opinion/212971/what-selma-meant-to-jews-like-my-father).

11. Heschel, *God in Search of Man*, 414.

12. Heschel, *God in Search of Man*, 417. The quotation has been edited to be gender neutral.

13. Heschel, *God in Search of Man*, 416.

13. THE TORAH

1. Cooper and Goldstein, "Festivals of Israel and Judah," 19–31.

2. There is some controversy as to the dating of Ezra and whether Ezra and Nehemiah were in fact contemporaries; Ezra himself does not refer to Nehemiah in his book. The more general point being made here—that the Torah is the work of Babylonian Jewry and represents an innovation to the native Jewish population of the Land of Israel—does not depend on exact dating of Ezra's return. With that in mind, the present author follows the account of their collaboration recorded in Nehemiah.

3. Ashdod is a coastal city so the reference may be to the Phoenicians, who eventually became a dominant Mediterranean sea power; Jews may have spoken Phoenician as a lingua franca much as English is spoken today. Although Ashdod was originally a Philistine city, Philistines seem to have disappeared from the historical record by 600 BCE; Ehrlich, "Philistia and the Philistines," 376.

4. See *Encyclopedia Mikrait*, "Ashdodit," vol. 1, 752. Also Myers, *Ezra, Nehemiah*: "All the evidence at present points to a linguistic and commercial continuum in this area, with the lingua franca Aramaic, though there may have been different dialects" (217).

5. The one reference in Malachi, "Remember the Torah of Moses" (3:22), seems so totally out of place within the total message of this prophet that almost all scholars agree it is a later addition to the text. This is all the more plausible as it is affixed to the end of the book. Indeed, if it is an addition, it is further evidence that the Palestinian prophets demonstrate total ignorance of any "Torah of Moses."

6. "That Ezra came up from Babylon, a scribe expert in the Teaching of Moses [*Torat Moshe*]" (Ezra 7:6).

7. "The Torah was forgotten, and Ezra reestablished it" (Babylonian Talmud, *Sukkah* 20a). The Talmud also ascribes to Ezra major extrabiblical innovations regarding synagogue practice, such as the reading of the Torah on Mondays and Thursdays and the calling up of three people for the reading.

8. Frequently in the ancient world, the apex of a given work appeared in the center of the text, not necessarily at the end.

9. Genesis 1:21 mentions that on the fourth day God created "the great sea monsters." These are entirely God's handiwork, not rival divine forces.

10. It is a good guess that the exile in Babylon broke the connection with the dead. Hundreds of miles away, one could no longer engage in the feeding of one's dead ancestors, as was the practice among Judeans before the destruction. Many Israelite graves from the First Temple period have holes at the top through which the living could lower food to the dead, and dried grain has been found in these graves.

11. Knohl entitles his book *The Sanctuary of Silence*.

12. Nevertheless, one can find traces of earlier "heterodox" beliefs, such as the goat sent out to the desert as part of the purification ceremony. By remaining silent as to their purpose, such beliefs could be mitigated.

FINAL THOUGHTS

1. This resolution of the difference is explicitly offered in rabbinic midrash, *Mekhilta of Rabbi Ishmael*, Bahodesh 7.

2. David Weiss Halivni's book *Revelation Restored* enunciates this thesis.

3. "By preserving four discrete and distinct documents, each of which relates its own version of the early history of Israel and argues for a particular

view of Israelite religion, the compiler has made an important theological statement. No one source, no one viewpoint, captures the entirety of the ancient Israelite religious experience. No single document describes the full panoply of ancient Israelite cultures. . . . The competing voices preserved in the Pentateuch are, in fact, complementary, even as they disagree. Only when they are read together is the picture complete." Baden, *Composition of the Pentateuch*, 228.

4. The Book of Jubilees, for instance, resolves the date on which the Passover is to occur. The Pentateuch sometimes refers to the fourteenth, and other times the fifteenth, of the first month. Jubilees ordains: "Remember, the . . . Passover, that you observe it in its time, on the fourteenth of the first month, so that you might sacrifice it before it becomes evening and so that you might eat it during the night on the evening of the fifteenth from the time of the sunset" (trans. by James Kugel in Feldman, Kugel, and Schiffman, *Outside the Bible*). The later (third-century) Mishnah adopted this resolution as well.

5. This resolution of the contradiction of the two Creation stories was adopted in rabbinic midrashic traditions. See *Avot de-Rabbi Natan*, version A, ch. 1:7 and Midrash on Psalms 92:2, among others.

6. There is no scholarly consensus regarding the dating of the Temple Scroll.

7. Geller, "Religion of the Bible," 2039–40.

8. The former Talmud was edited in the late fourth and early fifth centuries; the latter Talmud in the sixth and seventh centuries.

9. See Soloveitchik, *Halakhic Man*.

Bibliography

Adler, Rachel. *Engendering Judaism*. Boston: Beacon, 1998.

Andersen, Francis I., and David Noel Freedman. *Micah: A New Translation with Introduction and Commentary (The Anchor Bible)*. New York: Doubleday, 2000.

ANET. James B. Pritchard, ed. *Ancient Near Eastern Texts Relating to the Old Testament*. 3rd ed. Princeton NJ: Princeton University Press, 1969.

Baden, Joel. *The Composition of the Pentateuch: Renewing the Documentary Hypothesis*. New Haven CT: Yale University Press, 2012.

Berlin, Adele, and Marc Zvi Brettler. *The Jewish Study Bible*. Philadelphia and Oxford: The Jewish Publication Society / Oxford University Press, 2004.

Borowitz, Eugene. *Renewing the Covenant: A Theology for the Post-Modern Jew*. Philadelphia: The Jewish Publication Society, 1991.

Buber, Martin. *I and Thou*. 2nd ed. Translated by Ronald Gregor Smith. New York: Scribner's, 1958.

———. *Israel and the World: Essays in a Time of Crisis*. 2nd ed. New York: Schocken, 1963.

Childs, Brevard S. *The Book of Exodus (The Old Testamant Library)*. Philadelphia: Westminster, 1974.

Cogan, Mordecai, and Hayim Tadmor. *II Kings: A New Translation with Introduction and Commentary (The Anchor Bible)*. New York: Doubleday, 1988.

Cohen, Gerson D. *Jewish History and Jewish Destiny*. New York: Jewish Theological Seminary, 1997.

Cooper, Alan, and Bernard R. Goldstein. "The Development of the Priestly Calendars. I. The Daily Sacrifice and the Sabbath." *Hebrew Union College Annual* 74 (2003) [publ. 2005]: 1–20.

———. "The Festivals of Israel and Judah and the Literary History of the Pentateuch." *Journal of the American Oriental Society* 110 (1990): 19–31.

Crim, Keith, ed. *The Interpreter's Dictionary of the Bible: Supplement*. Nashville TN: Abingdon, 1976.

Cross, Frank Moore. "A Phoenician Inscription from Idalion: Some Old and New Texts Relating to Child Sacrifice." In *Scripture and Other Artifacts: Essays on the Bible and Archaeology in Honor of Philip J. King*, edited by Michael D. Coogan, J. Cheryl Exum, and Lawrence E. Stager, 93–107. Louisville KY: Westminster John Knox, 1994.

Dever, William. "The Silence of the Text: An Archaeological Commentary on II Kings 23." In *Scripture and Other Artifacts: Essays on the Bible and Archaeology in Honor of Philip J. King*, edited by Michael D. Coogan, Lawrence E. Stager, and J. Cheryl Exum, 143–68. Louisville KY: Westminster John Knox, 1994.

Douglas, Mary. *Purity and Danger: An Analysis of Concepts of Pollution and Taboo.* London: Routledge & Kegan Paul, 1970.

Ehrlich, Carl S. "Philistia and the Philistines." In *The world around the Old Testament*, edited by Bill T. Arnold and Brent A. Strawn, 353–58. Grand Rapids MI: Baker Academic, 2016.

Eisenberg, Richard. *Yeshayahu Leibowitz's Philosophy of Jewish Law: A Translation of His Essay "Ceremonial Laws (the Meaning of Halakha)."* MA thesis, Smith College, 1977.

Encyclopedia Miqrait [Hebrew]. 8 vols. Jerusalem: Mosad Bialik, 1982.

Feldman, Louis H., James L. Kugel, and Lawrence H. Schiffman. *Outside the Bible: Ancient Jewish Writings Related to Scripture.* Philadelphia: The Jewish Publication Society, 2013.

Finkelstein, Israel, and Neil Asher Silberman. *The Bible Unearthed: Archaeology's New Vision of Ancient Israel and the Origin of Sacred Texts.* New York: Free Press, 2001.

Fishbane, Michael. *Biblical Interpretation in Ancient Israel.* Oxford: Clarendon, 1985.

Freedman, David Noel, ed. *Anchor Bible Dictionary.* New York: Doubleday, 1992.

Geller, Stephen A. "The Religion of the Bible." In *The Jewish Study Bible*, edited by Adele Berlin and Marc Zvi Brettler, 2021–40. New York: Oxford University Press, 2004.

Goldschmidt, Daniel. *Mahzor for the High Holidays.* Vol. 1. *Rosh Hashanah.* Jerusalem: Koren, 1970.

Grabbe, Lester. *Ancient Israel: What Do We Know and How Do We Know It?* London: Bloomsbury, 2007.

———. *1&2 Kings, an Introduction and Study Guide: History and Story in Ancient Israel.* London: Bloomsbury, 2017.

Halivni, David Weiss. *Revelation Restored.* Boulder CO: Westview, 1997.

Hartman, David. *A Living Covenant: The Innovative Spirit in Jewish Tradition.* New York: Free Press, 1985.

Heschel, Abraham Joshua. *God in Search of Man.* New York: Farrar, Straus & Giroux, 1955.

——. *The Sabbath: Its Meaning for Modern Man.* New York: Farrar, Straus & Giroux, 2005.

Horowitz, Wayne, et al. *By the Rivers of Babylon* [Hebrew]. Jerusalem: Biblical Lands Museum, n.d.

JPS Hebrew-English Tanakh. 2nd ed. Philadelphia: The Jewish Publication Society, 1999.

Knohl, Israel. *The Bible's Genetic Code* [Hebrew]. Ḥevel Modi'in, Israel: Kinneret, Zimora-Bitan, Dvir, 2008.

——. *Biblical Beliefs* [Hebrew]. Jerusalem: Magnes, 2007.

——. *The Sanctuary of Silence: A Study of the Priestly Strata in the Pentateuch* [Hebrew]. Jerusalem: Magnes, 1992.

Levinson, Bernard M. *Deuteronomy and the Hermeneutics of Legal Innovation.* Oxford: Oxford University Press, 1998.

Maimonides, Moses. *The Guide of the Perplexed.* Translated by Shlomo Pines. Chicago: University of Chicago Press, 1969.

——. *Mishneh Torah.* Jerusalem: Hotzaat Shabse Frankel, 2001.

Mazar, Amihai. *Archaeology of the Land of the Bible, 10,000–586 BCE (The Anchor Bible).* New York: Doubleday, 1990.

Milgrom, Jacob. *Leviticus 17-22 (The Anchor Bible).* New York: Doubleday, 2000.

Moran, William L. "The Ancient Near Eastern Background of the Love of God in Deuteronomy." *Catholic Biblical Quarterly* 25 (1963): 77–87.

Myers, Jacob M. *Ezra, Nehemiah (The Anchor Bible).* New York: Doubleday, 1965.

——. *I Chronicles and II Chronicles (The Anchor Bible).* New York: Doubleday, 1965.

Paul, Shalom M. "The Book of the Covenant." In *The Jewish Encyclopedia,* vol. 4, 1214–16. New York: Macmillan, 1972.

Pritchard, James B., ed. *Ancient Near Eastern Texts Relating to the Old Testament.* 3rd ed. Princeton NJ: Princeton University Press, 1969.

Propp, William H. C. *Exodus 19-40 (The Anchor Bible).* New York: Doubleday, 2006.

Qimron, Elisha, ed. *The Dead Sea Scrolls: The Hebrew Writings* [Hebrew]. Vol. 1. Jerusalem: Yad Ben Zvi, 2010.

Quinn, Josephine C. *In Search of the Phoenicians.* Princeton NJ: Princeton University Press, 2018.

Rollston, Christopher A. "Transjordan: The Ammonites, Moabites, and Edomites." In *The World around the Old Testament: The People and Places of the Ancient Near East*, edited by Bill T. Arnold and Brent A. Strawn, 267–308. Grand Rapids MI: Baker Academic, 2016.

Saiman, Chaim N. *Halakha*. Princeton NJ: Princeton University Press, 2018.

Schwartz, Baruch J. *The Doctrine of Holiness: Studies in Priestly Law in the Torah* [Hebrew]. Jerusalem: Magnes, 1999.

Soloveitchik, Joseph B. *Halakhic Man*. Philadelphia: The Jewish Publication Society, 1983.

Sommer, Benjamin D. *The Bodies of God and the World of Ancient Israel*. New York: Cambridge University Press, 2009.

Sperling, David. *The Original Torah: The Political Intent of the Bible's Writers*. New York: NYU Press, 1988.

Stern, Ephraim. *The Archaeology of the Land of Israel*. Vol. 2. *The Assyrian, Babylonian, and Persian Periods (732–332 B.C.E.)*. New Haven CT: Yale University Press, 2001.

Weinberg, Abraham. *The Blessing of Abraham* [Hebrew]. Jerusalem: Yeshivat Beit Avraham, 2014.

Weinfeld, Moshe. *Deuteronomy and the Deuteronomic School*. Winona Lake IN: Einsenbrauns, 1992.

———. *Deuteronomy 1–11 (The Anchor Bible)*. New York: Doubleday, 1991.

Wiseman, D. J. "The Vassal Treaties of Esarhaddon." *Iraq* 20 (1958): 1–99.

Index

Italicized page numbers refer to illustrations.

Aaron, 33, 123, 188, 243
Aaronide priests, 72–73
Abraham, 5, 142, 253
Adler, Rachel, 48–49
Adonai (God): and the Asaph psalms, 261n9; and covenant, 45–49, 259n1; and the Covenant Code, 29–30, 34–37, 43; and governance, 192–95; and holiness, 180, 189–90; and Israel's chosenness, 136–39; and Jehu's revolution, 25–27; and Josianic reform, 165; and the land, 142–45; and mutuality, 43; and obedience, 156–58; and origin of the name of God, xxi–xxii, 6–7; and religious acts, 249–50; and the revelation at Sinai, 124–26; rhetorical devices used for, 150–52; and sacred places, 70; and the stranger, 205–8; and syncretism, 21; as ultimate monarch, 64, 147–53. *See also* commands/commandments; exclusive worship of God/*Adonai*; Sabbath
Adonai Ha-adonim (Master of all Masters), 147–48
adultery, 192–93
afterlife, 230–31
agency, 43, 46, 193

Ahab, 10–12, 16–20, 25
Ahaz, 52, 54, 57, 61–67, 80
Ahaziah, 15–18, 260n1
Ahijah of Shiloh, 233–34
Akhenaton, 5
Alter, Robert, xvi
Amaziah, 24, 52–54
Ammonites, 136
Amon, 65, 85
Amos, 20, 22–23, 26, 40, 56, 113–14, 196, 257n7, 268n10
apostasies, 68, 82, 132, 145–46, 171, 241
appreciation of the other, 216. *See also* stranger
appropriate worship. *See* proper worship
Aram, 11, 15, 56, 61–63, 260n2
archaeological evidence, xvi–xvii; of Assyrian influence, 81, 135; and the dead, 64, 230; of Deuteronomy, 109–11; of divine worship, 37, 261n6; of early biblical history in the Land of Israel, 3–5; of heterodox practices, 70–71, 90–91; and Hezekiah's rule, 75; and the House of Omri, 10; and Judea (Judah), 9, 19, 68, 81, 86, 140–41, 264n2; and the Moabite Stone, 25

Asaph clan, 73, 261n11
Asaph psalms, 73, 261n9
Ashdod, 270n3
Asherah (God's consort), 70, 81, 83,
    88, 261n6
asherah (sacred post), 72, 90
assassinations, 10, 15, 17–18, 51–54,
    65–66, 85, 263n3, 265n1
Assurbanipal II, 75, 80–81, 85, 87,
    109, 129
Assyria/Assyrian Empire: and
    Ahaz, 61–67; and archaeological
    evidence, 77–81, 261n16; and
    Assurbanipal II, 75, 80–81, 85, 87,
    109, 129; and Babylonia, 85–87,
    163–66; and Esarhaddon, 109–12;
    and exile, 234; and God's com-
    mands, 117–22; and Hezekiah,
    67–76; and Isaiah, 112–14, 263n4,
    264n4; and kingship, 111–12, 116,
    129; and Manasseh, 76–84, 140;
    and Northern Israel, 11–12, 69,
    109; and Sargon II, 74–75; and
    succession, 66–67, 85–86, 129;
    and the ten lost tribes, 135; as vas-
    sal state, 163; and vassal treaties,
    109–12, 136
Astarte, 19, 257n5, 260n4
astral worship, 81, 83, 88, 90, 126
Athaliah, 11, 23–24, 51–53
atonement, 205, 211, 260n4
authority. *See* earthly kingship;
    governance; kingship
Azariah. *See* Uzziah

Baal Hashamayim (Lord of Heaven),
    256n6

Baal worship, 5–6, 16–17, 18–21, 24,
    51, 67, 88, 256n1, 257n5, 262n2
Babylonia, 4, 74–75, 80, 84, 85–87,
    107, 146, 163–66, 169–70, 175, 195–
    96, 221, 265n2
Babylonian exile, 107, 146, 166, 169–
    70, 175, 183, 195–96, 199, 221, 223,
    226, 229–31, 234–35, 271n10
Babylonian Jewry, 227, 229, 270n2
Babylonian Talmud, 44, 155, 213,
    246–47, 269n3
Basha, 10–11, 22
Bathsheba, 2, 136
behavior(s), ethical, 16, 36–38, 42–
    43, 44, 48, 147, 155, 158, 161–62, 174,
    178, 182, 188–90, 209, 247
ben Zakkai, Johanan, 228
Beth-El, 28, 89
Beth Shemesh, 24, 62
beyondness, 150, 153
biblical criticism, xv–xvi, 243. *See also*
    contradictions in biblical texts
biblical information as historical,
    xvii–xviii
Biblical Interpretation (Fishbane), 266n4
biblical poetry, 236–37
blessings, 48, 148
Book of Jubilees, 204, 245, 272n4
book production, 158–62
booths, 224
Borowitz, Eugene, 47–48
boundaries, 103–5, 262n2
breastplate, 259n5
brit ahuvim, 49
brotherly hatred, 235
Buber, Martin, 215–16
burnt offerings, 89, 96, 231

Canaan/Canaanites, 2–6, 21, 202, 255n1. *See also* Baal worship

Carthage, 17, 90–91

casuistic law, 33–38, 97–98, 192–93

censorship, 149

centralization of worship, 95–96

characterological issues, 213–15

chariot of the sun, 90, 95

child sacrifice, 63, 88, 90–91, 107, 145, 165, 206, 260nn4–5, 262n3

Chronicles, xvi, 52–55, 80, 86–87, 262n1, 262n3, 265n1; in agreement with Kings, 24, 62, 66, 68, 91–92, 95

class distinctions, 20, 28–29, 32–33, 36–37

Code of Hammurabi, 32, 38, 116–17, 159

Cohen, Gerson, 48

commands/commandments, 194, 232, 234–35, 243, 249, 258n3; and Deuteronomy, 97–98, 118–22, 127–29, 132–33, 138–40, 144–45, 153–58, 214. *See also* Holiness Code

common law, 29

community, interpretive, 248–50

confession, 102

conquest(s): of Assyria, 67–68, 81–82, 104, 135; Babylonian policy of, 166; of Esarhaddon, 261n15; in Joshua, 201–2

contemplation of the Divine, 152, 214

contingent residence in the land, 119–20, 144–46

contradictions in biblical texts, xv–xvii, 3, 241–46, 252, 254, 272n5

counterrevolution, 82, 85

court systems, 29, 33–35, 38, 101, 137

covenant: contemporary theologies of, 45–49; and the Covenant Code, 43; defined, 31; and Deuteronomy, 110–11; and future generations, 129; and Kings, 93; and kingship, 259n1; and land, 144; and the law Judea inherited from Northern Israel, 118–19; and marriage, 45–49; mutuality, 43–45; and the people Israel, 121; in rabbinic and medieval Judaism, 44–45

Covenant Code, 31–40; and contemporary theologies of covenant, 48–49; and Deuteronomy, 97–99, 137, 179, 257n1; and eating of meat, 262n9; and exclusive worship of God/*Adonai*, 29–30, 36–40, 42–43, 147; heritage of, 41–57; historical setting of, 27–30; and holiness, 179, 189; implementation of, 251; and inclusiveness, 236; influence of on subsequent biblical authors, 41–43; and Jehu's revolution, 38–40, 57; and the later biblical story, 49–50; and the law of the sabbatical year, 104, 199–201; Near Eastern setting for, 32–33; and Northern Israel, 27–30, 38–40, 49–50, 56–57, 67; and religious and ethical teaching, 33–38

Creation, 197–99, 229, 245, 253, 272n5

creedal affirmations, 247–48

crimes, 182

Cross, Frank Moore, 262n3

cultic practice, 37, 71, 108, 180, 183–84, 216

curses, 110, 182, 200–201

Damascus, 63

Darius, 196

David/Davidic dynasty, 2, 7–10, 51, 54, 73–74, 76, 85, 91, 116–17, 136, 141, 232, 259n1

Day of Atonement, 205, 211, 260n4

the dead, 63–64, 102, 230–31, 260n4, 271n0

Dead Sea Scroll community, 245

Dead Sea Scrolls, 204

Deborah, 1–3, 21, 255n3

Decalogue, 98–99, 121–28, 160–61, 189, 191–95, 242, 243, 258nn2–3, 269n1

decline of empires, 4–6

democratization of holiness, 212–14

destruction of the Temple, 107, 173–76, 184, 226, 228, 230, 234, 252

Deuteronomic Code, 100–108, 133, 183, 236

Deuteronomy: authorship of, xvi; as the book, 158–62; and commands/commandments, 118–22, 153–58, 214; and contradictions, 241–42; and the Covenant Code, 39, 41–42, 97–99, 137, 179, 257n1; discovery of, 92–96; and earthly kings, 115–18; ethical laws in, 103–5; and exclusive worship of God/Adonai, 94–95, 100, 106, 113–15, 138; and exile, 171–73; and the Feast of Booths, 224; and God's voice, 122–29; heritage of, 147–62; and the Holiness Code, 189, 264n3, 266n4; and Huldah, 93, 165; and inclusiveness, 236–38; and Josiah, 85–96; and the Judeans, 49–50; and the land,

135–46, 192–93; law in, 97–108; and loans, 269n19; and Maimonides, 151–53; as practical, 251; and prescribed worship, 264n12; and proper liturgical time, 210; revelation of, 109–33; and royal scribes, 170–72; and the Sabbath, 195; and the sabbatical year, 199–200, 204; as scroll of God's teaching, 87, 92–93, 130, 158, 236; as secular in approach, 181–82; and the stranger, 205, 266n9, 269n20; and succession, 129–31

Dever, William, 91

Did God Have a Wife? (Dever), 91

difference of opinion, 247–50

diminution of territory in Judea, 68

direct experience of the Divine, 214, 216, 248

dissident priests, 51, 84, 178

distinguishing native and foreigner, 135

divine commands, 154

Divine/Divinity, 6, 21, 30, 46, 48, 71, 107, 112, 123–24, 132–33, 151–53, 156–57, 180–81, 190–91, 194, 197–99, 212, 214, 215–18, 231–32, 242, 248

divine will, 116, 154, 157, 159–60, 251

divine worship, 39–40, 55, 70, 71, 83, 89, 90–91, 117, 156, 171. *See also* exclusive worship of God/Adonai

division of the land, 201–2, 207–8

Douglas, Mary, 262n2

earthly kingship, 34, 38, 112–21, 133, 138–39, 146, 147–50

eating of meat, 35, 95–96, 137, 262n9

editing of the Five Books, 171–72, 183–84, 227, 236–38, 242–46, 255n2, 262n1, 266n3, 266n5, 268n13, 272n8

Edom, 53, 61–62, 68, 140

Egypt, 116–17, 138–39, 143, 163–65, 181, 194, 203–4; and Assyrian ascendancy, 85–86; and Babylonian dominance, 163–65; and Esarhaddon, 78–81; and Hezekiah, 75; and Josiah, 107; and origins of the people Israel, 4–6

Elah, 10–11, 22

El/Elohim, 5–6, 261n9

Eliakim, 107, 164, 263n4

Elijah, 12, 15–30, 38, 39–40, 50, 108

Elisha, 15–30, 38, 39, 50, 108, 259n13

elites, 55, 65–67, 100, 169, 172–73, 177, 191, 195, 221, 237, 244

Endor, 64

equal distribution of land, 201–2, 207–8

Esarhaddon, 75, 78–81, 79, 85, 109–11, 129, 261n15, 263n1

ethical and religious teachings, 33–38, 43, 48, 49, 209, 258n5

ethical behaviors, 16, 36–38, 42–43, 44, 48, 147, 155, 158, 161–62, 174, 178, 182, 188–90, 209, 247

ethical consciousness, 105, 190–91

ethical laws in Deuteronomy, 103–5

ethical sins, 173–76

ethics of neighborliness, 98

exclusiveness of the people Israel, 103, 175

exclusive worship of God/Adonai: and Chronicles, 53–55; and the Covenant Code, 29–30, 36–40, 42–43, 147; and Deuteronomy, 94–95, 100, 106, 113–15, 138; and Hezekiah, 82; and Josianic reform, 130; and Kings, 27; and kingship, 117; in the law codes, 147; and the prophets, 18–21, 100; and purity of Israel, 137; and religious reformers, 64–65; and vassal treaties, 110–11; and Zechariah, 176

exile(s): and Chronicles, 87; and Deuteronomy, 171–73; editing in, 244, 255n2, 266n3, 266n5; and jubilee years, 204; of Judea, 66–67, 82, 107, 169–70, 179, 233–35; and land as conditional gift, 145–46, 200–201; of Northern Israel, 69, 103–4, 135, 233–35; and preservation of tradition, 238; and redemption, 268n18; and reformist priests, 178–79, 183, 227; and the Sabbath, 195–99. *See also* Babylonia; Babylonian exile

Exodus: and Book of Jubilees, 245; and casuistic law, 97–98; and the Covenant Code, 27–30, 31–40, 41–42, 56–57; and expectancy, 253; and future generations, 131–32; and the Holiness Code, 194; and Israel's chosenness, 138–39; and the judiciary, 192; and law against usury, 103; and law of the sabbatical year, 104; and origins of the people Israel, 2–3; and reconciliation, 237–38; and redemption of the firstborn, 133; and revelation

Exodus (*cont.*)
   at Sinai, 123–27, 242–43; and
   the Sabbath, 195, 198; and the
   sabbatical year, 199–200; as
   secular in approach, 181–82; and
   the stranger, 206; and the Torah
   scholar, 213
Ezekiel, 123, 172–77, 184, 189, 196,
   227, 229, 255n2, 263n3, 268n11
Ezra, xv, 223–28, 238–39, 244–45,
   261n11, 262n1, 270n2, 271n7

Feast of Booths, 224
Festival of Matzot, 28, 37
Festival of Sukkot, 224
festivals, 27–28, 37, 195–97, 211, 224–
   25, 258n9
Finkelstein, Israel, 264n2
First Temple period, 65–66, 94, 99,
   145, 172–76, 226, 234, 237, 244–45,
   262n2, 271n10
Fishbane, Michael, 170, 266n4
Five Books of Moses (Torah), xv–xvi,
   241–54; and Babylonian Jewry,
   270n2; as the book, 158–62; and
   commands/commandments,
   154–57; and the Covenant Code,
   31–40, 258n3; and the destruction
   of the Temple, 230; and expectancy, 253–54; and Ezra, 271n7;
   and festival observance, 224–25;
   and the Holiness Code, 187–88;
   and ideal and the real, 250–52;
   injunction to study, 159–60;
   interpretations of, 244–47; as
   moral teaching, 176; and origins
   of the people Israel, 1–12; and

personal transformation, 212–14;
   as poetry, 236–38; and reformist
   priests, 178; and sanctuary, 228–
   29. *See also* Deuteronomy; Exodus; Genesis; Leviticus; Numbers
folk religion, 55
forbidden rituals, 206
foreigners, 36–37, 42, 98, 135, 205,
   269nn19–20. *See also* stranger
foreign influences, 71, 164
free-will offerings, 190, 232, 267n5

Geller, Stephen A., 246
gender distinction, 103
gender equality, 49
Genesis, xvi, 6–7, 28, 142, 157–58, 197–
   99, 233–34, 241, 245, 255n1, 271n9
Geshem the Arab, 225
Ginsberg, H. L., 27
goddess worship, 19, 70. *See also*
   Asherah (God's consort); Astarte
God of Israel. See *Adonai* (God)
governance, 100, 102, 191–95
The Guide of the Perplexed (Maimon-
   ides), 152, 156
Guide to the Duties of the Heart (Ibn
   Pakuda), 215

Haggai, 175, 226
Hakalir, Elazar, 148
halakhah (Jewish law), 121, 155–56,
   209, 212, 246–47, 251
Halivni, David Weiss, 244–45
Hammurabi's Code, 32, 38, 116–17, 159
Hartman, David, 45–48, 259n6
Hazor, 3, 255n3
Hebrew language, 225

henotheism, 258n8, 263n5

hereditary priesthood, 57, 228

Heschel, Abraham Joshua, 216–18, 270n10

Heschel, Susanna, 270n10

heterodox practices, 54, 64–65, 67, 70–71, 82, 88, 90–92, 170–71, 260n4, 271n12

Hexateuch, 254

Hezekiah, 65, 67–69, 71–77, 81–84, 106, 117, 140, 163

high places, 55, 69–71, 86, 108, 114

High Priest, 53–54, 123, 176, 211, 213–14, 228, 232, 263n11, 270n5. *See also* priests/priesthood

Hilkiah, 87, 93, 130, 158–59

Hittites/Hittite Empire, 2, 4–5, 32

Hittite treaties, 111

holidays, 36, 72, 195–96

holiness: and Abraham Joshua Heschel, 216–17; call to, 215; and the Covenant Code, 179, 266n4; democratization of, 212–14; and the land, 137; and personal behavior, 188–91; and reformist priests, 178–85; and the Sabbath, 196–200; of the sacrificial system, 190–91; and the stranger, 205–8

Holiness Code, 187–208; and booth building, 224; and brotherly hatred, 235; in contemporary Jewish thought, 215–18; and the Covenant Code, 41, 49, 257n1; and governance, 191–95; heritage of, 209–18; implementation of, 251; and inclusiveness, 236–37; Israel Knohl on, 267n2; and the jubilee year, 201–5; and land, 199–201, 264n3; and literary precedence, 266n4; and personal transformation, 212–15; and the priestly language of holiness, 188–89; and reformist priests, 178–85; and the Sabbath, 195–99, 223, 232; and the stranger, 205–8, 266n9

Holy of Holies, 111, 123, 171, 181, 214, 232, 248, 263n11

Horeb. *See* Sinai

Hosea, 22, 26, 40, 47, 56, 113, 196, 259n2

House of Hillel, 251–52

House of Israel, 184

House of Shammai, 251–52

Huldah, 93, 98, 158, 165

human agency, 43, 46, 193

human body, 154

Hyksos dynasty, 5

Ibn Ezra, Abraham, 267n4

Ibn Pakuda, Bahya, 214–15

ideal, 209–11, 250–52

idolatry, 34, 87–88, 92, 101, 106, 152, 156

Idumeans (tribes of Esau), 9

"If . . . then . . ." clauses. *See* casuistic law

image of God, 123–28, 150

impurity, 102, 178, 184, 210–11, 262n9

inclusiveness, 207, 236–38, 246, 250

individualism, 48

inheritance, 129–33. *See also* succession

inner life, 198–99, 213–14

instruction, 35–36, 97–99, 120, 128, 132–33, 159–62, 176, 179, 197, 237

intergenerational transmission, 132–33, 160

interhuman love and relationships, 216

intermarriage, 103, 136, 205, 226, 264n1

interpretative community, 248–50

Iraqi Jews, 265n1

Isaiah, 63–64, 68, 73, 112–14, 117–18, 173, 175–77, 196, 233, 235, 263n4, 264n4, 268n10, 269n24

Isaiah of Babylon, 229–30

ish ish, "each person," 212–13

Issachar, tribe of, 10

Jacob, 1, 28, 233

Jehoahaz, 22, 107, 263n4

Jehoash (Joash), 22–24, 26, 51–53

Jehoiachin, 164–66

Jehoiada, 51–52, 259n1

Jehoram, 15–17

Jehu, 15–19, 21–27, 29–30, 38–40, 51, 56–57, 257n8, 259n13

Jeremiah, 107, 132, 139, 142, 144–46, 164–65, 170, 179, 235, 238, 260n5, 262n2, 263n9, 268n12

Jeroboam I, 10–11

Jeroboam II, 22–23, 56, 233, 257n7

Jerusalem, 11, 53, 61–62, 68–76, 89, 95–96, 101–2, 112, 140, 145–46, 166, 170–72, 221–25, 238–39

Jerusalem priesthood, 55–57, 64, 69–70, 83, 99, 231

Jerusalem Temple: Assyrian altar in, 67, 80; and centralization of worship, 95–96; destruction of, 107, 173–76, 184, 226, 228, 230, 234, 252; and Deuteronomy, 99; and divine worship, 89, 91; and festival law, 197; and local priesthood,

102; and purity, 164, 260n4; and reform, 68–71, 83, 107; restoration of, 172–77; and ritual, 255n2; and the Sabbath, 195–98, 223, 268n14; and sacrifices, 237; and Temple worship, 90–91, 178–79, 183–84, 227–29, 269n24; and tithing, 101–2

Jewish assimilation, 48, 169

Jewish law (halakhah), 121, 155–56, 209, 212, 246–47, 251

Jewish mystics, 214

Jewish self-understanding, 45, 209, 241, 246

Jews. *See* people Israel

Jezebel, 10, 12, 15–20, 22, 25, 257n5

Jezreel plain, 18

Joah, 73

Jordan River, 1, 7, 135, 241, 257n15

Joseph, 5, 28, 233–35

Joshua, xvi–xvii, 1–3, 171, 201–2, 226, 253–54, 255n3, 266n3, 269n5

Josiah, 50, 65–66, 85–96, 101, 106, 107–8, 117, 130, 139, 141, 145, 158–59, 163–65, 170–71, 237, 263n3, 265n1

Jotham, 52, 54

Jubilees, Book of, 204, 245, 272n4

jubilees/jubilee years, 201–5, 209, 245, 267n3, 268n18

Judea (Judah): and Assyria, 61–67; and Assyrian vassal treaties, 109–12; and Babylonia, 163–66; and burial practices, 63–64; and the Covenant Code, 27–30, 39, 49–50; and Deuteronomy, 98–99; and exclusivism, 135; exile of, 66–67, 82, 107, 169–70, 179,

233–35; expansion of, 264n2; and the Hebrew language, 225; and Hezekiah, 67–76; and historical conclusions, 25–26; independence of, 23–24, 238; and Josiah, 86, 96, 107; in Kings, 51–57; and kingship, 259n1; and the land, 140–46; the last kings of, 65; and Manasseh, 80–82, 92; map of, 8; and nationalism, 91–92, 104–6; and Northern Israel, 19, 23–24, 67, 118–19, 233–35; and origins of the people Israel, 3–12; polytheurgy in, 260n4; population of, 236n12; and prophets, 175; rulers of, 52; and sacred places, 88–89; and wars of succession, 66–67

Judges, xvi–xvii, 1–3, 171, 202, 256n14, 266n3

judiciary/judicial process, 34–38, 101, 191–95

justice, 18, 41, 65, 99–101, 147, 174–76, 216, 269n18

Kaufmann, Yehezkel, 231, 261n7

Kenites, 2

Kings, book of: and Ahab, 16, 19; and Ahaz, 62–63; and astral worship, 83, 90; and the Covenant Code, 38; and Elijah and Elisha's prophetic ministries, 15–30; and exile, 145–46; and Hezekiah, 68–69, 74–76; and high places, 70–71; and Hilkiah, 130; historical conclusions of, 24–27; and Jeroboam II, 56, 233–34; and Jezebel, 16, 18; and Josiah, 91–96,

107–8, 158–59, 164–65, 265n1; and Judea, 51–57; and kingship, 266n3; and Manasseh, 77, 80–82; and Micah, 263n4; and Northern Israel, 25–27, 67; and reforms, 87; and sin and punishment, 171; and Solomon's Temple, 231–32; and Zedekiah, 166

kingship, 100–101, 111–12, 115–17, 129, 148–49, 232, 238, 259n1, 266n3

Kings of Assyria. See Assurbanipal II; Esarhaddon

Kings of Northern Israel, 11, 16

Knohl, Israel, 4–6, 128, 231, 266n5, 267n2, 269n22

land, 1–12, 119–20, 135, 140–46, 169–70, 175–77, 192–93, 196, 197, 199–208, 221–27, 229, 252–54, 264n3, 268n18, 270n2. See also return to the land

language, Hebrew, 225

law codes. See Covenant Code; Deuteronomic Code; Holiness Code

Law of Moses, 87, 92

laws: casuistic, 33–38, 97–98, 192–93; in Deuteronomy, 97–108; ethical, 103–5; of festival observance, 224–25; and the Holiness Code, 209; as realist or idealist, 251–52; of the recalcitrant city, 137; of the sabbatical year, 104, 199–201; of sacrifices, 190; against usury, 103; of war, 102

Lebanon, 90–91

legal rhetorical style, 33

Leibowitz, Yeshayahu, 157

leisure class, 20, 28

Levinson, Bernard M., 101

Levites, 6, 69, 72–73, 102, 160, 223–26
Leviticus, 41–42, 55, 72, 96, 128, 178–
    83, 187–88, 200–201, 224, 231, 242,
    262n5. *See also* Holiness Code
liberation, 203–4
liturgy, 45, 210, 264n12
A Living Covenant (Hartman), 45–46
loans, 35, 42, 104, 205, 269n19
local priesthood, 101–2
love, 47, 114–15, 132, 138, 181, 184, 189,
    191, 193, 205, 209, 213–16, 250, 251,
    266n9, 270n7

Maimonides, Moses, 150–53, 156–57,
    214, 247–48
Malachi, 175–77, 226, 229, 271n5
Manasseh, 2, 65, 73, 76–84, 85–
    86, 92, 98, 117, 140–41, 163, 178,
    261n12, 261n15
marriage, 46–47, 49. *See also* inter-
    marriage
meat, 35, 95–96, 137, 262n9
medieval Judaism, 44–45, 48
medieval mystics, 153
Megiddo, 163, 263n3
"*Melekh Elyon*/The King on High,"
    148–49
Melekh Ha-olam ("King of the
    World"), 148
Melqart, 19, 21, 257n4
Mesopotamia, 111, 143
Micah, 71–72, 263n4
Milgrom, Jacob, 180–81, 266n7
Mishnah, 155–56, 209–12, 213, 246–
    47, 265n7, 269n1, 269n3, 272n4
Mishneh Torah (Maimonides), 151,
    156, 247

Moabites, 136, 264n1
Moabite Stone, 25
monarchy, 22, 39, 115, 117, 138
morality, 21, 35–36, 41, 104, 175–77
Moses: and authorship, xv–xvi;
    and books, 160–61; and com-
    mandments, 120–21, 154; and
    continuous exile, 241; and the
    Covenant Code, 31–40, 43, 258n3;
    and covenant in the Babylonian
    Talmud, 99; and the Decalogue,
    258nn2–3; and the discovery of
    Deuteronomy, 93; and Elijah, 26;
    and the exclusive worship of God,
    94–95; and exile, 145; and the
    Exodus, 138–39; and expectancy,
    253–54; and knowledge of law,
    206–7; and the land, 143–44; and
    Leviticus, 187–88; and the name
    of God, 5–7; and the priestly
    breastplate, 269n5; as prophet,
    232; and reforms, 92; and the
    revelation at Sinai, 105, 121–28,
    242–43; words of to future gener-
    ations, 130–31, 238–39
Mount Sinai. *See* Sinai
musar (genre of Jewish literature), 215
mutuality, 43–45, 111, 119–21

Naboth, 15–20, 25
Nachmanides, 183, 194
Nadab, 10, 22
name of God, xxi–xxii, 6–7. See also
    Adonai (God)
national consciousness, 28–29
nationalism, 17, 71, 74, 91–92, 98,
    103–5, 118, 226

native and foreigner distinctions, 135

Near Eastern law codes, 32–33. *See also* Covenant Code

Near Eastern treaties. *See* vassal treaties

Necho II, 107, 164–65, 263n3

necromancy, 63–64, 192

negative theology, 151, 248

Negev, 7, 9, 23, 61, 68, 140–41, 163

Nehemiah, xv, 221–27, 239, 261n11, 262n1, 270n2

Nehushtan, 70

Nineveh, 77–78

non-Israelite. *See* stranger

Northern Israel: and Ahaz, 61–62; and the Asaph clan, 73; and Assyria, 11–12, 69, 109; Baal worship in, 17; and the Covenant Code, 27–30, 38–40, 49–50, 56–57, 67; and Hezekiah, 67–69, 83–84; and Jehu, 18–23; and Judea, 19, 23–24, 67, 118–19, 233–35; and Kings, 25–27, 67; kings of, 11, 16; and the land, 140–41; map of, 8; origins of, 7–12; population of, 256n12; and royal power, 53–54; and sacred places, 89; and the ten lost tribes, 135, 166; and theology of covenant, 47

Northern priests, 69, 72

Numbers, 72, 178, 183, 187–88, 201, 203, 206–7, 257n1, 262n5, 267n2, 269n2, 269n5, 269n22

obedience, 106, 118–21, 133, 156–58, 190, 227

objects of worship, 18, 40, 94–95. See also *asherah* (sacred post); astral worship; chariot of the sun; the dead; Nehushtan

obligations and responsibilities, 35–36, 43, 44–49, 91, 119–20, 154–55, 178–85, 188–91, 212, 266n9. *See also* covenant; Holiness Code

observance, 121, 156–57, 172, 178, 190, 215, 270n7; of festivals, 211; of the jubilee year, 205; and plurality of viewpoints, 236, 249–50; of the Sabbath, 200–201, 223–25

Omri, 10–11, 15–19, 22, 23, 25, 39, 51, 258n12, 259n13

oral teaching, 156, 161

ordained worship, 55

origins of the people Israel, 1–12

the other, 216. *See also* characterological issues; love; stranger

pagan worship, 36, 87, 100, 184

paschal celebration, 96

passing a son through the fire, 63, 81–82

Passover, 28, 49, 68, 206, 236, 242, 272n4

penitential prayer, 45

Pentateuch. *See* Five Books of Moses (Torah)

people Israel: and the Covenant Code, 42–43, 50; exclusiveness of, 103–4, 175; and exclusive worship, 40, 110–11, 113–14; God and, 106, 122–25, 147; and holiness, 178; and the Holiness Code, 181, 189–90; and instruction, 160; and Israel's chosenness, 138–40; and Jerusalem, 89; and kingship, 116;

people Israel (*cont.*)

and the land, 201–4; and marriage, 49; and nationalism, 17, 71, 92, 103–5; and obedience, 119–20; and obligations and responsibilities, 46–47; origins of, 1–12; in Rabbinic Judaism, 44; and reformist priests, 184–85; and religious reforms, 71; and self-definition, 135; and the stranger, 206–7

People of the Book, 161–62

Persia/Persian Jews, 175, 221–22, 225, 239

personal and religious ethics, 33–38, 183

personal transformation, 188–91, 209, 212–15

Philistine gods, 19, 26–27

Philistines, 4, 62, 68, 256n14, 270n3

philosophers, 214

Phoenician gods, 20–21, 51

Phoenicians, 4, 10–11, 17, 25–26, 61, 91, 270n3

piety, 48, 165, 212, 238

pilgrimage festivals, 27–28, 197

Plains of Moab, 121, 130, 177

pluralism, 250

poetry, 127–28, 236–37

pollution, 106

polyatric religious practices, 64, 66, 91, 260n4

polytheurgic religious practices, 64, 66, 91, 260n4

popular religious practices, 72

portable sanctuary, 188–89, 198, 228, 231–32

pottery, 81, 261n16

prayer, 44–45, 102, 128, 148, 152, 210, 252

preexilic practice, 179, 183, 204, 235, 244

prescribed worship, 231, 264n12

preservation of traditions, 238

priestly breastplate, 259n5

Priestly Code, 72, 262n9, 267n2

priestly materials, 197–98, 255n2

priestly theology, 123–25, 188, 229

priests/priesthood, 51, 54–55, 57, 64, 69–70, 72–73, 83–84, 91, 99–102, 169–85, 187–92, 210–14, 226, 227–29, 231–32

proper liturgical time, 210–11

proper worship, xv, 37, 54–55, 68–69, 72, 100, 107, 128, 132–33, 172, 178–79, 183–84, 189, 211, 226

prophets: and contemporary theologies of covenant, 46–47; and the Covenant Code, 39–40, 42; and the Deuteronomic reformers, 170–71; Elijah and Elisha, 15–30, 39–40; and ethics, 104–5; and exclusive worship of God/*Adonai*, 82, 100, 114; and exile, 145–46; and the Holiness Code, 188–89; and idolatrous practices, 88; and Isaiah's vision, 112–14; and Jeremiah, 268n12; and Josiah's death, 165; and the jubilee year, 203–4; and the later prophets, 226–32, 243; and legal portions of Deuteronomy, 99–101; and Malachi, 271n5; in Northern Israel, 67; and priests, 83, 123–24, 178; and proper worship, 183–84; pun-

ishments for, 100; and religious reform, 65, 71–72; succession of, 196; and the Temple, 172–77
prose poetry, 127–28
Psalms, 64, 73–74, 116, 259n4
punishments, 32–35, 100, 144–45, 170–71, 181–82, 191–93, 200, 206–7
pure monotheism, 107, 147, 244
purges, 89–92
puritan theology, 123
purity, 103–4, 105, 123, 137, 150–52, 155–56, 164, 171, 174, 177, 178–80, 183–85, 190, 210–12, 231–32, 262n2

Queen Mothers, 18
Qumran community, 204, 265n7

Rabbinic Judaism, 44–45, 155–56, 162, 192, 228, 243, 251–52, 265nn8–9, 269nn2–3
Rabbis, 160–61, 192–93, 197, 204, 234, 246, 252, 265n8, 268n14
Rashi, 267n3
reconciliation, 232–36, 238
reconstructed Temple, 172–77, 178–79, 227, 229
redemption, 56–57, 175, 235, 268n18
redemption of the firstborn, 56–57, 133, 258n7
reform. *See* religious reforms
reformist priesthood, 91, 178–85
refugees, 6, 69, 73, 102, 104, 135, 244. *See also* exile(s)
Rehoboam, 10, 12, 71, 233
religiosity, 199, 216–17
religious imagery, 149–50

religious purity. *See* exclusive worship of God/*Adonai*
religious reforms, 55, 64–66, 67–76, 83–84, 86–87, 91–92, 94–95, 98–99, 107, 163–65, 178–85, 194, 223–26
religious responsibility. *See* obligations and responsibilities
remittance of debts, 104
Renewing the Covenant (Borowitz), 47
reordering of the Temple schema, 72
repentance, 93, 184, 211
responsibility. *See* obligations and responsibilities
restoration, 99, 146, 166, 170, 172, 175, 177, 184
return to eclectic religious practices, 107
return to the land, 169–70, 172–77, 183, 199, 201–4, 208, 227, 234–35, 244, 267n12, 268n18
revelation, 44, 98–99, 105, 121–28, 131, 160–61, 187–88, 189–90, 242–45, 258nn2–3
rhetoric and language, 127–28, 150–51
ritual(s), 35, 37, 64, 72, 88, 102, 178, 184–85, 187, 190, 206, 211, 217, 223–25, 227–28, 249–50
ritual objects, 88–90
royal power, 16, 19–20, 29, 53–54, 113, 137, 172. *See also* kingship
royal scribes, 107–8, 170–72, 177
rulers of Judea, 52
Ruth, 136

Sabbath, 38, 195–99, 207–8, 217–18, 222–26, 227, 232, 268nn10–15
Sabbath of Sabbaths, 201, 269n18

Sabbath of the land, 199–201

sabbatical year, 104, 199–200, 201, 204, 205, 267n3, 269n19

sacred males, 88, 90, 94–95

sacred places, 70, 88–89

sacrifice(s), 37, 54, 63, 88, 90–91, 96, 102, 107, 128, 137, 145, 178–85, 188, 190, 231, 237, 260nn3–5, 262n3, 262n9, 267n5. *See also* redemption of the firstborn

sacrificial law, 206, 262n3

Saiman, Chaim, 162

salvation, 71, 139, 252

Samaria, 10, 17, 19–20, 135, 221–22

Samuel, 2, 22, 57, 64, 100–101, 258n7, 266n3

Sanballat the Horonite, 225

sanctuary, 37, 73, 95–96, 102, 174, 180–81, 187–90, 196, 198, 206–7, 228–29, 231–32, 236–37, 252, 262n5, 267n12, 268n15

Sanctuary of Silence (Knohl), 266n5, 267n2, 269n22

Sargon II, 74–75

Schwartz, Baruch, 193

scribes, 227–28, 244

Sea Peoples, 256n14

Second Temple period, 204, 228, 234, 252, 263n6

sectarianism, 250

secular laws, 33, 101, 108, 181–82

secular realm, 137, 180–81, 205, 217, 251

secular slaughter, 96, 100, 237

segulah (treasure), 136

Sennacherib, 75–76, 135, 261n12

separatist identity, 169

seventh year. *See* sabbatical year

sexual crimes, 182

Shema, 93, 114, 127, 132, 143–44, 210–12

shemitah. See sabbatical year

shofar, 205

Sidon, 10, 17, 19

Simlai, Rabbi, 154, 156

Simon the Maccabee, 228

Sinai, 26, 105, 121–28, 131, 152, 160, 187–90, 194, 242–43, 253

Sinai desert, 5–6

single central sanctuary, 95–96, 99–100

sins, 44–45, 170–71, 174–75, 182, 192, 253

slavery, 104, 133, 195, 234, 242

societal life, 22, 153, 178

sole worship. *See* exclusive worship of God/*Adonai*

Solomon, 7–9, 74, 76, 141, 165, 233, 256n11, 263n7, 264n2

Solomon's Temple, 231–32, 267n12

Soloveitchik, Joseph Ber, 251

speech, 128–29

stranger, 36–38, 181, 205–7, 255n9, 269n20

succession, 66–67, 85–86, 129–31, 196

suffering, 175–77

synagogue, 197, 271n7

syncretism, 18, 21, 26, 53, 67, 107, 260n4

tablets, 109–11, 121–22, 258nn2–3

Talmud, 44–45, 160–62, 212, 246–47, 271n7, 272n8. *See also* Babylonian Talmud

Talmud study, 251

Temple. *See* Jerusalem Temple

Temple priests, 54–55

Temple schema, 72

Temple Scroll, 98–99, 245, 272n6

Temple worship, 90–91, 178–79, 183–84, 227–29, 269n24

temporal circle, 201–2

ten lost tribes, 69, 135, 166

Tent of Meeting, 124, 188

territorial expansion of Judea, 140–41

thanksgiving offering, 262n9

theology of the land, 199–201

theophany at Sinai, 123, 127

Tibni, 10–11

Tiglath-pileser III, 61–63, 75, 80

tithes, 72, 101–2, 210–11

Tobiah the Ammonite, 225

Torah. *See* Five Books of Moses (Torah)

Torah scholar, 213

Transjordan, 140

treaties. *See* vassal treaties

tribal society, 3, 10, 21, 28, 202, 233

Tyre, 19

Ugarit, 111

unification period, 7

universal monotheism, 231

urbanization, 10, 23, 99, 105, 143

usury, 103

Uzziah, 52, 54, 112

Valley of Hinnom, 107

vassal treaties, 109–12, 119, 121, 129, 136, 263n1

victory stele of Esarhaddon, 79

wandering in the desert, 131–32, 207, 238–39

wars of succession, 66–67, 85–86

Weinberg, Abraham, 157–58

Weinfeld, Moshe, 111, 121, 136, 263n10

women, 20, 103

word of God, 121–22, 127–28, 133, 138, 159–62, 165, 247

worship: astral, 81, 83, 88, 90, 126; of Baal, 5–6, 16–17, 18–21, 24, 51, 67, 88, 256n1, 257n5, 262n2; centralization of, 95–96; divine, 39–40, 55, 70, 71, 83, 89, 90–91, 117, 156, 171; objects of, 18, 40, 94–95; ordained, 55; pagan, 36, 87, 100, 184; prescribed, 231, 264n12; proper, xv, 37, 54–55, 68–69, 72, 100, 107, 128, 132–33, 172, 178–79, 183–84, 189, 211, 226; Temple, 90–91, 178–79, 183–84, 227–29, 269n24. *See also* exclusive worship of God/*Adonai*

Written Law, 161, 265n8

written tradition, 228. *See also* scribes

Yod-Heh-Vav-Heh, 5–6

Zechariah, 22, 175–76, 226

Zedekiah, 65, 166, 260n5

Zerubbabel, 226–27

Zimri, 10–11, 18, 22

OTHER WORKS BY EDWARD FELD

The Spirit of Renewal: Finding Faith after the Holocaust
Joy, Despair and Hope: Reading Psalms
Mahzor Lev Shalem: Rosh Hashanah and Yom Kippur (senior editor)
Siddur Lev Shalem for Shabbat and Festivals (senior editor)
Siddur Lev Shalem for Weekdays (forthcoming) (senior editor)